# RUTHLESS COPYWRITING STRATEGIES

By **T.J. Rohleder**
(a.k.a "The Blue Jeans Millionaire")

## Also by T.J. Rohleder:

*The Black Book of Marketing Secrets (Series)*
*The Ultimate Wealth-Maker*
*Four Magical Secrets to Building a Fabulous Fortune*
*The Ruthless Marketing Attack*
*$60,000.00 in 90 Days*
*How to Start Your Own Million Dollar Business*
*Fast Track to Riches*
*Five Secrets That Will Triple Your Profits*
*25 Direct Mail Success Secrets That Can Make You Rich*
*24 Simple and Easy Ways to Get Rich Quick*
*How to Create a Hot Selling Internet Product in One Day*
*Secrets of the Blue Jeans Millionaire*
*Shortcut Secrets to Creating High-Profit Products*
*How to Turn Your Kitchen Table or Spare Bedroom into a Cash Machine!*

FIRST EDITION

ISBN 1-933356-27-8

# TABLE OF CONTENTS:

# INTRODUCTION:

Welcome! My name is T.J. ROHLEDER, and I'm the co-founder of M.O.R.E., Inc. and the Direct-Response Network, both of which are headquartered in Goessel, Kansas. In this book, I'm going to introduce you to what I believe is the single greatest marketing skill that anyone can ever learn. It's a skill that's brought in more than *$110 million* for my companies over the past 20 years. Let me assure you, I don't say that to brag: I say it as a fact, to show you that it really is possible, as a way to help inspire you to compile the kind of wealth you could and should be enjoying.

The crucial skill I'm talking here about is *copywriting*. It's the ability to effectively put words down on paper, or to create them electronically in email or on a website, or to dictate them as part a sales presentation. However you create and present them, these are words that make people take action and give you money.

This book was adapted from a three-day seminar that I presented to members of the Direct-Response Network in October 2008, with the assistance of my good friends and colleagues Chris Hollinger and Chris Lakey. Everything you're going to read here is based on our direct experience: none of it came out of some textbook written by an obscure business professor who's never actually been out in the trenches. We're not professional speakers or communicators — we're professional entrepreneurs, people who are out there doing, on a daily basis, what I'm going to show *you* how to do.

I've titled both the original seminar and this book *Ruthless Copywriting Strategies* for a very good reason — so before I get started with the meat of the program, let me explain that title, and a few main ideas you'll encounter here. I realize that in most circumstances, "ruthless" isn't such a good word. Look it up in the dictionary, and you'll see that in its most extreme usages, the term "ruthless" means that you're able to hurt someone else without being bothered by it emotionally. But look here — that's *not* the way I use that word. The word "ruthless" has less-brutal meanings, and the English language is constantly evolving. Anyone who's ever tried to understand what the younger generation is trying to say knows what I'm talking about. The language is constantly in motion. A good synonym for the way I use "ruthless" would be "aggressive." In business, an aggressive person is bold, audacious, and doesn't necessarily care what other people think about how he conducts his business.

A ruthless marketer does things that are aggressive, things that are bold, things that are assertive — and doesn't worry about anyone except the people who are going to give him money. When you're a marketer, those are the only folks who really matter. When you're writing copy, you're only writing to that person who's going to give you money. Nobody else counts. You're not trying to please everybody; you're only trying to please those few people who are your best customers. It's all about adopting the strategies that let you do that in the most effective way.

One of my favorite quotes comes from Abraham Lincoln, who once said that if he only had three hours to chop down a tree, he'd spend the first two hours sharpening the ax — so he wouldn't have to work nearly as hard that last hour. Some people might just pick up that dull ax and start whaling away at the tree without bothering with a strategy, using brawn rather than brainpower. That tree might come down, but only after the expenditure of a great deal of effort. A smart person focused on strategies would do what Abraham Lincoln did: they'd get the axe real sharp first, so they wouldn't have to chop much before the tree came falling down.

Put simply, ruthless marketing brings you the greatest results in the shortest amount of time. So when you think "ruthless," think about being bold, audacious, about focusing on the precise buyer you want to reach. Copywriting is your way to do that. It's the ability to put words on paper that make people take action, that inspire people, that influence people, that cause them to give you money. The best strategies are the ones that will give you the biggest results for the least amount of effort.

Let me give you a good example of ruthless copywriting. As I'm writing this, we're heading into a tough economic period, something that's worrying millions of people. Recessions come and go, but some of the experts out there — you know, the Ph.D.s and MBAs and the other folks on TV with those initials after their names — are saying that things are going to get a lot worse before they get better. Some of those experts are telling us that this may be one of the worst recessions we've seen in 50 to100 years. Those comments are scaring a lot of people — but some of my marketing friends want to pretend none of these things are happening. Their marketing materials don't even address these issues, because they don't want to bring up anything negative; they don't want to scare people. But hell, people are scared already!

I've decided to take a completely different stance on the issue. I've decided we won't try to ignore the problem, or pretend that it's going to go away soon, or make believe that are our customers aren't thinking about it. Because they *are* thinking about it. It's *essential* in their thinking. They're worried about it; many of them have lost a lot of money. Hell, I have myself; and I'm sure you have too, if you've got your money invested in mutual funds or the stock market. Here at the DRN, we've decided to face the problem head on, so we're producing a program we call the Recession-Proof Wealth System. As of this writing, six marketers are involved (including my colleagues in this endeavor, Chris Lakey and Chris Hollinger), and we're about three-quarters done.

Why are we bothering? Because we want to show people how they can make huge sums of money in spite of whatever happens in the economy. We're trying to give them the skills and the knowledge and the ability to go out there and make money, no matter how bad things get. We're promoting it right now; we're being very aggressive, because the crashing economy is something that's on people's minds, and we don't want to pretend it's not. We're finding something good in what's normally bad, whereas the media is spitting out all this fear. They're just trying to scare people; but we're taking people who are *already* scared and showing them how they can survive whatever comes.

We're selling them something that will empower them, something that will help them. We're taking on the problem head on. That's what I would call a ruthless, aggressive marketing strategy; not just burying your head in the sand, not just pulling back and trying to pretend the economic situation doesn't exist, or that it's not a central issue for your customers and the people you're doing business with. We're facing it head-on. *That's* the boldness and audacity, the ruthlessness, that I'm talking about.

But we're not stopping there. We're putting together a distributorship for this product, so that other people can go out there and sell it. We're also putting together a Master Distributorship that gives the distributors who want to make the most money even more opportunities to do so. And it doesn't even stop there! We're continuing to develop products and services that are all directly related to this terrible, terrible situation that other people are trying to run from or ignore. We're busy creating all kinds of solutions that are built around helping people make more money in this traumatic period.

We're using certain strategies that I'll go into more detail on later, specific strategies that let us be excited, rather than fearful, about the future.

When you have the ability to go out there and apply these aggressive copywriting strategies, you have power and strength; you take control of your destiny and don't let the tough times hold you down. Power, literally defined, is the ability to take action. The more you possess the ability to take action, the more power you have. If you take to heart these marketing strategies I'm going to teach you in the following chapters, you'll have a lot of power. You won't be held down by fear, caught up in your frustrations and worry. I realize that those are just words right now — but when I unfold some of the specific strategies here, you'll realize that it's almost like creating money out of thin air. You're almost like some medieval alchemist, trying to turn base metals into gold. A lot of our modern science was actually developed through the processes explored by those greedy people! What we, as marketers, do is turn *words* into gold. We put together sales letters that cause people to give us money.

Our good friend Russ von Hoelscher is famous for saying that all it takes is one good sales letter to make a million dollars. He told us that back in the winter of 1989, when we first got started with him. We picked him up at the airport in Wichita and were driving him back to Goessel, and he mentioned that during the course of our conversation. So here's Russ; he's a big guy, and we had this little car. Russ is all crunched up in the back of that car, and I'm driving and watching Russ; I'm talking to him and trying to keep one eye on the road while trying to keep the other eye on Russ as we're having this conversation. At that time, we were making about $16,000 a month, which was pretty good money for us, because we'd been broke for so many years. Just as I was turning off the Interstate onto the K15 Highway toward Goessel, Russ said, "Yeah, all it takes is one good sales letter to make a million dollars." Man, I got so excited! I said, "What did you say?" And he goes, "All it takes is one good..." and I just about drove right off the road!

The idea that you can write words that can cause people to give you hundreds of thousands or even *millions* of dollars was exciting to me. It was only nine months later that I wrote my first sales letter — with Russ's help. He also helped put the product together that it sold, too. We generated over a million dollars with just that one sales letter. It took me three months to write it, and I worked on it every day. I usually don't have to do that anymore, thank goodness! I only work on a sales letter about a week or two, and then I'm done with it. But back then I spent three months working on this sales letter — and it generated over a million dollars for us.

I'm not saying that to brag on *us*. I'm saying that to brag on the idea that you can put words together and inspire people to send you cash, checks, money orders, and credit card authorizations for millions of dollars. That should excite everyone reading this! Every one of you has the ability to do it. And as I hope to prove to you in the coming pages, you don't even have to be that good to make a lot of money. If you have any little doubt in the back of your head saying, "I could never really be good at *that*," well, you're wrong... and I'll prove it. That's my promise to you.

# CHAPTER ONE:

# Study the Lively Art of Copywriting

I love to talk about copywriting, because it's something I absolutely love to do. While it's just one part of the direct marketing strategy that we teach to our clients, it's supremely important, because it's what brings in the money directly. Now, all the other things that go along with marketing are important, too; I can and I have spent whole books, not to mention countless seminars, discussing those subjects. But copywriting is extra special to me.

I'm glad that you're reading this book, and I hope you'll get a lot out of it. I hope you'll read it more than once, in fact, and take a lot of notes, too. Write in the margins, scribble in the end pages, highlight specific passages, do whatever it takes to help you internalize this material. All modesty aside, there's a lot of great stuff here, advice that can literally make you millions. (I know I say that a lot, but only because it's true.) And the truth is, I've had to pare down all the knowledge I could potentially share with you, in order to present it in an easily accessible format. I could always produce the marketing version of *War and Peace* here, but how many folks have ever read *War and Peace* itself? Damn few, and for good reason — it's huge! In order to give you something you can read in a reasonable amount of time, I've whittled down the complete library of things I could discuss to the most valuable items, things you should be able to start putting into use immediately.

I'm going to give you a broad overview of some very specific things, which I'll go into in detail as I go along. There's a lot to learn, but you can learn the basics fairly quickly. As with chess, good copywriting basics can take a day or two to learn, but a lifetime to master. Along the way, you'll learn how to leverage your knowledge into undeniable success — if you just keep at it, and keep learning. I've been at it a good 20 years, and I can tell you that I haven't mastered it all yet. But don't let that get you down; as I've said, I've made a lot of money at it along the way.

My Director of Marketing, Chris Lakey, recently reminded me of something called the 10,000-hour rule. According to business author Malcolm Gladwell, while talent and intelligence have their place in any endeavor, it takes you about 10,000 hours to really become good at anything. Mastering something doesn't necessarily have anything to do with your skills or your education level, it has to do with how many hours you put into practicing it. Gladwell uses the example of athletes who start at age 3 or 4, like Tiger Woods. By the time they're teenagers, they excel at their sport, because they've spent about 10,000 hours practicing it. Musicians are the same way. A kid who sits down at the piano at age 2 and starts learning to play ought to be able to play the piano as well as any adult, after putting in their 10,000 hours. That's about five years at 40 hours a week — ten years if you look at it more as a hobby and just spend a few hours a day at it.

Chris and I have passed our 10,000-hour marks for marketing already, so we can safely say that, yes, we're experts — but we're still learning. Reaching our level of experience at copywriting just takes getting out there and doing it. But guess what — and this is really exciting — you can still make money as you learn! I'm here to give you the foundation to help you get started, even if you've never written a sales letter before. You've got to start at some point, no matter how amateurish you think that first effort might be. You've *got* to do it. I won't lie to you here: if you want to make any significant money as a marketer, you're going to have to get started and really work at it. If you already have, I congratulate you — you're on the right track, and I hope this book helps! If you haven't, start practicing what I preach immediately.

I'll be blunt here: I know from experience that some of you will see that word "work" up there in the previous paragraph, and that'll be it — this book will go back on the shelf. Others will read the book all the way through with the best of intentions... but won't try anything I've said here. That's fine. This book is for the rest of you: the ones who aren't afraid of rolling up your sleeves and jumping right in. I encourage you to take what I share with you here, and let that be your foundation. Use the resources we give you, learn more about writing sales copy, and put all that into practice — because it's in the doing that you'll get better at it. You'll discover things when you get down in the trenches, so to speak, and start actually putting copywriting principles into practice.

You don't even need to start with full-blown sales letters. A classified ad is a good way to start learning how to write sales copy, simply because it's short. It doesn't require many words. Once you feel you have a good grasp of writing a decent classified ad, from there you can go on to writing a small display ad, or maybe a postcard — just several hundred words — and make that work. And then you can start working on long-form sales letters. We've occasionally written sales letters that were as long as 60 pages.

You might think, "Wow, how could I write a 60-page sales letter? It's hard for me to write just one page of copy!" Well, the way you get to the point of writing a 60-page sales letter is to understand all the concepts that go into writing a *one*-page sales letter — and just expand them to the new length. The strategies I'm going to teach you will work whether you're writing a Yellow Page ad, a postcard, or a 60-page sales letter. Just start small, and build from there.

So just take some notes; write down the main ideas that excite you. Do more research on the Internet. Ask other marketers questions. I want to help you be the best copywriter you can be. I guarantee you that I can use the competition, and there's plenty of room in the field. You don't have to be the best copywriter ever; you don't even have to be good. You just have to be *good enough*. You just have to understand a few basic things to write sales letters... and those sales letters can make you good money.

So I'll be sharing some basic strategies with you as a foundation that you can start with. It's up to you to take that and run with it.

Let me emphasize, again, that this is not rocket science. Just about anyone can learn to be a decent copywriter, if they're willing to work at it. The strategies I'll show you here are the most important things you need to know. When you decide to become a good copywriter, you start out with several things in your favor. For example: the writing part of it is something you all know how to do. You're already a writer, every time you take notes, write a letter, or put together a grocery list. Trust me on this. You *know* how to write! It's the *strategies* that make you the most money. It's the things that you do with the words that you write that matter, and I'll be focusing heavily on those things.

Here's something else I want to say again: Copywriting is exciting! When you put words together that cause people to give you money, when you get an idea and get excited about it, and you write sales copy during that moment of excitement — *that's* where most of your money comes from. Even if you're not a Pulitzer Prize-winning writer, when you convey that excitement in your writing, it's contagious. I try to write only when I'm excited, and I try to make sure I'm excited every morning at 5:37 AM. I drink a gallon or two of coffee and I get all animated, and I have a big stack of legal pads that I attack, and I just write like crazy. Later, I review it and have it typed up. When that copy goes out to people, they get excited about it too — and they give me money!

Copywriting is one of the most enjoyable things that I do in my business. My colleague and friend Ted Ciuba likes to say that writing copy is better than sex. I'm not sure I agree, but I do know that it's exciting and profitable. It's also something I do well, so it's one of the few things I do in my business — which is another thing you absolutely have to take to heart if you really want to succeed. You need to farm out the extra jobs that you're either not good at, or that are unprofitable for you to do personally. Hire people to do some things on a part-time or full-time basis, so you can concentrate on the things that make your business the most money — like copywriting.

The strategies that I'm sharing in this book are directly applicable to any business you may be involved in. We've all been taught that business is a highly competitive environment, right? You've got to have your ducks in a row, and mind your P's and Q's, and you've got to know what you're doing; and if you *do* know what you're doing and you build a better mousetrap and you have integrity, then people are going beat a path to your door. That's true to a certain degree. However, copywriting gives you an added edge, which is something you *must* have. Why? Well, let's look at it with a ruthless analogy: Does the wolf shed a tear when the caribou it's been eying goes down? Of course not. As Americans, we're all taught that we live in a competitive world. We provide for our families by going out and being in business.

Most businesses say they're competitive — and yet the

majority of people in these businesses are running around like caribou in a herd. They're all doing the same thing, whereas a direct-response marketer using good copywriting strategies is the wolf amongst the caribou. You're not following the herd; you're directing it, taking down your competition at your leisure, at will. You're using these strategies because you're in touch with your inner wolf as a marketer, as a businessperson. I'm using the wolf analogy because a wolf can be ruthless. It can be very aggressive — but the wolf is very selective in what it targets. It doesn't want to waste its energy, time, and money spinning its wheels while trying to earn a living for its pack. In a similar way, that's what we, as ruthless marketers, are doing. We're using copywriting to focus in on the specific prospects who are most likely to do business with us; to hell with the rest. We use our copywriting skills to convince those prospects that the money they're giving us isn't *anything* compared to what they're getting — and then we prove it. We have to use our words to get them to do that. These strategies are powerful and exciting, and they're *fun*.

When I started my business, this was a whole new world to me. I could write, of course; I could construct sentences with proper subject/verb agreement. I knew where punctuation went, for the most part. But copywriting is different. It has less to do with proper grammar and punctuation than with grabbing people by the emotions, getting their attention, and using human nature to get them to act. But so many businesses out there don't do that! They just say: "I've been in business for 25 years. I'm the best there is." And to some extent, that's worked for them. But a ruthless marketer, using ruthless copywriting strategies, will out-perform those bland ads every single time. The guy who understands ruthless marketing — because he's sharpened his ax carefully by learning these strategies — is going to raise fat kids because he's going to have lots of money.

I urge you to immediately start using these strategies. Start writing small ads — little classified ads, small space ads — and start learning how to get someone's attention, to keep their attention, to make it exciting. It's all about learning how to make an effective call to action, to get your prospects to take that step toward rewarding you with their money. I guarantee you'll find that you get better and better at it. Practice, practice, and practice some more, and you'll become familiar with how to weave these strategies into a sales letter, a classified ad, or whatever it is you're working on.

Why is this important? Quite simply because *copywriting is the engine that makes the whole marketing process work.* It's those words, and the ideas they manifest, that get people to do what we want them to do. As a business person, what you want them to do is become your customer, and keep coming back.

Again, it's all about emotion, and how much of it you can inject into your work. Get pumped up before you start writing. If I'm a little sleepy, if I'm tired, or if I've had a hard day, my writing reflects it; it's not so good. But when I'm fresh or I put on some music and drink my coffee, I'm all pumped up, and then that emotion — that super-charged feeling — comes across in the words I use. I lose track of time when I'm really "in the zone," as the athletes put it. Hours can literally go by and I'm like, "Oh, crap! I had all this other stuff I needed to get done, but I got caught up in writing this sales letter!"

Have you ever had a time in your life when you found that you were pretty good at something, or at least you had a lot of fun doing it — and then time would just fly by? Let's take algebra. My colleague Chris Hollinger, who used to be a teacher, has told me that he remembers well the day he finally realized he was good at math. It was his freshman year in high school. Up until then, he says, he was average at best. He always struggled with math. And then, in his freshman year, he was inspired by his algebra teacher, a mathematician who had once worked for NASA. The way she taught algebra that year caused Chris to pick it up and learn it, bam, bam, bam. It came so easily for him that he got straight A's in math from then on. It felt good to do math; it was exciting.

That's how copywriting can be. For me, copywriting — putting words down on paper that can lead to heaping piles of mailbox money (as Chris Hollinger calls it) — is fun and energetic. All the truly successful marketers I know feel the same way. If you take one thing away from this book, it should be the enthusiasm to sit down and write something, even a little classified ad you can put in a local newspaper, to get someone to take action and call a phone number or go to a website. Take something from here, and apply it. When you see it turn to money, you're going to say, "That's so cool!"

I want you to be in touch with your inner wolf, as a marketer and as a copywriter. If you keep that in mind, you're going to go far.

# CHAPTER TWO:

# Practice These Basic Strategies

In the next few chapters, I'm going to share a wide variety of basic strategies that you can use to become a profitable copywriter. I'm going to start by unfolding just a few very crucial ideas, four or five strategies that I think are the most important I have.

Let me get the first one out into the open immediately. It's something I already promised you in the previous chapter: that you don't have to be all that good to make good money. This is a strategy that's so easy that most people just miss it altogether, though I have to admit that it does presuppose one factor on your part: that you know your marketplace, the people that you're communicating to, very well. The better you know those people — the more intimately you know who they are, what they're excited about, what turns them on, what they're spending their money on — the more money you will make, period. You need to understand exactly what they like about the products and services they're buying right now, and what *don't* they like. What problems are inherent in their lives? What gets them excited? What drives them crazy? What angers them? What frustrates them? All marketing is, basically, is selling to people the first time, and then re-selling to them. Every successful business does that. The more you know about the common denominators of the people you sell to, the more money you'll make.

From the very beginning, this was the biggest strength Eileen and I had. When we met Russ von Hoelscher in 1989, we'd been in the business for six months, so we were babies in the business. We didn't know anything back then, except for this one thing — we knew the people we were selling to, so we were making about $16,000 a month. Not bad, right? We knew who we were marketing to because they were just like us. They were people who habitually bought one moneymaking program after another, and that was my story, too. I understood how they felt; I was frustrated. I was angry. I was confused. I was disappointed by all these programs, and I was getting all kinds of criticism from my friends and family. My friends mostly just laughed at me. Most of my family laughed at me, too, but some of my family members, those who really cared about me, begged me to stop. In fact, my Dad, who was not a violent man, got so angry with me one day that he threw me up against the wall and shouted, "Look, give up these crazy ideas that you're going to get rich someday!" I was in my early 20s when he did it, and I was living at home — so obviously, I was broke. After being on my own for about eight years, I had to go live with him for a while, that's how broke I was. I was eating his food. I was under his roof. I wasn't paying any bills. I was running up his long-distance phone bill, and I was sending away for one get-rich-quick program after another. All I was doing was dreaming about making millions of dollars — when according to the normal scheme of things I should have been out looking for a job like the average person does. According to my dad, I should have resigned myself to the fact that I was never going to make any significant amount of money, and that I had all these things against me.

So he shoved me against the wall one day and said, "Get rid of these crazy ideas that you're going to make millions of dollars, because you're not going to do it. You're *never* going to do it." That's the same general mindset millions of other people are dealing with right now — though maybe not as extreme as what I went through. Maybe they don't have somebody who actually throws them against the wall. He was trying to get my attention, you know? And he did! But I was determined more than ever after that.

I didn't know it then, but there are millions of people out there who fit that demographic profile I just expressed to you. They're habitually buying one moneymaking program after another. They're addicted to buying these programs. They've got a strong ambition and they want to do *something*, so they keep buying programs — and they're frustrated and confused when those programs fail to deliver.

When we finally put together a moneymaking system, it was called *Dialing for Dollars*. This was our first little publication, based on a couple of programs that really worked for us. We weren't getting rich, but we were steadily making hundreds of dollars a week, and it was the first time ever that we'd actually done that. So we wrote a little booklet about it. I was on all these mailing lists and I was getting all this stuff in the mail and I thought, "You know what? I betcha there are other people out there just like me." What I didn't realize was that there were *millions* of people just like me! So we decided to try to sell this little pamphlet, which cost us maybe 40 cents to print up, for $12.95. It was worth at least that, we figured, because it worked — it was a proven plan.

Before long, we were actually making about $16,000 a month from selling this plan — because we understood the market. We *knew* that, even though some of my family members looked at this thing and said, "Man, this is crap. This is total crap. You're selling this thing for $12.95? Look, you can't even write. It's filled with the worst sort of writing. It's terrible." It was a proven program, but they thought we were ripping people off. My dad's wife even threw it across the room one day when I showed it to her. She said, "That's crap. You're ripping people off."

But we *weren't* ripping people off; we were helping them. We understood the marketplace; and because of that, we didn't have to be that good to make good money. So I want you to realize this; if you forget everything else you read in this book, just remember this one thing, and let it be your foundation. Let it be your source of inspiration. Just know that as long as you're writing to people that you already know about, people you understand at a basic level, you'll succeed. You have to know what they like and dislike, who they are and what they're excited about. That was our strength, and it can be yours. Do this, and you can make a lot of money without having well-developed skills at all. You just have to *really understand* the people to whom you sell.

Your first few tries don't have to be great — just honest, enthusiastic, and good enough. *Dialing for Dollars* is a good example. I'm embarrassed by that little booklet today. I mean, it was written 20 years ago. I'm still not that good a writer today, but back then I was really bad! Yet it was good enough to launch a company and get some serious money coming in, if only because it was the right product for the right market.

You may be reading this and thinking, "Heck, I don't have the time, energy, or the skills to become a great copywriter." Well, come on — it doesn't have to be *great*. My friend Chris Hollinger tells me that when he was a teacher, one of the things he tried to do early on was to put an example out there for his students regarding what he was looking for in a particular assignment. And the students would close down, because they'd say, "I can't write that well. I'm not as good a writer as you are yet." His examples were intimidating to them. A lot of people are like that; when they see a piece of copywriting they just close down, saying, "Well, I'm never going to be good at it," so they just stop. But you don't have to be a prize-winning writer the first time around!

One of the best things you can do with copywriting is to copy the ideas and structure of the best copywriters you can find. Don't plagiarize, but use their work as a model. Pretty soon, you'll find that what you produce is passable. Keep writing, and you'll get better — though I'll be the first to admit that there's a never-ending learning process when it comes to copywriting. But good enough is good enough.

Knowing your market is absolutely crucial. If you're going to fire a missile at something, you'd better have an idea that it's at this longitude and latitude and this range, and that it's the second adobe building on the left; you want your missile to be guided. Any guided, targeted marketing campaign using ruthless copywriting strategies starts with knowing your market. Whether your market is the home-based opportunity market, or if you're a plumber wanting to take away your competitors' shares, you've got to know what's going to motivate your customers to act.

How do you do that? How do you get to know your market? In my case, I *was* the market. That's the best advice I can give to anybody who's just getting started: go with what you know. The time to experiment — the time to go into other markets that you think are cool but don't know anything about — is when you have a few million in the bank. Become a customer of the kinds of businesses you want to emulate. Collect their ad copy and study it closely. Always go with what you know.

And don't be satisfied with that, either. Be aggressive. Here's an example, again from Chris Hollinger. One of the things he did when analyzing the market was to call customers up and interview them — basically, he asked them directly what they wanted. For a while he ran space ads, doing a lot of advertising and marketing; he was generating a lot of leads and prospects, and he qualified those prospects and made some sales. But, quite frankly, he wasn't satisfied with his conversion rate. So he picked up the phone to ask people, "What are you looking for?" That gave him a very good feeling for what the prospects he was going after really wanted. It wasn't easy, but it was worthwhile.

Spending that time putting yourself in the prospect's shoes, understanding and thinking critically about their needs, is like Abe Lincoln sharpening his ax before cutting down the tree. It's critical to really understanding that what you're doing needs to be laser-guided toward the specific prospects you want to convert into sales.

Our *Dialing for Dollars* booklet speaks volumes about what I'm talking about here. It's a thin booklet; there aren't even page numbers. It *wishes* it could be a book. It's a little thing that hopes someday, maybe, it will grow up and be a book. And it did! But in its original form, it was a tiny booklet — and it still did the trick. It got us started. It made us money. And more importantly, the system described in our booklet made money for the people who used it. Its value came from the information it offered, not its size, not the materials it was made from. Sure, I'm still a little embarrassed by it, even though there's no reason to be. Just like with my early sales letters, when I read it I think, "What was I thinking? What was I *not* thinking? Why did I write that?"

We do that sometimes. We're allowed to have those moments. The point is, this book got us started, and we were on our way at that point. The important thing is to make that start. If you never write a sales letter, if you never get started — well, there's nothing to analyze later. There's nothing to critique. There's probably also no money to be had, so you've got to do *some*thing. It's a journey, just like being a star athlete is a journey. Even if that person makes it to their sport's Hall of Fame, they didn't *always* play like a Hall of Famer. Most likely, when they first got started, they made some rookie mistakes. Everyone has a journey to success, and nobody looks back and says, "Okay, I did everything right along the way." In fact, those who succeed are usually the ones who simply manage to outlive their failures until they achieve success. Today, *Dialing for Dollars* is a representation of what it took for Eileen and me to get started. Even though it embarrasses us now, it's a part of our journey to success — just as what you do to get started today will be a part of *your* journey to success. Everybody looks back and critiques their early work, whatever it is. Artists, musicians, copywriters... everybody does it. But it's a starting point and a foundation, and you've got to have those in order to succeed later, to get to those works that you're proudest of.

We have sales letters we look at and say, "Wow! This one was right on target." It was the perfect message to the perfect audience at the perfect time, and everything about that offer was right on the money. We know that because it worked like a charm and made lots of money. But we also have the ones we look at and say, "Hmm, I don't really understand why I did it this way or why I did that," and hopefully, as you're learning, you continue to have fewer of the kind that you shake your head at and wonder what you were thinking, and more of the ones where you say, "Yes, I did it right," because you're using these strategies I'm showing you here. You're learning from them as you go.

There are writers I adore, people whom I know in my heart that I'll never be able to write like. I don't care if I live to be a hundred and if I work at it for hours a day, there is no way on God's green earth that I'm ever going to be able to write like some of my favorite writers. Let's face it: they just have more writing talent than I do. But what they do is inspire me to want to be better, so that's a positive thing. I read their work and I say,

"Man, I've got a long way to go," so it helps move me forward.

But again, the point I want to make is that you don't have to be that good to make good money. You just have to really, *really* know your market well. So find a market that you know very well and get to work!

One of the people who attended the real-life seminar that this book is based on is a man from Maryland named Paul Daniels — and he's deaf. He brought a couple of interpreters from Wichita to translate what I said into sign language. I'm trying to sell him on the idea that he needs to go out and work with other deaf people, because if there's one group who will read those sales letters, it's deaf people. If you write a 60-page sales letter, they're a lot more apt to read the whole thing than most people are. Reading is the main way they get their information, and Paul could be an excellent spokesman for that marketplace. It's a niche market, and it's one he understands well — as you only can if you grow up deaf. When he goes out to speak to that market, if he does what I'm asking him to do, he's going to be able to communicate with those people in a much stronger way than anyone else ever could. They're going to pay attention to him. He knows what to say to them that will help him connect with them at an emotional, heartfelt level. So do like I'm suggesting Paul should do. Find a market full of people you understand at a visceral level; if you can do that, you don't have to be very good at copywriting. You just have to focus on them. Marketing begins and ends with the prospect.

Let's move on to another strategy, one that took me a while to realize. It's related to a big mistake that a lot of new copywriters make. In a sense, they're trying to drive their car down the road with one foot on the gas pedal and the other on the brake; in other words, they're trying to write and re-write at the same time. I do my best copywriting as a two-part process. The first part is when I just write and don't really think about what I'm writing about. Instead, I try to think about the person I'm writing to, and what's most important to them; I try to present the benefits of the product or service that I'm selling, in such a way that they'll get enthusiastic about them, will appreciate them and find them valuable. That's all I'm thinking about, the person I'm writing to — just like when I write a letter to my mom. I don't necessarily think about what I'm writing. I love my mom, I'm thinking about her, I know what's important to her, and I just sit there and write her a letter. I don't think much about it; I just do it.

Writing and rewriting are two entirely different processes that require two entirely different frames of mind. When you're re-writing you're critical. You're looking for all the misspellings, the poor word usages. You have a critical analytical mind that's focused on details, and focused on looking for things that are wrong and things that could be improved. When you're writing, you're just writing. You're focused on the overall goal, and you just put it all out there. You can edit it later. Some of our best sales letters, the ones that have made us more money than any other sales letters, started out being 30 pages long before they were edited down to size.

The mood to write can strike at any time, but it's best to make sure you can write at a specific time every day. I've already told you how I do most of my writing: I get juiced up on coffee early in the morning. That's my only real vice: I love good coffee. Now, I'll get a buzz if I drink too much. My wife tells me to quit drinking — she says, "T.J., you've had enough coffee!" It's almost the way you'd you tell an alcoholic they've had enough booze. I usually have to drink coffee for about 90 minutes before I ever write my first real word. Oh, I'm writing little things during that time, but mostly I'm just doing other stuff. I'm reading and getting myself in the proper mental framework, preparing myself. When I do start to write, I just let it all out. I'm not critical of myself at all. I'm focused on what I'm trying to do, which is selling. *It's all about selling.* You're trying to convince people to buy by giving them the benefits of your product or service.

I do my rewriting mostly at night, because I'm tired and I'm sitting next to my wife while she watches all these dumb TV programs that I pretty much hate. But I do want to spend time with her, because I'm trying to have a happy marriage and they tell me you have to spend time with your spouse to do that. And so, she'll be sitting there on the couch and I'll be sitting right next to her pretending I'm watching the show, but I'm really just doing my editing work on my laptop. It's a relaxing thing. When I'm writing, I'm not really relaxed — I'm putting a lot of energy out there. So, one of my best suggestions is, don't try to write and re-write at the same time. It's using two different sides of your mind; it's using two different mental frameworks, and all you're going to do is make it frustrating. Not that writing isn't a little frustrating anyway, but if you try to keep these steps separate, it'll be much more enjoyable for you.

Also, you have to set regular routines. There are exceptions, but for the most part I only write at a certain time every day, and that's it. I do all my writing in the early morning. That works for me. My friend Jim Brewer writes all his stuff at one or two o'clock in the morning. You may have another time of day when it's easiest for you to write. The point is, there's that one time that's *your* time, whether it's in the morning, night, or afternoon. It's a time when your energy is highest; it's when your mind is working the best. I try to make sure I write every day during that time, because if I don't, I'm just not as effective. It's something that I like to do seven days a week, too.

Here's another tip that took me years to figure out, and I touched on it earlier. I used to look at other copywriters' work and tell myself, "Man, those guys are a hell of a lot better than

I'm ever going to be," and I'd get very discouraged. What I didn't realize at the time — and what I want you to consider deeply right now — is this: they may want you to think that they just sat down and wrote those things, but the truth is, they do what I do all the time now. They keep writing and rewriting until they just absolutely have to put the copy out to meet a deadline.

Consider a sales letter that we were working on while hosting the seminar this book is based on: it's for a $5,000 package. We want to sell a lot of them, of course; and to get somebody to give you $5,000, you have to do a lot more selling than you would to get them to give you $500. So with the letter I'm talking about, we kept trying to make it perfect. Every time we went through that sales letter, we made significant changes — though eventually, we had to stop, because we had a deadline to meet. The point I want to make to you is that somebody who doesn't know better is going to look at that letter when it comes out and they're going to say, "Man, that guy can write his butt off." And maybe they'll be intimidated, because it's a really good letter. It's powerful. But they're not going to realize that it went back and forth and back and forth and just drove me, Chris Lakey, and my assistant Keli crazy. It's grueling work.

One night recently, I worked on an order form for close to four hours, and when I went to bed, I was almost ready to send it to the graphic artist — but there was something inside me that said, "No, wait. Take one more look at it tomorrow," even though I'd just worked on it for four hours. It was a little over a page long. It started out being three pages, but then I narrowed it down and re-wrote it and re-wrote it and re-wrote it. Well, the next morning I woke up thinking, "Oh, maybe I'll find a couple things wrong with it." But you know what? I found quite a lot wrong with it, and I made even more changes to it that morning — for probably a total of five and a half hours worth of work. Five and a half hours to write a little over one page on an order form!

## RUTHLESS COPYWRITING STRATEGIES

Most people don't understand this secret. They think that somehow the copywriters who produce all the ad copy they see are just gifted somehow, and they write it all perfectly from the start. Well, there might be some of those people out there, but I ain't one of them... and I'm thinking most people aren't either. There are a lot of people out there doing just what I do all the time, every day. They write it, then they rewrite it, and then they re-write it again and they keep going over every sentence until, finally, they either run out of time or view it as perfect. They've done everything they can possibly do.

This idea of writing sales letters is funny to me, because if you're just looking at a sales letter, you might think it was written from front to back — that the writer sat down to stare at a blank screen, before all of a sudden coming up with a pre-header (that's the smaller print at the very top of the letter that goes right before the headline). And then you've got an idea for a headline, and you write that. And then there are a few words below that, and then you've got the "Dear Friend," and then you start writing the sales letter and several hours later you sign it and you write a P.S. and send it to the printer.

But that's not how most sales letters are written. Most letters are just bits and pieces thrown together in a way that makes some organizational and reading sense, and they might be written backward for all you know. The money is made in the editing, not in the writing. The first time you write, you're just dumping ideas on paper — and that's the best way to describe it. You're taking everything and anything that comes to your mind, and you're dumping it all out onto paper. I write it up on stacks of yellow legal pads, and poor Keli gets to type them up. I only get a few words down per page, because I write really big and fast, and that's really what it's all about. I freeform it, dumping it all on paper, writing anything that comes to mind. I'm thinking about the clients that I'm writing to, knowing in the back of my mind what I want the offer to look like (in general, anyhow), and I'm just writing longhand on legal pads. Maybe something else works for you — Chris Lakey is a typer. He grew up typing, so he's always done everything on a computer. Whichever way you do it, the first process is getting those ideas down; a paragraph here, a paragraph there. Maybe all of a sudden as you're writing you'll get an idea that might work for a headline, so you write that, and you make a note that it might be a good headline or a sub-head. Maybe you sit down and you write a string of bullets. You think about the prospect who'll receive your letter, you think about your product, and you think about the main benefits you want to convey to them — so maybe you spend an entire day just writing bullets down, documenting all the benefits you're offering.

When you're done with all that, you go back and try to piece it all together. You might say, "All right, this block of copy *here* would be better towards the front of the letter," and so you cut it and paste it where you want it to go. Then you look at something else and think, "Man, that would make a great P.S.," so you drop that piece down to the end of the letter. You just mix and match, cut and paste, and write new copy as you need it — because of course it's choppy at that point, so you have to bridge things together. You might say, "Hmm, these two paragraphs don't really flow that well. How can I write a new sentence between them to make them flow together?" and so you do that. It's a process of constantly patching and patching.

When I say "the money is made in the editing," what I mean is that, again, your first time through just involves dumping your ideas onto paper. It never comes out smoothly — unless you're doing it wrong. There may be some people out there who write sales letters front to back, but I don't know of any. In my opinion, the best way to do it is get those ideas out, and then edit. When you're editing you're looking for the clarity; you're looking for multiple reader paths; you're looking for all the things that make your sales letter something that makes you money. Sometimes the rewriting can take a week or two; sometimes it take a month or longer.

And let me be honest — there are times when we would never finish a sales letter were it not for deadlines. There's *always* something to change. Every time we look at a sales letter, we find something to change. Every single time. So at some point you just have to say, "I'm done. That's it. It's going to the printer." And even then, if you find out that it works, there's time to go back and edit it again for the second run. But there would be an *endless* number of things you could change. Sometimes we'll spend hours going over a letter word-by-word, sentence-by-sentence, looking for better adjectives, better ways to describe the product, more flowery language that simply sounds better. We do that line-by-line, and it's tedious work. But in the end, when someone reads your sales letter, to them it doesn't read like you did that.

I've never written a novel, but I imagine a novelist writes much the same way. They have their main story line, and they piece it together — and all of a sudden they've got it in chapters and it's all formatted and then it goes out the door. But there's always something to change. How can they make that character come alive a little bit better? How can they describe what's happening in that character's mind, and make it a little more flowery to the reader so that it's more exciting to read? We want that in our sales letters. We want them to hang on every word. We want to make each word have a maximum impact as it relates to the entire sales letter. Whether it's a four-page lead-generation sales letter or a 32-page back-end sales letter that asks for big money, we want to make sure every word counts. If you're editing sales copy and you find useless words in there, take them out. If there are words that aren't descriptive enough, change them. And if you need to add more words, just do it. You look at every phrase, every sentence, every word along the way — front to back — and that's all done in the editing process, which is what makes your letter make you money.

Here's one more tip I'd like to share in this chapter: the swipe file. That's a collection of all the so-called "junk mail" you've received. *This mail is not junk to you.* All that unsolicited bulk sales copy is like a textbook; it provides models for writing, certain ideas that you can use over and over. Now, I'm not talking about plagiarism; I'm talking about recycling ideas. I'll be writing something and I'll think, "Oh, hey, I remember this one guy, he wrote *this*," and I'll run over and check my swipe file, where I've kept a copy of that particular ad, sales letter, brochure, or whatever. I try to keep those as organized as I can, because there's a good chance I'm going to use it someday.

I might look at how he worded his guarantee, for example, or try to determine what made his headline powerful. Maybe it was just word choice, or the way he strung these emotionally charged words together that struck me as something that I really wanted to use. So I'll say, "Okay, I'm going to now take my swipe file, and I'm going to look at this headline. I'm not going to copy it verbatim; I'm not going to plagiarize it, but I'm going to try and generate the same effect." Having that swipe file full of things that you've identified as pretty good writing, going through and getting that idea, working that idea into your own... that's a powerful creative process that helps you synthesize the power, the emotion, the passion, the effect of a headline or a sub-head or even a guarantee into a great new offer.

# Chapter Three:

# Realize the Importance of Relationships

When writing copy, it's important to create the best, most grammatically correct copy you can — but you must never, ever forget that the overall effect is more important than anything else. Does it sell? Does it convert? Does it get people to take action? Does it strike a chord with someone so that they'll connect with you, so that a relationship can be built between you, as a marketer, and your prospect? That's paramount above anything else. Successful marketing requires constant and consistent relationship building.

The idea that you can have a relationship with your customers is just a concept until you actually live it; in fact, all of this stuff I'll teach you here is, really. You have to actually experience it to understand it. But one of marketing's strengths is that if you do it right, you can enjoy wonderful relationships with your customers, relationships where people feel they know you and you know them, because you *do* know a lot about them in advance. Remember, that was the first thing I told you: you don't have to be all that good, you just have to really understand your audience. As long as you're writing directly to your prospects about things that interest *them* the most, and as long as you're doing things to let them get a sense of who you are, then you're going to grab their attention. That's the basis of what I call "relationship building."

Some people take it to extremes. I'm trying to, when I tell my customers my personal story. Many of my customers know my story — and that's part of the way you develop a relationship, by just telling your story first off. You use things in your story that are common denominators with your customer's stories. You try to let them get to know you; you try to be personable. Every business should be in the business of developing relationships with their customers — whether you have a little restaurant and you want people to come back again and again, or you have a huge company that grosses a billion dollars a year. You're trying to establish bonds of trust and rapport with people. Those are strategies that you incorporate when you write copy, so you're never writing "down" to people. I know you've read stuff where the writer was writing down to you; and we've all spoken with people who spoke down to us, who weren't really trying to make a connection. These are people who are always keeping themselves at a distance, always keeping something from you. They're usually too polished, too professional.

I'm a jeans-and-T-shirt guy. That's just how I am. Sure, I could go out and buy a $5,000 suit, or get a haircut from somebody who charges hundreds of dollars an hour to snip every little hair just right. We've all been around people like that — people who are too perfect, too slick. I don't want to name him, but I have a person in mind that everyone in the marketing field knows. He always dresses in expensive suits, and every hair on his head is always perfect. He watches his words very carefully, so that when he talks to you, you get the feeling that every word was well-chosen before it ever came out of his mouth. He says all the right things. And yet, the way he delivers it, the way he presents himself... well, I don't trust the guy at all. I know that some of my colleagues feel the same way, because there's just something that's too polished about him, too perfect.

REALIZE THE IMPORTANCE OF RELATIONSHIPS

I feel that as a good copywriter, what you're trying to do is make connections with people. You can't do that if they can't relate to you. You have to win their trust. All copywriting is really selling. That's something I've said before in these pages, and yes, you're going to keep hearing that over and over. And what is salesmanship? First, it's winning people's trust before you win their money. People who don't trust you are going to be much less inclined to give you money — and most of the time they won't give you money at all. Even if they do, it'll just be token amounts; they're never going to commit to anything large. You have to first let them know that you're somebody they can trust, somebody looking out for their best interests. So you do things to build a true relationship with your customers. You're personable with people, you tell them your story, you tell them the things that you have in common with them — because common denominators are part of rapport building. After all, all friendships are built on either two things: a mutual enemy, or commonalities — things you share with someone else.

A lot of people are afraid to write in a warm, personable way. They're trying to be too careful, too perfect, too polished. In real life, those are folks we often run from or never fully trust. The same thing is true for all forms of communication with your customers. Just be yourself. Don't be afraid to tell your story; don't be afraid to show your picture. You're a real person. Don't make your copy too perfect. Oh, we talk about writing and re-writing to *try* to make it perfect, but you also need to have a likeable, humanistic element to your writing. If your copy's too polished, that part of your writing dies.

Chris Hollinger often kicks his copy up to his wife, who happens to own her own company, to proofread. Well, she's a stickler, so she changes certain words to make them more grammatical. Unfortunately, that sometimes makes them less effective. We direct-response marketers drive English teachers crazy! We violate the rules of the English language on a daily basis, because we write the way we talk. We're trying to sell, so we try to do things to build relationships. If people don't feel they can trust you, they're not going to re-buy, so you have to write in a way that makes things feel personal to them.

Here's an example. As of this writing, I've got almost two weeks invested in a 20-page sales letter. The problem with this letter is that it's been rewritten so many times that it's almost *too* careful. So what I've done is had the graphic artist put all these handwritten comments — hand marks, I call them — throughout the letter using a big, black magic marker to make it look more like it was just done off the cuff, and less like it was written carefully over a two-week period. And we're trying to make it more personal, so we're personalizing every page. The letter has the person's name at the top of every page, and on the P.S. it mentions their name specifically. We're paying extra money to have it done that way — thank goodness for modern technology! When the customer gets this letter — a 20-page letter with their name on every page, with hand marks all throughout it, with their name on the order form — they're going to feel like it was written *just for them*.

That's just one example of relationship building. There are many, many more. Here's the gist of it: don't be afraid to tell your story. Don't be afraid to get personable with people. Don't worry about being perfect. People will forgive you for a lot of things, as long as they feel you're looking out for their best interests, and as long as they feel they can trust you. We forgive our friends all the time — and what you want to do is create friendships with your customers. I know that that's just a concept for you right now, but it's a reality for the marketers who make the most money. Think about the relationships that you've had in your lives: what made them good, what made them great, what made them crumble, or what kept them from growing — whether those relationships were romantic, friendships, or family. The same principles apply to all. The easiest way to connect with someone is to be open and honest, to be yourself. Be willing to go ahead and open up to your prospects, to your customers — because it does turn to dollars.

Look at network marketing in particular: it's a multi-billion dollar industry built on one simple concept — relationships. How many companies say, "Okay, all you have to do is go get three of your friends or family in on this?" They're building their fortunes on the backs of other people's relationships. Well, if you're using the right copywriting techniques, what you're doing instead of exploiting personal relationships is going out there and building new professional relationships with people, getting to know them through your copywriting. They're getting to know us, too. There's got to be a give and take — and that happens within a framework that we, as marketers, can control through the copy we produce for our prospects. Of course, it could involve more — it could be popcorn, or cookies. Food's a great relationship builder!

However you do it, you need to find ways to make your business relationships "sticky," so your customers never want to leave. Serve them well, help them be more successful, so they keep coming back for more and more. Chris Hollinger reminded me recently of a seminar we did up in Hillsboro, Kansas, at Tabor College, where two marketers did a very good job of making their sales stick — because they had an ongoing continuity program where people were paying a considerable amount of money every month for their services. They would take a nice chunk of that money and put it back into food, into gifts, into good quality information that they were feeding back to their customers, because they wanted to keep those customers paying that big chunk of change every single month. That all goes to building relationships and being creative. And here's the neat thing about it: most marketers don't even think about making their sales sticky!

Why is that so neat? Because it leaves you an opening to steal their customers away! That may sound ruthless, sure, but that's what good marketing is all about: capturing a significant part of the existing market share. Most people don't even think about doing creative things to make their sales stick. So if you just go out and spend $200 on a bunch of popcorn and sent it to your customers, then a month later maybe your customers are sitting there and they're thinking, "Okay, I could go to XYZ for this item... or I could go there. Well, this guy sent me popcorn; I'm going to go there!" It's just human nature, and it's things like that that will get you ahead, because so many of these other businessmen and entrepreneurs are out there acting as part of that caribou herd, just doing what everybody else does. All you did was send someone some popcorn!

Now, I want to talk a little bit more about making sure you're not too perfect. None of us is perfect — though we feel bad when we're not. If we could just all be real, the world would probably be a lot better place, and that's true in marketing, too. Just be yourself. If you look too perfect, people will think something's not right.

Chris Lakey recently bought a car on eBay from a dealership in another city. It just so happened that he had a friend who lived in that city, so he asked this friend to go look at it for him. Chris got a report back that said, "Well, it's a nice-looking car." It's a little older and has a lot of miles on it, so Chris was concerned about it. If it was brand new he wouldn't think twice, but it's a well-used 2002 Suburban, so he wanted to make sure that the pictures he saw online matched what he saw when he was actually there looking at it. So his friend emails him and says, "It looks nice. It looks real clean. There are some scratches on it," which you'd expect. Nothing major, but this

40

guy also said, "When I looked at the engine, it looked really clean." He was concerned that this meant maybe something was wrong. Was the engine new? Had it been replaced recently? The engine was too clean, and in his mind, that was a concern — because it looked too perfect.

I think people in general have that perception. If something looks too good, if it looks too perfect, they question it. Whereas if there are some flaws, if things look rough around the edges, it looks real. People believe it because it seems more authentic. It's just like if you have a relationship with someone, and they seem like a goody-goody perfect person... well, something's wrong with that picture, because no one is perfect. If someone seems too glossy, too slick, you're less likely to trust them. People think that way of your sales letters, too. If your copy looks too perfect, then they don't trust it.

Now, you can do things to make your sales letter look what we call "dirty." Earlier, I told you about a letter we're creating that has handwriting throughout. By putting handwriting on it, it looks dirty — that is, it just doesn't look as polished. You can also use different sizes and types of fonts. You can have some stuff in smaller print, and some in giant print. Some writers have even gone so far as to make their copy actually look a little dirty... like the paper doesn't look clean and sharp. I happen to think that's going too far, but the point is, people do it. Some people even put typos in there on purpose, because a typo makes it seem like it was written by a real person — by someone who pounded it out on the computer in a state of excitement and sent it out immediately. Having a typo in your letter makes it look more recent. It looks like you wrote the letter, put it on the press, and sent it right out.

Using improper English is a big way to make your sales copy look more real, more immediate. Now, English teachers and others who are super-critical about writing are going to look at your sales letter, and they'll either do what my stepmom did to my original *Dialing for Dollars* book or they'll *edit it for you.* We've had people actually send back sales letters with red ink all over them, like they were proofreading for us! But most people won't do that. You want your letter to read like people think, and like they speak. They speak differently than they write, if they're writing proper English. So forget all the English rules and "dirty it up" a little, so when people are sitting there with your letter in their hand and reading through it, it sounds like they're hearing you speak to them.

You don't want it to sound like you wrote a proper English paper. It should sound like they're reading it as if they would *speak* it. One of the ways you can help with that is to actually read your sales letter out loud, and have someone else sit there and listen to it. Or have someone else read it, and listen to it yourself. Does it sound like something you'd hear yourself say? If it doesn't, change it. If it *does* sound like you would say it aloud, then you know you're on the right track. Some people actually dictate their sales letters onto tape or a CD and then transcribe them, because the way you talk is simply different from the way you write. You want people to read your sales letter and hear it in their minds as if it were something you were saying, because it comes across better in their mind. So don't be too perfect, because perfection is never real. People are more likely to trust something that seems authentic, even if it's not perfect. That's one of the reasons I fell in love with my wife 21 years ago: She's just an extremely real person. She doesn't B.S. in any way, shape, or form. She tells the truth, no matter how much it hurts.

And that's a good thing to do with your copywriting, because you need to keep in mind how skeptical people are these days. A big mistake many copywriters make is that they fall so much in love with whatever it is they're writing about that they have the delusion that other people are naturally going to fall in love with it, too. Nothing could be further from the truth. People are very skeptical, even if they don't express it. It's an unconscious thing for most, but we're all holding back. All of us are. Every time you see a claim, you're wondering in the back of your mind, "Can I really trust that person?"

Because people are always skeptical, you need to write to that skepticism. Assume that when you're writing copy, you're writing to the most skeptical person on the planet. You can't just accept they're going to believe anything that you say. You have to try to remember that, and use the strategies I'll teach you in this book to help get around that natural skepticism. I'll go into that in more detail in later chapters.

I'll wrap up this one with an old quote, well worth repeating: "In the land of the blind, the one-eyed man is king." You don't have to be perfect; you just have to be a little better than everybody else.

# CHAPTER FOUR

# Hone Your Salesmanship

Copywriting is nothing more than salesmanship, as I've already mentioned several times. And what is salesmanship, if you really think about it? It's the ability to present your products and services well, and to get people to exchange their money for them. The best copywriters are the best salespeople. They're people who know how to present their products, who know how to convince their prospects that what they have to offer is worth more than the money they're asking for in exchange. That's salesmanship in general — you're asking people to give you their money. Well, they worked hard for that money, and they're not going to just give it up that readily, especially in trying economic times. People always tighten up on their spending during hard times.

So you're always looking for effective ways to make offers to people. That's what we sell, really — we don't necessarily sell products and services. What we sell are *offers*. And what is an offer? It's all the things that you do to package up whatever you sell in an attractive way, to help get people to make that buying decision. Here's an example: there's a man named Mike who attended the workshop this book was adapted from. One of the things he does is make wonderful soy candles, made from agricultural products grown right here on American soil. I bought a hundred dollars' worth a few months before the workshop, and just before he came down, he emailed me and said, "Hey, T.J., do you want some more candles?" Well, I still hadn't used the ones I had yet, so I said, "No, I'm good. Thank you."

But Mike's a salesman, and as a salesman, he wasn't going to take no for an answer. So a couple days later he came back at me with this other idea. He said, "Hey, T.J., I know how you always give out free popcorn to your customers in order to make them feel appreciated and to let them know how important they are." He said, "I'm coming down here to this seminar. Why don't I just make up a little candle that you can give to each and every person, to let them know just how much you appreciate them. You're already doing it with popcorn; why not do it with one of these healthy soy candles that I personally will make for each and everybody at the seminar?"

It was an offer! He made me an offer! I already liked him, and I was already sold on the soy candles. And then he made me an offer, and he wasn't going to take no for an answer. So I said yes. Something tells me that if I would have said, "Oh, Mike, that's a good idea... but no, thank you," a couple days later he would have found a new way to come at me with something a little bit different, and he would have kept bugging me and bugging me until finally I said, "Oh, why not. Let's give everybody a good healthy all-American soy candle." I think Mike's case is great example, a perfect illustration of the things that salesmanship is all about.

Remember, the copy you write isn't nearly as important as the strategies that you use. And one of those strategies is that you've got to stay on top of people until they buy. You've got to keep going after them again and again. New marketers often make the mistake of thinking that just because somebody doesn't buy the first time they send them the stuff, or the second time, or the third time, or the fourth time, then that somehow means they're not interested and they're never going to buy.

Nothing could be further from the truth. It all starts with a qualified prospect, of course — nothing can replace that. You have to find somebody who really wants what it is that you sell. As long as you have a prospective buyer you know is serious and they really do want what you offer, you've got a good chance to sell to them eventually — even if it takes a while. As long as they're very qualified, you can keep trying. Sometimes it takes as many as 15 tries — so you keep coming at them again and again.

But let me caution you here: Don't come at them in such a way that you're bothering them too much. The best approach is to be altruistic in your approach. Try to express the benefits; try to show them a self-serving advantage. That's what Mike did for me. He tried to show me the advantage, using an argument I found hard to say no to. And he gave me a good price, because price is important.

Salesmanship is a subject that a lot of people know about, but few have ever given much thought. That is, they've never tried to actively apply it to their lives and businesses, though they know it's there. Worse, some salespeople aren't really salespeople at all; they're really criminals, con men. A few bad apples have poisoned the whole batch for us. For this reason, a lot of people have the wrong idea about what salesmanship is, because they've fallen afoul of cons who claim they're salespeople, but don't care one bit about their product or the people they're selling it to. They couldn't care less about trying to deliver things that are of real value. All they're trying to do is get your money.

Consequently, the whole art of salesmanship has largely been ignored. People haven't focused on it. Nobody wants to be a salesman! Why be a salesman, when the whole concept is that you've got to be some cold-hearted, manipulative, greedy jerk? And just because the title of this book is *Ruthless Copywriting*

# RUTHLESS COPYWRITING STRATEGIES

*Strategies*, don't think that I'm advocating treating your customers badly. Being a ruthless marketer is more about just being aggressive — "ruthless" just sounds better. We chose that word because it paints a different word picture than "aggressive." If you're being truly ruthless to anyone, it's to your competitors, not your customers.

As long as you've got a product or service that people can benefit from, as long as what you're selling really *does* have value that delivers on the promises that you make, and as long as you're targeting a qualified prospect who really wants what it is you're offering, then in some ways, you're doing them a disservice by *not* doing everything possible to make that sale. You really have to put yourself in that mindset. You have to convince yourself first that what I just said is true, and then you develop the strategies necessary to aggressively go out there and make as many sales as you can. And you use strategies that let you multiply salesmanship.

Earlier in this book, I discussed a letter that I've been reworking for a month; and as of this writing, I'm probably going to work on it for another month. It's a powerful sales letter. Once it's done, we're going to blast it out there to as many people as we can, using as many different media as we can. In this case we're going to use it in print form, and we're going to post it on a website that Chris Lakey's building. So it's salesmanship multiplied to reach as many people as possible, to make as many sales as possible. But here's a question you may be asking yourself: "With something like this, how do you know when to stop before you alienate your prospects?" That's a great question, one I've asked myself and my teachers plenty of times. The thing is, *everybody* is worried about going too far. Everybody! How far is too far? The short answer is that you have to let the numbers tell you what to do. As long as you're still getting sales, then you haven't alienated your prospects; you haven't gone too far. You may not have gone far enough!

It all starts with two-step marketing, which is a very simple, fast way to qualify prospects and *know* that they're qualified. In the first step, you get them to raise their hands and express an interest in what you're offering. They prove to you through that action that they're serious, that they really do want what it is that you sell. This first step can involve a small sale, so they're not just raising their hand saying "Send me your free stuff" — because sometimes people who send away for free stuff aren't qualified at all.

From that point forward, you have to watch your numbers and let them tell you what to do. Let's say, for instance, that I mail out 10,000 postcards to get people to take that first step to prove they're qualified. Suppose I get 400 prospects who say, "Yes, send it to me." They're showing me they're serious, that they want the offer I put out there in those 10,000 postcards. Now I'll go after them on a sequential mailing system, where I continue to follow up on that initial offer. If I get people calling me up and saying, "Hey, quit sending me all that stuff," then I've got to take a look at the numbers and see what they tell me. It may be that no matter how angry these people are, I find that every time I mail to that group of 400 people, I'm getting more and more sales. If that's the case, you ignore the angry people. Part of being a ruthless marketer is that you listen to the people who are giving you money — and you don't necessarily listen to those who aren't.

You have to be willing to take a little criticism and you have to be willing, as long as you're making good money, to keep going out there and keep applying the pressure. You don't have to apply that pressure in a negative way, though. You don't have to be pushy. You can be altruistic in nature; and when I say "altruistic," what I'm talking about is a situation where you're really trying to serve people. That's one of my definitions for selling, by the way. Selling is serving. You're trying to help people; you're trying to give them something that will benefit them.

Mike might have seemed a little pushy if, every time I said, "No, Mike. No thank you," he came at me two or three days later with a different offer. But he would have kept coming at me with a way of showing me why it was in my best interests to go ahead and write him a check and have him make these candles. He would have kept coming at me knowing what's important to me, which is keeping my clients happy. He would have kept coming at me saying, "Hey, I'm not trying to sell you anything, T.J. I'm just trying to help you get something that's important to you." You have to keep coming at people with that angle — and you have to be willing to have some people get angry with you. If you're going to maximize your profit, you have to be a little thick-skinned. As long as the numbers are still good and holding out, just take the complainers off your mailing list and keep mailing to the rest of those people.

I've mentioned many times in my other publications and workshops that the people you chase off this way are probably the people who aren't going to buy your item in the first place. That's a good point that I believe I should re-emphasize here. From the standpoint of marketing and business, there are just two types of people: those who count and those who don't, and you've got to be able to separate the two. If someone's not giving you money, if they're complaining and giving you nothing but trouble, then they don't count. Now, if you've got a bunch of good customers who are complaining, then you've better wise up!

One thing that took me a little time to learn early on was the whole follow-up thing. I'd write a sales letter and launch it out there and maybe get some sales. But I hadn't learned the whole art of the follow-up and the sequential mailing. Following up on interested prospects and on completed sales is vitally important.

When we're talking about copywriting, we're talking about space ads, we're talking about classified ads, and we're talking about sales letters. But a good part of the copywriting you need to do in your business involves following up with prospects who have identified themselves as serious by raising their hands and saying, "Okay, send me the packet" — especially if that packet cost money. That's how you know you've got a real, seriously qualified prospect in this business. When you get a whole list of people who've sent you money, that's a pretty serious list. You need to spend some money to focus in on those people, and try to generate as many sales as possible. You do that with a follow-up campaign. I usually do it with direct mail; my colleague Chris Hollinger uses email. If he has a list of email addresses, or a phone blast to drive them to, maybe, he uses a conference call that he's got planned — anything he can do to get people to raise their hands and respond to his offer.

Chris tells me that one thing he did early on in his business — something he learned the hard way about — was blasting out more mail pieces than was prudent all at once. We've all done that. What you should so is test that mail piece first before spending a whole bunch of money on printing and postage. I've been guilty of this myself; I've sent something out there and the sales weren't where I wanted them to be, and I was like, "Crap, that was a bad list!" Actually, it very well could have been my poor copy! Or it could have been a lot of different variables. The point is that I gave up and moved on to something else, where maybe what I should have done was tested more carefully, and tailored my primary offer to results of that test. All that matters is results. If you don't get the results you want, then take a really close look at your copywriting and at the systems you had in place. What can you change to produce more sales? That's what testing is all about. Not only does it save you a lot of money, but it also helps you refine your approach to converting those sales, because in the end it doesn't matter how big a prospect you have. The only thing that matters is conversion: How much money you make versus how much you spend.

If you're smart, you'll test. I've lost a lot of money by not testing. Sometimes I get an idea and I'm all excited about it and I'm so confident it'll work that I think I don't have to test — I just throw it out there. And it sinks, despite my false sense of confidence. Remember, just because you're crazy about it doesn't mean that the people you're presenting it to are going to be crazy about it. It's easy to get caught up in your own hype.

Earlier, I mentioned two-step marketing as a way to really qualify folks. With direct mail, you can do that with mailing lists. There are hundreds of lists out there that you can rent. When you're researching those, you can usually find a little synopsis that will tell you about a particular list you're interested to try. Are those the prospects you think would respond well to your offer? If you think so, then you design that sales piece and you test it and get people to raise their hand and say, "Okay, yeah, I want to know more." You're basically sifting and sorting, paring that big list down to the people who have identified themselves as those who want to hear what you have to offer. Once you've done that, you're able to spend more money on that smaller group to convert sales.

There's no better way to make money than two-step marketing, where the first step is *always* to get people to take a smaller, simple action. People have sales resistance. Remember, everybody is skeptical; I talked about that in the previous chapter. We're all careful; we're all cautious, and we should be. We know that if we're not, we're going to get taken advantage of. You never really know people. No matter how hard you try, there will always be some people that you just can't read. So skepticism is necessary, and you should always expect it. In a perfect world, if it weren't for skepticism, you could just go to a cold prospect — somebody who's never done business with you — and sell them something for thousands of dollars right out of the gate. But because few people are that trusting, we have to use two-step marketing as one of our strategies to separate the smaller group of the people who are qualified and interested in what we have to offer from the larger group that isn't. It costs money to do that. You've got to advertise, and you've got to do something to get people to take that first step. There's always going to be some expense there; but once you get that smaller group defined, you're able to tailor your offers to them in ways that make you money.

Now your whole strategy is to spend even more money per person, though less overall, of course, because the list now is so much smaller. That smaller group of people has proven worthy of your attention. They've proven that they're serious. Now you can afford to go after them in a more assertive way, and you can try to do everything possible to make the largest number of sales to that group. It's a great strategy; not only is it the most proven way to make money, it's also the safest way. As long as you never try to make people do too much too fast, you're guaranteed a profit.

Consider one of our current offers (current as I write this, anyway). We start with a $39 sale as our first step; we're not just giving away free information. Then, on the back-end, we offer them a $495 package. So we take the people who give us the $39, and we immediately up-sell them on a $495 package that's very closely related to the $39 package. It's a natural up-sell; it's a perfect fit, because it was designed that way. Then, from that $495 sale we've got a multitude of other items that we offer to that smaller group. Once someone has given us $495, we know that they're very serious. The question of whether they're qualified or not goes right out the door. You still have to wonder at $39, of course, because $39 isn't a lot of money. But $495... that's a lot of money to most people. When they give you hundreds of dollars, what they're really telling you is, "I'm serious about what it is that you offer." So you have to have more things to offer to those people. You may not be able to go from $39 to $3,900 in one step (though sometimes you can), but you can stair-step your prospects from one price up the ladder to more profitable products and packages.

Two-step marketing really is the best way to make sure you're spending your money in the right place. It's tough to try to make a cold sale to people who have never met you before or don't trust you, even if you're using a list that you're already familiar with. If you'll first get them to raise their hand and say they're interested, you've got a much better opportunity to turn that lead into a sale. Send them a short letter and tell them that you've got something exciting to show them and you want them to request it; maybe for free, maybe for $5, maybe for $39. By making them do something, they've expressed an interest. Once they respond, they can find out the whole story.

Not only does this qualify them, it gives you a chance to talk to them as someone who has requested information. You can be more firm with them. You can say, "Hey, I'm sending you this because you requested it." When you do follow-ups with them, you can remind them that you're only communicating with them because they *asked* that you communicate with them. This gives you a stronger position to approach them from, to try to get them to convert from a lead to a sale. It puts you at an advantage over them.

Now, I want to point out that you don't need to get hung up on the idea of two-step, because it really could be five-step marketing, or six-step marketing, or ten-step! Again, that's the whole secret. Consider the restaurant business; that's my best example. Now, if you're one of my frequent customers or have ever heard me talk in public, I'm sure you're sick of me talking about the restaurant business, because I always do it; but it's a damn good example. If you've got a little restaurant — a business all of us can understand, because we all have our favorite restaurant — your goal is to get people to come back again and again, to keep sitting in the same seat they sat in last time. In some bars, they have one bar stool that's reserved for just that one person. A good restaurant's the same way. The idea is to get you to keep coming back. You understand how that works in a restaurant business.

What you also have to understand is, that's exactly how things should work in *every single business*. If you want to make the most money, that's how it *has* to work in your business! So, it's not just two-step marketing; it could be 222-step marketing. The idea is to get people to come to you to show that they're serious, and then your job is to do everything possible to develop relationships with those people and to provide additional products and services that give them more of the things you know that they're interested in. Get them to keep coming back again and again, helping them to get more of what they want — so that you, in turn, get more of what *you* want.

You can take these copywriting and marketing skills and directly translate them into any business that you want to be successful with. Maybe it's the restaurant business; maybe it's the plumbing business. A plumber could start by applying a strategy to target a specific area of a town, simply because the gas prices are so high that he doesn't want his vans and service people having to travel all over the city. Maybe it's an affluent area of town that he specifically wants to go after. He wants to concentrate his marketing in this one area, and he wants to get as many of the people as possible in this one area of town to be his customers. He's applying a specific strategy he's devised to do

RUTHLESS COPYWRITING STRATEGIES

that, whether it's through mailers, or his ad in the Yellow Pages, or emails, or little refrigerator magnets — or whatever else he can think of. Now, once he gets that established and he's got that area locked up, he's forced his competitors to be the ones who have to spend the money and gas to drive all over town to do their business, whereas he's right there.

The point is, you can apply the strategies and direct-response marketing to any business. But it's something that, as I mentioned earlier, many businesspeople and entrepreneurs *aren't* doing. They're not using the kinds of headline writing and copywriting and marketing that I'm teaching you here to develop a selling system — because ultimately, that's what we're talking about. We're talking about a *selling* system. Whether it's a lead-generation sales letter, a follow-up offer, a Yellow Pages ad, or a space ad in the local newspaper — it's all part of your system for selling. Once you have a system for selling, it takes a lot of the guesswork out of making money. If you don't have that system for selling, then you're at the mercy of your customers' system for buying — if they have one. Even if they do, they'll buy things haphazardly, sporadically, only when they're really in the need for whatever they're looking for.

If any business is having sales problems, the answers to those problems can be found in their selling system. How effective their selling system is has a lot to do with overcoming sales resistance, as I've mentioned, because people are skeptical and don't want to be sold. Some companies use very manipulative, aggressive ways to sell you their products. For example, consider vacuum-cleaner salesmen — or better yet, people who sell water-purification treatments. These are some pretty savvy marketers, and I've had the pleasure of having them in my front room of my house, where I'm sitting there and actually taking notes on their system of selling, and what pressures they're putting on me. One of the pressures they use is fear. They have this little chemistry set they carry with them, and they'll take your water right out of the tap and add these chemicals to it. You see all that stuff start popping out of your water, and you're like, "Oh, I don't want to drink that!" That's their system; they want to scare you into buying this high-dollar water purification system... and it works for them! If they get in your house, they know they have a system that closes sales. The numbers tell them if they can do enough prospecting to get in front of enough people, they're going to make sales, because their selling system works.

So a good, solid marketing system solves your sales problems. Even better, a good, solid marketing system can be systemized to the point where it can be actually automatic. It contains, first of all, something that got them to raise their hand the first time. With our current promotion, we ask for $39 in exchange for a package that we promise to deliver to them on a particular subject matter, which has to do with the recession and the nature of our economy, and all the associated things they're worried about. Once they buy, we have an automatic back-end up-sell that goes out to them immediately, trying to make that $495 sale. This is all brand new; we're just developing it right now. But based on other models we've developed in the past, the people who don't give us that $495 and take that up-sell right away will receive a series of postcards and phone blasts trying to make the sale. Maybe we'll do another tele-seminar for them. Those people who give us the $495 will receive a series of sales letters and postcards and other attempts to get them to move to a higher level with us and buy our additional higher-dollar products and services. We'll just keep doing anything and everything we can possibly think of until the numbers tell us that people just aren't buying, that we've already taken as much of the profitable business out of that list as we possibly can.

This is how marketers think. I'm not trying to reduce this to absolutes, but at some level it's all about the numbers. It's also about the people, of course, but you keep have to following up and following up and following up. We create this marketing system once, and from that point forward it becomes automatic and systematic. Felicia Crosby, our shipping manager, keeps all this organized. She knows that if it's Follow-up Letter #7, it's got to go out to *this* group on *this* day. All Chris Lakey and I had to do was design it once, and it becomes salesmanship multiplied. It works for us automatically.

This promotion could last a year or two, so that for a couple years we might have thousands of people sending us the $39. And then hundreds of those people might send us the $495, followed by five or ten follow-up offers until it stops being profitable. This organized, systematized marketing system is designed to do one thing, which is to sell. It's all about salesmanship, and the best salespeople are the ones who are the most aggressive. There was a book written by Zig Ziglar's brother called *Timid Salespeople Raise Skinny Kids*. You don't want your kids to be skinny, do you? Of course not. Salesmanship is all about the person who's the most aggressive, the most assertive, the one who won't let you go — the one who keeps bugging you until finally you say, "Okay, Mike, I'm sold. Bring the candles, and we'll give one out to everybody."

CHAPTER FIVE:

# Develop Your Own Writing Routine and Style

To be an effective copywriter, you have to develop a writing routine — and then you have to stick to it, just like you'd stick to an exercise program or any other form of discipline if you wanted it to be effective. Make your writing routine a part of your lifestyle, because it's the one common denominator that all the best copywriters have. The thing is, no one can determine what routine works best for you except you.

Writing is a personal thing. Nobody writes the same way; everybody has different habits, large and small. Your writing is an extension of who you are, so you should experiment with many different ways until you find what's comfortable for you. Once you do find what works best, my best advice is to set it in stone. Every day, at that particular time, you *must* write new copy. At M.O.R.E., Inc., we try to have about four or five sales letters going at one time. Part of the reason is because we get bored of working on the same things all the time, so we try to have different projects available to work on. This helps fight the boredom a little. But boredom or not, the copywriting has to be a part of your schedule every day. You have to find a "best time of the day" that serves you best; not just the writing part of it, but also the editing part of it. I treat it almost as a religious ritual that I perform every single day.

Discipline yourself to do this. None of this will come easily to you if you're not already a writer who does it on a daily basis. It's a skill-set, and by its very nature a skill-set is something that has to be developed. But it's also something that's fun, creative, challenging, stimulating. It's a beautiful thing... but it also can be a lot of work sometimes. I don't want to paint an unrealistic picture for you. It's challenging, which means that it's frustrating occasionally, and can be difficult at times, too. So anybody who tells you it's not any of those things isn't telling you the whole story — and I don't want to be like that. Yes, there *are* times when you're going to be frustrated. It's going to be somewhat challenging. When you run into those times, there are models that you can work from to get you through, particularly the copy of people whose work you admire. Remember what I said earlier about swipe files? This is where they come in handy.

Chris Lakey was talking to his son the other day after school, about why he needs to learn cursive handwriting. And Chris thought to himself, "You know, I don't think I've ever used cursive." Chris hates writing in cursive; as he puts it, his handwriting is a mishmash of all the ways he learned to write, and it's barely readable even to him. And let's get real — is there any practical purpose for writing in cursive anymore? Yet it's important to learn it, because it teaches discipline. If you're disciplined enough to learn to write in cursive, then that helps you in other areas of life, simply because you're learning discipline. You don't really *need* to learn how to write in cursive these days — it just teaches discipline. I think that's what having your own copywriting style and sticking to it is about.

Earlier, I talked about making sure you write at the same time every day. A lot of these strategies I'll discuss in this book really come down to being disciplined. I get up every morning and drink a pot of coffee before I start writing; that's part of my style, part of my discipline. I write everything out on legal pads first — longhand — and then I have it typed for me, and I edit it from there. It's the system that I've developed. It means that I have a system in place that helps me be disciplined enough to keep writing every day. Maybe a discipline for you would be to write so many words or pages per day, or write for so many hours. Maybe, for starters, it's just 30 minutes. If you don't have a lot of time you could say, "Well, I'll devote 30 minutes every day — from *this* time to *this* time — to writing. I'll learn to write sales copy by spending 30 minutes a day writing sales letters or writing ads." It doesn't matter exactly what that discipline is. Does it matter whether you get up every morning and write at 5:00 AM, while someone else does it better at 10:00 PM? No. Both of you could be excellent copywriters. It's not the actual time you write, or even necessarily how much time you spend at it. What's important is being disciplined, and what that gets you.

Let's take a look at personal style. Style is something I liken to a movie producer, or maybe a fiction writer. Each has a style. When you see a movie made by a certain producer, you can peg it. You say, "Oh, I can tell that's a Spielberg movie," or whatever, because you know their style and that their movies tend to have the same flow; the feel is similar from one movie to another. A fiction writer sometimes can have the same thing; for example, John Grisham writes legal thrillers, and there's a certain style there. You, as a copywriter, can also have a certain style.

Many marketers produce newsletters that have a certain feel to them. They've got a noticeable writing style, and people get used to that. Having a discernable style is important, because it helps people get comfortable with you. They get to where they know and like your style, and that's one reason why they do business with you. So continuing to write in that style becomes important; it can be a benefit to you from the relationship-building perspective.

Having said that, one thing that you can do to start on your road to becoming a better copywriter is to find some really good sales letters and copy them out in your own hand. As you go through this exercise, as you're actually physically writing out each word, you start to think about the elements that made this particular piece of copy good. This gives both your muscle memory and your brain time to absorb the strategies and concepts that went into developing a particular sales piece.

For example, you may see a huge headline in 38- or 42-point type and ask yourself, "What emotions is that headline stirring in me personally? Why is it such a big headline? What's it saying? How is it saying it?" Do that enough times, and things are going to come together for you. Connections are going to be made in your mind as to how you can then go back and write your own copy and innately incorporate the elements that you've learned from somebody else's writing. Because you took the time and were disciplined enough to do that, the exercise in and of itself is the reward — because there will be things your mind absorbs that you don't even know you're learning as you're copying. It's an exercise in discipline, because who really wants to copy something in their own hand, over and over? It takes some work to do that. But this is work that eventually puts money in your pocket — heaping piles of mailbox money.

Is it worth it to spend that time? Of course it is. Do you want to do it? Is it hard? Yeah, it's hard. Chris Hollinger used to be a basketball player and coach. But every time the season would start, season after season, from Bitty Ball all the way through grade school and college, he was always out of shape at the start of the season. He didn't want to do what it took to be in shape at the start of the season, without the coach there, pushing him and his teammates to get in shape for that first game. None of it was fun, but they were better for it.

I've read a couple of books on Oliver Stone's filmmaking.

In one of the books, they interviewed Michael Douglas about the movie *Wall Street*. Douglas said that Oliver Stone made his life a living nightmare for almost four months, because he kept making him re-shoot shots over and over. He would give his best performance and Oliver would say, "That's terrible. That sucks. Re-shoot that." He made Michael Douglas' life a nightmare for four months, re-shooting shot after shot after shot. He was so glad when that four-month period was over; he said, "I hate this guy. I hate him!" Then he won an Academy Award for his role in that movie. And as he got up to collect his Academy Award, he told the story about how Oliver Stone just drove him crazy for four months and made his life a living hell by making him re-shoot all these scenes over and over again... but they got it *right*. That's the good thing about discipline.

As an entrepreneur, when it's your business and your butt on the line, can you get motivated to be disciplined enough to do the kinds of things that you *need* to do, to improve yourself so that your bottom line improves? The answer had better be yes.

This is how I feel about discipline: It never feels good as you're doing it. But it always feels good afterwards, once you've paid the price and profited from it. There's some discipline involved in writing; all the writing teachers will tell you that. It does require routine. That strategy I told you earlier, where you repeatedly write the same good ad over and over again until you internalize it? The famous Gary Halbert wrote about that in his newsletter 15 years ago. When I did it I chose Joe Carbo's "Lazy Man's to Riches" ad, which is a full-page ad that made Joe millions and millions of dollars. I knew it was a proven ad, so every morning for 45 days in a row, I spent a little less than an hour just re-writing that whole ad, word for word. I did that every single morning until I could almost do the whole thing by memory. And what I found was, there's a language to it all. There's a rhythm to good advertising. I see similar metaphors in the music world. If you study the lives of some musicians, you'll find that no matter how famous they got, no matter when they ultimately achieved their fame and fortune, they all started out by playing other people's songs first. First they learned how to play the Beatles songs, or the Rolling Stones songs, or the other popular songs of the day on the radio. They learned the chords, they learned how to play other people's songs, and then slowly, over a period of time, they developed their own style.

When I took drum lessons 27 years ago, the very first day the drum teacher showed me this drum pattern to play and recorded it for me. He showed me exactly what to do and then he said, "Look, I want you back here one week from today. Every day I want you to practice for at least an hour, just playing this little drum pattern. Every single day, try to match what I just did, what I showed you how to do. You can call me if you have problems during the week." So I called him every day! I could never do what he tried to show me, but he just kept encouraging me, saying, "Just keep going... keep going... keep going."

Eventually, months later, I told him, "You know, Keith, I never *have* been able to play that pattern." And he replied, "Well, I knew you never would be able to play it, because it was a little too advanced." As it turned out, it took him years to learn how to play that pattern himself! He said, "But through the process of *trying* to play it, I knew you'd develop something that was your own, that was based on something sort of like that." And sure enough, that's still the only drum pattern I can really play 27 years later. It never did sound like it sounded with him — but it's my own style.

Good writers have their own style. We used to have a freelancer who did a bunch of work for us before I was good enough to do my own new-customer acquisition, which is the hard part of our business. This freelancer copywriter out of Denton, Texas wrote the same sales letter over and over again.

That's all he did his entire career (he's retired now). You could take a hundred sales letters, where just 10 were his, and put them up on the wall — and if you knew him at all, you could walk along and say, "That's Luther's. That's Luther's letter. That's his letter. That's his letter." He just kept re-writing the same sales letter over and over again. Now, his sales letters all worked. They all produced profits, and that's really the only thing that counts in the end. But he had his own style; he had his own way of writing. It's something that anyone can achieve, but it does take time, work, effort, energy — and that's the bad news. You get it through daily routine.

That's one reason I want you to get rid of the words "junk mail." It's true that some of the stuff you'll get really is junk mail; some of it's not well-written, and it doesn't look good. But a lot of what some people call junk mail is treasured by us copywriters, and we save it in our collections. One of the best compliments anybody ever gave me was when I met this famous marketer in Jacksonville, Florida, in 2002. I'd never met him before. He came up to me, shook my hand, and he said, "I've got a whole box at home with just your stuff in it." That's the ultimate, supreme compliment a copywriter can get. We save back the well-written sales copy because we look at it, we study it, and we get ideas from it. If you look at enough of it, you'll get an eye for what's good and bad. It's just like my printer, Steve, is with stuff in his field. He can look at any piece of printing and he can say, "Oh, this is terrible. This is just terrible." Whereas we might look at it and we say, "Hey, it's not terrible. It looks pretty good to me." And he says, "No, no... look at this, and look at this, and look at the fuzzy lines over here. Man, that's not right. And look what they did there." He has a trained eye, and that enables him to see things that a person who's not in the business can't see. It's the same thing with good copywriting. If you read enough sales letters, you'll see the same ideas over and over, the same themes, the same language — and that's a good thing, because you realize that it really *is* simple.

I drink a lot of coffee in the morning when I'm writing. I have one brand that I really like. I've tried others, but this is the one that really works for me. I know just how to make it, and just how much of it to drink, and I get that good caffeine buzz. After about 90 minutes of drinking coffee, I'm ready to start writing. I grab the legal pads and start writing as fast as I can. I know what I'm going to write about and I know the general ideas, but I don't think about it too hard in advance. That's where I take a page from Neil Young, one of my favorite musicians. He's written five or six hundred songs, and he says, "When you think, you stink." What he means is what I said in an earlier chapter, when I told you that you needed to view writing as two separate processes.

Process one is where you just write and don't edit. You just don't even think; you just let it all out. That's what I do. I drink my favorite coffee, I grab my favorite legal pad and my favorite pen, and I start writing as much as I can as fast as I can. The reason I do that is because that's how I used to see Russ von Hoelscher do it. Back in 1989, Russ used to come to our home for the weekend to work. He always told us, "Whenever I come to your house, make sure you have a big stack of legal pads for me, and plenty of pens!" And Russ drank a lot of coffee! I sat and watched him, and we would talk about these different ideas for promotions and things we were going to sell and things we were going to do, and different product ideas. And then all of a sudden, Russ would get all excited and start writing real fast and I'd shut up (which is hard for me to do!). Russ would write like crazy until he finally ran out of steam, and then we'd just talk. We'd eat and we'd drink some more coffee and we'd talk a little bit more — then Russ would get excited again and he'd start writing again! Then, when he left on Sunday, we'd take that big stack of legal pads over to our typist, who would then type them all up into sales letters. We'd put them out there, and people would send in their money.

It's simple! You write the copy, you put the letters out, and people send in the money. I learned it by watching Russ. I developed my own style of writing by copying him, and I didn't even know that until about 15 years later. We talk a lot in this business about the importance of models, and not only in this sense, where I picked up my style from Russ — as a child will model after their parent in so many ways. There are other models. There are sales letters that are already written by other people that you can model yourself after. Now, you can copy the structure; you can't plagiarize, because that's illegal and immoral, and shows no creativity on your part. You're taking little bits and pieces from a lot of different people, and you're finding your own unique way to combine them. There are lots of models out there.

The way to do that is to get on the other side of the cash register. Stop thinking like a consumer who only buys stuff. A consumer buys mostly in an unconscious way, and they just keep buying. There's a certain mentality to being a consumer, but there's another mentality of being the marketer, where you're thinking about how to go out there and reach consumers. So start looking at ads and sales letters for themes and ideas and structures, and start trying to see them as a businessperson sees them. Then model accordingly, and start developing your own styles. Past that, you're simply doing what Luther did. Once you develop your own style — once you've got some experience under your belt, and you have a bunch of sales letters that you've already written — now you're just copying yourself over and over again. A lot of our sales letters look the same for this reason, because at some level, they are. We're copying from ourselves now — and you can't steal from yourself, really. As long as it makes money, why reinvent the wheel?

Models can be anywhere. Anytime you see something that looks interesting, put it into your swipe file. Of course, you need to make sure your swipe file contains good models only; there are bad models, and you don't want to get caught using one of those. Be sure, when you're swiping something, that you know it worked. You can find models for your swipe file in all kinds of places; just keep studying the media that reaches the same marketplace you reach, or that you're trying to reach. If you're in the business-opportunity market, for example, look at ads running in the business-opportunity magazines. See which ads are repeating month after month, and use those as models.

You may have a different opportunity than they do, but you can use their models. If you see a lot of ads that have the same kinds of headlines, then obviously they're working, still bringing in money. Just as an example, if the headlines that keep working over and over again use the same font, then you can make your headline match that font. In a similar vein, you can do other things to make your ads look like the others. It can be completely different copy, but it can have a similar look and feel if you know that look and feel has produced results. If you see someone mailing a sales letter in a certain type of envelope and making money at it, then put your sales letter out in a similar envelope. That way, you're using a model that mimics what's already proven to work.

Of course, if you've run a successful ad yourself, you can use your own model: you can make your new ads look like your old ads, or your new sales letters look like your old sales letters. It's all about finding something that you know worked, and then modeling your new offer after it. Maybe it's something in the offer. Maybe it's just the way the sales letter looked, the size of the letter, the font, maybe the color of paper, or maybe you're matching an envelope. You can model all kinds of things. There's so much out there that's already been done that creativity is overrated in direct-response marketing. There's so much good stuff out there to sample that to sit down with a blank paper or screen, with no idea of what you're going to write, is a big waste of time. It's a hassle, and it slows you down. Use models to your advantage, and it can be really profitable.

There are so many things out there to borrow ideas from. Take a look at the advertising and marketing that's going on around you, almost on a 24/7 basis. Wherever you're at, there's someone out there with a sign, with a headline, with a teaser, with something to grab your attention, something that's designed to get you to do business with their company or pay attention or invoke some curiosity. Before I got into the field, I didn't pay much attention to most advertising, as most people don't. Most of us are so inundated with advertising that we tune out the vast majority of it. As a marketer, though, my antennae are always up to catch an idea or a headline or something that I can use — and I really like what some newscasts and media outlets do.

Tonight, while you're watching the news, note how the anchors do it. At the start of their program, they'll give you a little teaser to keep you hanging around till the end, won't they? They'll say, "Stay tuned for details on..." and they won't give it to you till the end. But what did they do? They just used one little blurb to pique your curiosity. I've even sat there for the whole hour, getting mad because I know that they've totally manipulated me to sit and watch the entire newscast just because they've piqued my interest — and they're not going to give me that payoff until the end.

The trick is that when you see a teaser, you can turn the TV off for about 50 minutes. You know that if they "tease" it, they're not going to show it until later. Sometimes they'll tease at the top of the hour for the bottom of the hour. Generally, it's either at the very bottom of the hour or the very end of the program. If you see a teaser, you're going to wait.

Now, how can that be applied to your copy? Can you start developing your skills to generate people's curiosity? Can you use a headline where the only intention is to get your reader to go, "Hmm, that makes me curious"? When someone is curious, they'll have an innate desire that compels them to satisfy their curiosity. That's an element of human nature that you can start weaving into your copy, whether in a headline, a sub-head, a pre-head, or in the body itself... to the point where you get them curious, you heighten their curiosity even more, and then they're absolutely compelled to read the rest of your copy so they can satisfy their curiosity. It's just another element you can use to sweeten your copy. So look for how other marketers have used curiosity, fear, greed, love, and any other human emotion to get their reader or viewer to pay attention and take that desired step. With a teaser, you're telling them to "stay tuned" for this life-shattering information that you're only going to receive here.

This is a strategy that's used over and over again by good writers. Once you become aware of it, you'll see it repeatedly. The writer will say something like, "And in a minute, I'm going to show you..." and then they make you some wild promise and get you all excited and they say, "More on that in a moment. But first..." So you have it in the back of your head — and then they keep doing things like that to keep you getting involved, taking you by the hand so that you don't lose your interest. In face-to-face sales training, they tell you that the idea is that you're supposed to try to get people to nod their head and agree with you on all kinds of simple, easy things — so when it comes time for them to ask you for the order, you're continuing to nod your head. You see it all the time.

Once you become aware of this, when you consciously start trying to see how other people are trying to sell to you all the time, you think to yourself, "Why do I do what I do?" You know, most people buy in an unconscious way. The factors that cause them to spend their money are emotionally based. So the idea is that the more you can understand yourself and why you buy what you buy, the better you'll be at understanding why other people buy things. What is the motive here? Why are you so excited about all this stuff? Understand that, and you'll understand other people, too.

One of Chris Hollinger's favorite movies is about Beethoven — *Immortal Beloved*. There's a part in the movie where Beethoven is describing to the guy who will become his secretary and life companion about what music can do. He asks the guy, "Now, what's this piece of music all about?" And this guy starts to describe very superficial things about the music itself. But Beethoven comes back with, "No, music is about taking the listener into the mind of the musician." That's where Beethoven starts talking about how he wrote this particular piece because his carriage was bogged in the mud when he was on his way to a rendezvous with his love, and he couldn't get to her because of the mud, and he tried to express the angst and frustration that he felt.

It's our job as copywriters to enter the conversation that's already going on in the minds of our prospects. That's the art I'm talking about. Once we've entered that conversation, it's up to us to take them where we want them to go — which, ultimately, is to get them to buy what we have to sell. So you've got to consciously be aware of the fact that the habits and routines that are involved in developing your art form are critical. I don't consider myself an artist by any means, but I'm involved in an ongoing process of discovery, of learning, and of discipline. Like any creative person, there are days where it's hard to write anything that I think is even remotely good; and then there are other days where it just pours out of me.

So be mindful of all the things that you can draw from — whether it's a teaser on a letter or an example from big business.

RUTHLESS COPYWRITING STRATEGIES

Hell, you can learn a lot from big business. Microsoft, for example, is very good at letting mavericks go out there and do the testing for all their new technology. And then they come in after the market has already been somewhat created and tested, and do the originators one better. They've seen what's working out there, and then they take it to the next level. You can do the same with your models. See what's working, and borrow some aspect of it — whether it's an envelope or a headline or a particular genre. Don't just come in there and try and capitalize on it just because someone else is doing well with it. Sure, if you see a bunch of marketers doing something and making money with it, that means there's money to be made in that market; but you can do even better. Come in and capture more of that market than they have, by using more of the same but better. Infuse what they're doing with better ideas and new elaborations they haven't thought of. Be mindful of all the marketing and advertising that you can use to capitalize on and reach that entire market.

Chris Hollinger told me about a church near his house that's really packed every Sunday. They have a big marquee out by their parking lot, and the pastor posts the best headlines up there. He does a really good job with headlines, and I want to share some of those that he's used — because obviously, the church is successful. It's been there a long time, and Chris has noticed that they have a good mix of older and younger congregation members. One week the headline was, "If God is your co-pilot, swap seats." It's always something catchy like that! Chris says he giggles every time he drives by it, even though he doesn't agree with this particular denomination. Once the headline was, "Stop, drop, and roll doesn't work in Hell." It's not like I'm going to use that particular one in a sales letter or anything, but it was a great headline! See, my antennae are always up, looking at billboards, looking at signs, and all the advertising that I hear, see, and feel. What's going on around me hopefully translates into making me a better marketer. I think that that's a good point to remember: to always be looking for ideas you can use. That's not just true of copywriting, it's true of marketing in general. Just being in tune and having your radar up and watching for what other people are doing, just being receptive to other advertising messages and noticing them and seeing how you can incorporate them into your business, can make you a lot of money.

I got something in the mail recently that I was completely surprised by. It was a political letter. It was a guy running for a local office... except that, in the end, he decided *not* to. When he wrote the letter, he was expressing concerns that he thought he could fix if he won the office. At the end he had an attachment that said, "You know, after thinking about it and verbalizing all of my concerns, I've decided that the best person to do this is me. So I want you to write me in. It's too late to be on the ballot officially, but I want you to write my name in." What was really weird was what I found on the back of the envelope, a sticker that he put there after it was sealed. The sticker said, "I changed my mind. I don't want to run for office, but I think all my points in here are still valid, and I'd like you to just look them over — so I thought I'd go ahead and mail this to you."

First of all, I thought that was funny. It was interesting. Here he is, running for this small township office, and there's this sticker on the back where he says, basically, "Ignore what I said about running for office at the end of this letter." But all the rest of this stuff in the letter was valid, and he wanted people to consider it. He listed 10 grievances he has with the current administration, and how they're blowing our money. He decided he was the best man to fix it, and asked us to write him in on the ballot. But then, on the sticker, he says, "On second thought, I don't want to run for office. But still, these are concerns I had, so I thought I'd share them with everybody before the upcoming election." The sticker became the tease!

And I thought, "Man, I don't know how exactly to use that, but I've got to find a way to use it. Here you've got a letter that's sealed up, and then on the envelope is a sticker that offers a last-minute thought or something like, "Here's something I couldn't get this inside the envelope," or "Ignore what I said on page 18," or something like that. That's a great tease. It struck me that something like that will make you open the envelope. Otherwise, if I would have recognized it as political letter, I might not have even bothered opening it up. He put *personality* into it. That made me open it and find out what he was talking about inside.

You just have to be in tune for unique, useful things. Normally, you might not think such a thing would have any application for business. But I saw it as a way to get people to open the envelope. Just stick something on it that points to something inside. It makes people curious; it makes them want to open your envelope and read your letter to find out what it is that you want them to ignore. It's going to get people's attention. The point is, if you're just being watchful and mindful of what's going on around you, ideas for copywriting will come from all over the place. So keep something with you where you can note them down — a legal pad, or little notebook, or even a cheap voice recorder. When an idea strikes, record it so you can use it later. You never know when one of those ideas will hit you, or when you'll remember it as you're working on a new idea or a new letter. You may suddenly, unexpectedly, find the perfect place to implement that strategy.

# CHAPTER SIX:

# Embrace News-Style Advertising

Let me hit you with a nice little headline: News-style advertising gets up to *500%* greater response than image advertising. That's a fact. If you've got a business of any kind and you're thinking about doing some marketing, don't skimp on the news-style advertising, because it gets up to five times the response of plain image advertising. And these are industry-specific statistics — there have been plenty of studies on what works and what doesn't. Obviously there are a lot of big companies out there that spend millions of dollars on image advertising, basically protecting their brand. They're not asking for anything specific, they're not selling anything specific, and they're not asking the prospect to do anything specific; they're just saying "This is my brand," so no one else will lay claim to it. Unless you're a multinational, you probably don't need to do that.

News-style advertising gets up to 500% greater response than color brochures, business cards, and all other forms of product or image advertising. Why? Simple — news-style advertising doesn't look like advertising. It looks like news. Very few people read advertising, but a lot of people read news. If it looks like advertising, most people won't read it. The reason's simple. We're all inundated with advertising, so we have to tune it out. News-style advertising gets by this filter. When you see a news story, you see a pre-head, a headline, a sub-head, a story. A good news-style ad will have all the same elements — just like all the sales letters I've been talking about throughout this book.

Let's take a look at a popular form of advertisement: the Yellow Pages. You can go to any Yellow Pages in the country today, rip out a page, and you're going to see a bunch of ads that look exactly the same. You could literally go in there and swap out the names and the telephone numbers in a particular category, move them from ad to ad, and those people wouldn't notice a difference in their business.

But after hearing the statistic that news-style advertising gets up to 500% greater response, don't you think that maybe if you paid attention to some of your copywriting and made your ad stand out dramatically from your competition, then you might come out on top? This is where people compete with their ads. But all the Yellow Pages guys want to do is sell ad space; they don't care about the real ad. And they want it to be homogenized, too. That's the whole thing about traditional Yellow Page advertising: they don't want to upset any of their other advertisers. They want to make all those ads look exactly alike, and they're ineffective because of that.

So take the next Yellow Pages ad you're planning to run and start applying some of the copywriting strategies I've explained in this book. Try using a news-style headline that's benefit-laden for the customer — or maybe a unique selling position, built into your headline, that's automatically going to out-perform all the other guys on the same page, because it's proven to work. We know that we are, by and large, employing proven strategies. Recently, Chris Hollinger sat down and wrote a headline right off the top of his head, based on some of the things I've been talking about. More than likely it's going to change during the editing process, but I think it's great, and it's easy to imagine and prepare in a news-style format.

Here's the headline: "This May Be Your Only Opportunity *Ever* To Lock In Your Spot At The Top Before The Big Boys Blast Their Way To A Fortune." Notice how all the words are capitalized. You can juggle some of the elements of the headline to make them stand out; for example, in Chris's original headline, the word "Your" was a lot bigger than the other words. He's saying "This may be YOUR only opportunity ever…". Now, why would you want to use a word like that? Because you want to make it benefit-laden to the person reading it. You want to get their attention — so you make it bigger, or maybe you underline it. You're trying to make the person reading it see the benefit of locking in their position before the big boys do. It's YOUR turn to be on top, right? Below is a subhead and a piece of the copy that says, "With this economy, wouldn't it be great for you to make heaping piles of mailbox cash automatically, by being at the right place, at the right time, ahead of some of the biggest and best marketers in the world?"

This is based on the news-style advertising that I'm talking about in this chapter. Chris has no idea, at the moment, whether he'll use this headline. It'll probably change — and doubtless will have by the time you read this. But it's still a great example of news-style headline writing and copywriting, of the kind that's proven to be more effective than image advertising. It's considered news-style because it talks about something that's brand new. It uses a new angle on a brand new upgrade that they're going to be able to lock in before it really gets up and going. It's a beta-tester deal. But by calling it news-style, we're talking predominantly about how we use news-like headlines, sub-heads, body of information, and more. This is the news-style print that gets people's attention and then, ultimately, asks for action of some kind.

Our job as salespeople — or as copywriters — is to get people to trade their money for what we're offering. That's what it's all about. Our job is to give people what they want. There are few things people really want, and one of them is whatever's new.

If you look at the word "news" and you take off the "s" at the end, you have what people really want: something that's *new*. They don't call it "the news" for nothing. My wife is addicted to the news, so she's got it on all the time — and they always have "Breaking News." Once I said to her, "What happens when there *is* no breaking news? What happens when there's nothing to report?" Well, you need to ask yourself the same thing; and if this occurs, realize that you still have to come up with something. That's what they do on CNN and the networks. They've got their market to serve, and their market *always* wants something new. So there's got to be breaking news, even if there *is* no news! That's what you have to do as copywriters, too. The process of getting rich is based on reselling to your customers again and again, so you've got to keep giving them something new, something that's different... or at least something that *sounds* different.

So, I like the idea of editorial-style ads. But I like the general theme behind them even more — and that general theme is that if everybody is zagging, then you've got to zig. If everybody's zigging, you've got to zag. You've got to be different from other marketers. You have to separate yourself somehow from the crowd. If your ad looks exactly like theirs, if everything you're doing looks exactly like what they're doing, then you're going to get the same poor results that everybody else gets. So when you start looking at ways to separate yourself from the herd, ask yourself first what people want. The best answer I can think of, besides "something new," is this: they want what I call an irresistible offer. They also want that offer made to them by somebody they feel is honest and trustworthy — somebody who feels real in a phony world. Because after all, we're living in a world that's pretty phony. As a copywriter, I think you should write to that. You should write to peoples' skepticism. They want something that's real, something that's new and interesting, in a world where all copy is homogenized. It's too similar. It's too bland. Since it's your job to separate yourself from everybody else, don't be afraid to be real, to be raw, to be honest, to be truthful with people. Don't be afraid to *upset* some people. Go out there and try to do it in some unique way.

For a good example of what not to do, let's look again at the Yellow Pages. Most Yellow Pages ads are watered down, dumbed down; they all look the same, and they're all pretty boring and bland. Most don't use direct-response-style copywriting at all. It's kind of funny; you'll notice that almost all of them lead with the name of their business, as if that's going to make me pick up the phone and call them. I don't care who they are; I want to know that they'll do for me what I want them to do for me! If I need a plumber, I want a headline that specifically tells me why that plumber is a good one to choose. If I need someone to do some electrical work, I want to know other things besides that they're called XYZ Electric Company. I always ask myself the infamous WIIFM: What's In It For Me? Because that's what people want to know when they read your ad. Having a plain ad with the name of your business as the headline isn't going to produce any kind of results. Having an ad that looks like everybody else's isn't going to produce results. You have to be *different*.

Again: if everybody else is zigging, you want to zag. And if everybody else is zagging, you want to zig. It's not necessarily what you're doing or specifically the style you use that's important — it's that you want to be different. You want to stand out. You want to do things that are unique and creatively unlike what everybody else is doing. If you look like everybody else, why should someone choose to do business with you? They'll probably just close their eyes and point to the page and say,

"Okay, *that's* who I'm calling!" Or, otherwise, you'll be in the fight to name your company AAA Whatever. If you look in the Yellow Pages under certain industries, you see them: there'll be A Company, AA Company, and then AAA Company, and maybe someone comes along and they're AAAA. They do this to try to get to the very top of the listing alphabetically, thinking that by doing so they'll be called first. And that is such delusional thinking! If that's the best they can do to make themselves different from everyone else, they're in way over their heads.

I started this chapter by telling you that news-style advertising gets you up to 500% more response than traditional advertising. Here's another good point to remember: news-style advertising looks editorial. It looks like it's information, and not just an ad. Therefore, it stands out among all of the other "me too" ads. That's what makes it so valuable as a model. And, yes, it can also be newsworthy! Look at what we're doing right now with our Recession-Proof Wealth promotion. This nasty recession is in the news right now; it's on the top of people's minds. The media is blasting away at it, with one bad story after another. They're having a field day with this whole thing — and they're scaring the crap out of people. We're aware that people are already in that mindset. We didn't create it; we're just cashing in on it. We're hitching our wagon to something that they created — and in the process of making money, we're helping other people. There's not a thing wrong with that.

CHAPTER SEVEN:

# Follow These Five Steps to Copywriting Success

In this chapter, I'll outline a five-step process that you can start using right now to improve your copywriting. These steps form a sort of formula, a blueprint for writing better copy. Taken together, they're something like a recipe that you'd use in the kitchen to cook something. If you follow a recipe exactly as it's laid out, you'll come up with something that tastes very good. The same's true here.

I suggest that you give yourself at least one day for each of these steps. So if you've got a sales letter that you want to write, give yourself a minimum of five days to write that sales letter — and then, every day, focus on one of these steps and write as much copy as you can that's focused on achieving that step. In five days, you'll have a whole bunch of interesting copy, and then you can spend another five days editing it down and rewriting it. This is a formula that works!

**Step One**

Samuel Johnson, the 18th-century British writer, once said that a big promise is the soul of an advertisement. That's as true today as it was 250 years ago. You've got to start with a big promise, and it has to be a promise that's custom-tailored to the type of person you want to reach. It has to offer a big benefit.

Take the one thing that's most compelling in your offer, focus in on it, and try to make it as big and as bold and as audacious a promise as you possibly can. That becomes your lead. If you write copy the way I write copy, you're going to spend one whole day on that. Whatever you write, however much time you spend on it, all you're doing is focusing on your big promise.

Now, this process can take a while to really get moving, which is why I prefer to take a week, or even longer, on my sales letters. During that week, if I'm just focused on writing that one sales letter, my mind becomes obsessed with the whole idea. I start getting ideas on the second and third day, and by the fifth or seventh day my mind is on fire! It's all flowing by that day, whereas the first day it may have been slow; and then, the second day, I did a little bit more; the third day I was writing a little bit more; and by the fifth, sixth, and seventh day, I'm jamming that copy out! By that time the copy is flowing like hot lava, it's a hell of a lot better than the copy I started with on Day One. That's because by late in the week, I was obsessed! I'd been working on it for a whole week — and I get my best ideas when my brain is alive and on fire.

However it works for you, you're starting with the big promise. One of the things you absolutely, positively have to do when copywriting is to grab your reader's attention from the very beginning. You've got to put a stranglehold on it and not let go. As soon as you let go of that attention, they're gone, like a fish that breaks your line. A big promise helps you to grab their attention and pique their curiosity — or scare them, or invoke some other emotion that's going to keep them charged up enough to make it through to the next headline that grabs their attention and moves them forward through the copy.

Begin by writing down some of the biggest features, benefits, and values that your product, service, or opportunity offers to the consumer. Of those, pick the biggest and create a solid headline that really synthesizes a big promise. That big promise launches the rest of your sales material or sales letter; it grabs their attention and forces them to keep going with your copy. That big promise is really the big picture, and the whole big offer is synthesized in that big promise. From a nuts-and-bolts perspective, it's the big promise that first grabs their attention and won't let go. That being the case, you need to determine what it is in your offer that's the most exciting. Which benefit is the most compelling, the most interesting, the most stimulating? What one thing is going to grab people and take them away from everything they're doing so they'll focus in on what *you're* trying to do? I've mentioned several times one problem that can make this difficult. It's simply the immunity that people build up for advertising messages. As prospective buyers, we've got all these marketers trying to get our attention all day long, screaming and shouting in almost every medium we're exposed to. We've learned to filter it out; it becomes white noise. Like at home, where my wife has the TV running all the time. From the minute she gets up in the morning till the minute she goes to bed at night, that television is on. The only peace I have from that TV is three hours in the morning!

But really, I don't listen to the TV. It just becomes white noise. That's how a lot of the marketing messages are for the customer: white noise. Nobody's paying any attention, because they've built up an immunity towards it. People are so inundated with their own problems, their own challenges, their own situations, that nobody's paying attention. That's why you start your sales letter with the biggest, boldest, most audacious, most compelling promise you can possibly make: because you want to cut through the clutter.

In order to find that big promise, you need to spend that whole first day of writing carefully examining your offer. Once you've got that promise, keep writing it down in as many different ways as you can, because eventually you'll find a set of words that sound better than any of the others. Keep trying again and again. Focus on the features. Focus on the benefits. Keep looking for the things that are the most exciting, the most unusual, and the most interesting.

It's very, very difficult to go over-the-top with a big promise, no matter how hard you try. People in this field are always worried about that, but it's not really possible. The truth is, despite the fact that you have this recipe, this five-step blueprint to writing sales letters that quickly make you millions of dollars, it's very rare that you'll write a big enough promise or headline on that very first day. You can't be big enough, no matter how over-the-top it may seem. Never be afraid to blow it up and make it as big as you possibly can, because if you don't grab their attention, then your sales letter is done.

It's hard to go over-the-top because people buy with their emotions. One of my best stories illustrating this took place in 1997, when we had our second big, expensive seminar. We charged $6,700 for that seminar. That first day, right before the seminar, Eileen, Russ von Hoelscher, and I were upstairs at the Broadview Hotel, mapping out some strategies on how we could open this thing in the best possible way. Russ said, "Look, let's not go out there and talk about making millions of dollars. Let's first tell people the simple truth — which is that you don't make millions of dollars overnight. First, you start with $50,000, and the next year you try to make $150,000, and the next year you try to make $400,000 — and then eventually, by your fourth or fifth year, you're into the millions. So let's go out there and tell them how it really is."

We thought, hey, well, he's got more experience than us. We had a hundred people in the room, and they'd all paid big bucks to be there, and we wanted to start it off on the right tone. Well, we went out there and I said, "Who here is interested in making $50,000 this year?" It fell flat. You could've heard a pin drop — and things were very uncomfortable and kind of scary. And then all of a sudden, after a couple of very awkward minutes, I quickly said, "Now, who here wants to make millions of dollars?" and everybody jumped up and started yelling and screaming and hollering and whooping... and *then* we got the seminar started right!

From a logical standpoint, Russ was correct — and everybody knows that logically. People know they can't go from zero to millions right away, that there are some intermediate steps. They've pretty much got to crawl before they walk, and they've got to walk before they run, and they've got to run before they learn how to slam-dunk basketballs. But they don't care. *We're selling to people's emotions.* You can't try to think logically when you're working in matters of the emotions. Emotion knows no logic, and you can see that in the most extreme examples of marketing. And certainly, when you're trying to sell in a market that's overcrowded, and you're trying to get people's attention, you do have to go over-the-top sometimes with your promises — as much as you can. You have to watch things from a legal standpoint; you can't make promises you can't deliver on. But you do have to go over the top. The person who makes the biggest, boldest promise usually is the person who wins out.

**Step Two**

The second step is painting the picture. This is a metaphor, of course, because we're really talking about words here. But it's the images that we create with our words that matter. We want people to visualize our offer and its benefits. We want them to see themselves using our product or service. In the business opportunity market, which is where I've worked for 20 years, one of the number one rules of selling is that if people can't see themselves doing it, they're not going to get involved. So you need to do things that make it real. You're using examples; you're telling stories.

Take, for instance, this new Recession-Proof Wealth program that we're promoting. Some experts say this recession we're entering could become a full-fledged depression. So we try to paint the picture. We make it real. We remind them of all the news they've been subjected to. We give them quotes from famous talking heads, credible experts that they've seen on the three major networks and CNN and FOX News. This is how we're painting the picture; and while it works better with some products than others, it's something you should always try to do. You should always try to put yourself in the shoes of the prospect, to see how they visualize the picture you're trying to paint.

There are several different ways you can do that. Obviously, getting them to imagine themselves being successful with your product, your service, or your opportunity is vital. Getting them to see the benefits that they'll enjoy is important. Also, they'll respond to concrete examples of how your project will do that. Infomercials are pretty good at providing that imagery, showing what your life is going to be like with that new product, or once the money comes rolling in.

Also, the process of explaining in detail how you make money with your product or opportunity is very effective. In the process of the hows and the whys and wherefores of showing them how it works, you're giving them the opportunity to place themselves into the equation so that they can visualize their own success at whatever it is you're offering. So you have to use the type of language that helps paint that picture. Maybe you can do that in a page, or half a page; or maybe it requires a 20-page hand-marked letter with big quotes and large type.

Here's an example from my Recession-Proof Wealth sales letter, which we're already generating leads for. This line of copy illustrates what I was saying above: "Imagine waking up every Monday morning to a mailbox that is stuffed full of cash, checks, and money orders for this powerful Recession-Proof Wealth System, which is desperately wanted and needed by millions of people who are very worried about their financial futures. All you have to do is let our simple marketing system make money for you — automatically. This takes as little as 10 minutes a day, and your day is over. Now you're free to go anywhere. You're free to do anything you like. This is the kind of life that's possible when you're using this Master Distributorship, and I will help you cash in with it." And then it goes on to give them some income projections down at the bottom, based on certain numbers of sales.

What we're trying to do is make it real for them. We're trying to paint them a picture. We're trying to get them to see themselves actually using this product and benefiting from it, so they'll say, "Yeah, that's great! That's the opportunity for me!" That's part of that process of painting the picture. Those income projections I mentioned can be very powerful, especially when they're backed up with proof. I show them what happens if they make this many sales, or what happens with that many sales. Then I show them copies of actual commissions or sales checks, and/or testimonials that backup the idea that "if you do this, this happens." By using income projections, you're painting that picture very vividly, making a direct causal connection in their minds.

Be absolutely sure to give them proof of your claims. This is very important because, again, I feel that people are more skeptical now than ever before in history. I firmly believe that. They're constantly bombarded with advertising and news, and so they're forced to filter it out, to grow so skeptical that they don't believe anything. That's why you've got to do something to show them proof. You can't expect people to be sold on something just because you are. Why should they believe you? Show them proof: copies of real checks, or better, testimonials. Testimonials are very powerful. However you do it, prove to them you're telling them the truth, the whole truth, and nothing but the truth. In the past, we've spent page after page trying to do just that.

As part of that proof, we also tell them that we back our product up with a guarantee. And we tell them that we don't blame them for being skeptical... that it's *good* to be skeptical. We acknowledge the fact that they already have that in their minds; we don't try to run or hide from it. We just tell them, "Of course you're skeptical. Of course you don't believe me. But here's why you should... And in case you don't at the end of the day, if you're still not happy, you can get all your money back."

I was watching TV recently, and I saw an infomercial for an Internet guy. He had, literally, ten minutes straight of nothing but testimonial after testimonial, videos of people saying, "I'm using this and I'm making this," and "I went from zero to $15,000 a week," and it just went on and on and on. It was very persuasive. Although I thought the whole infomercial was cheesy, the testimonials did a very good job of offering social proof and getting people's attention. This works with written media as well as TV. People read testimonials, and it helps take it to their exact level. They think, "Well, if he can do it, I can do it!" That's what social proof does for your product, service, or opportunity.

**Step Three**

Next, tell them why your product is unique. What we're doing with our Recession-Proof Wealth System that makes it unique, that really gets people stimulated and makes them curious to want to know more, is that we're telling them a simple story that happens to be true. We point out that during the

Great Depression, when unemployment was 25 percent or higher in some cities, there was still a small group of people who did extremely well — even when everybody else was struggling and barely making it. That's true of any great social change, by the way, whether it's good or bad. There's always a group of people who do well. Some are exploiting the problem; some are just trying to do something positive.

Anyway: we tell people that during the Great Depression, there was this group of people who, because they had a secret, were able to make excellent money when everyone around them was suffering. Now, 80 years later, we're faced with a similar situation that may end up being worse that what we suffered through then. But we've discovered a new way to capitalize on something that enabled that group of people back in the Great Depression to become very, very wealthy, and we've got a whole new way of doing it now. That's our hook. That's our angle. That's what makes it unique.

There has to be something that sets you or your offer apart, and that's just an example of how we're doing it. Everybody likes something that seems different, whether a little or a lot. And in reality, it may be that what you have isn't *that* much different. Most things aren't. Take my example from earlier: plumbers. How much different could one plumber really be from another, honestly? I don't know that much about plumbing, but I'm pretty sure that the work isn't much different from one plumber to another. Yet can your marketing be different? You bet! Your marketing can be the part about your business and your company that makes you stand out. You may be in a bland, homogenized industry, but that doesn't mean that your marketing has to be that way. So for purposes of this five-step blueprint, spend some time on identifying things that you can put in front of people that makes your offer look unique and special and different. You might have to get pretty creative. You have to ask yourself constantly, "What is it about this that makes it unique?" Or, "What can I *do* to make this offer unique?

There's this great Jackson Brown song that goes, "You take Sally, I'll take Sue. There's really no difference between the two." I love that line, because that's just the way the market is! There's no real difference from Company A to Company B; you might as well flip a coin. There's nothing that's unique. If you're in that kind of business, you have to be the one to *create* that uniqueness. You have to be the one to find that angle, like my friend Mike did with the soy candle. You can go to Wal-Mart and pick up a candle for a dollar that's made in Vietnam or Indonesia — but you can't find a soy candle at Wal-Mart. I know because I checked; it's unique.

In order to know what's unique, you have to know what's out there in the marketplace — especially what's being done on a regular basis by other companies. You can't really have something that's totally unique until and unless you know what's out there, what's the norm, what people are buying. Then you look for points of differentiation, things that mean the most to your customers or your market. That goes back to the very first thing I told you in this book: that you can be the world's worst copywriter, and *still* make really good money if you just know your market. If you intuitively and intimately understand who it is that you're selling to and what excites them, what interests them, where their passions are, what frustrates them the most — then you don't have to be a good copywriter, because you're locked in on the exact type of person you're after. At that point, coming up with something unique is easy, because you really understand them.

**Step Four**

The next step is to close your argument by telling your customer why they must act now. Not doing so is a big mistake that a lot of marketers make; in fact, it's a big mistake that I make sometimes, too. I've made every mistake there is to make when it comes to marketing, so don't ever think I'm coming at you from an angle like I've got it all figured out. I constantly make mistakes, and this is a mistake I've made many times.

I've talked about people building up an immunity towards advertising and marketing, to the point where they just tune it out. Well, one of the things that people tune out all the time is those ads that say, "You must respond in the next 10 days!" *Click*. Nobody believes that. They're thinking, "Yeah, right. I could respond *10 months* from now and get the same deal." If you don't give people a compelling reason why they should take action right now, then the chances are good that a lot of people *aren't* going to, and you're going to lose money that could and should be yours. They're qualified prospects, they truly want what it is that you have to offer — but they're holding onto their money. So you have to find a reason; if necessary, you've got to create one. After all, there's no reason why they have to give you money — they don't care about your bills!

So close your argument by telling them why they must act now. One thing that comes to mind is scarcity or limited resources. It's one thing to say "You must act now!" and another to prove why they should. People get inundated with a lot of those offers, and they know that this is, in fact, a marketing tactic. It is a strategy to get people to act. They know that 99 times out of 100, marketers who tell them this are pulling the wool over their eyes. You need to give them a good reason why it's true in this case, or they're not going to believe you, and you're going to lose credibility.

So if you tell them to act fast before it fills up, tell them *why* it's going to fill up quickly. Give them a good reason to want to be in there before it does. You'll turn them off or lose credibility by not giving them a compelling reason to act. Just to go back to this promotion that we're finishing up now: it's limited to only 250 distributors. If our prospects want to respond to our offer, it's for them and for 249 other distributors *only*. Period. We tell them that after that we may terminate the program forever, and that's the truth. On the order form, it says the offer expires on November 1, 2008, or when all 250 positions are filled. And then we give them the incentive: if they order now, "Plus, I'll get all the private secrets behind this amazing new wealth-making opportunity, at least 100 days *before* all of the other distributors. This gives me a huge head start to make even more money." We tell them in the sales letter that it's all brand new; and because it's brand new, that's the good news. But because it's brand new that's also the *bad* news, because we're still developing things — that's how new it is.

Then we're telling people that as distributors, they need to watch their mailboxes, because over the next hundred days we're going to give all this to them. And because we gave them that distributorship at such a low price, they can either tolerate waiting another 90 days, *or* they can become a Master Distributor immediately. We're going to give them all the secrets right now, right away; they're going to be the first to get them! That's a reason for them to step up to the plate, to go ahead and upgrade their position. There's a Money Back Guarantee. They can upgrade their position and then, if they want to back out later, no problem. No questions asked. It's a reason for them to take action.

Make them that special offer to get them to respond now. You've seen it time and again: "But wait! That's not all. If you act now, we're going to throw in this XYZ special gift." It does get people to go ahead and respond. Obviously, with our copywriting and our Direct-Response, we're writing and pushing for a response. In this case, we're pushing for that sale. We're stacking all these benefits and bonus gifts and everything up until they're saying, "All right! I get all this? Okay, I'm done. Where's the order form?"

You also need to offer an upsell — something associated with your product or service but better, something that interested clients can purchase for a higher price. Remember the Master Distributorship I mentioned earlier? That's the upsell with our new program, and it's got some unique aspects that really draw people's attention. We're taking people who are already distributors, and now we want to upsell them to a Master Distributorship. Since we've appointed them as distributors already, it's easy to take them to that next step. It's a logical upsell; it's directly tied to the first offer that they bought. They get a wonderful, unique bonus when they trade up: right here on the front page it says, "Plus, you'll also receive the world's greatest free bonus gift, guaranteed to have an honest value of $33,248.20." Now, if that's not over the top, if that's not unique, I don't know what is. You're selling something for $495 — and that's a half-price sale, by the way. The regular price is $987, but we're letting people come in early at half price. For $495, we're going to give them something that's worth $33,000. When they get to the last five pages that explain the world's greatest bonus gift, there is a headline that says: "How Can We Give You A Free Bonus Gift That Is Guaranteed To Be Worth A Total Of $33,248.20?" And then it says, "Listen, I don't blame you for being skeptical. After all, getting 50 powerful recession-proof websites..."

See how we tied the websites in with the whole offer? They're not just websites; they're *recession-proof* websites. We did that for a reason. We wanted to maintain cohesiveness with the whole thing, to keep it all locked in to the original offer. And then we explain to them that the websites are also brand new, they're still being developed, and that they need to go through extensive testing — which they do. It's all true. Nobody is lying.

There's no dishonesty here. We tell them that these websites, if they went out there and tried to build them all on their own, would cost them every bit of $33,000 to put them all together... but we're doing it all on our dime. What we don't tell them is that we then collectively give the whole group the same basic replicated websites. That's the secret we don't tell people, but it's true that the sites do have that type of value.

Next, we show people how it's possible for us to give them such a valuable bonus gift for just $495. What we're trying to do is create that irresistible offer, such that the $495 we're asking them to give us pales in comparison to everything they're going to receive in exchange for it. It's all part of stacking and building that offer. It's a fact that those websites have an honest value of $33,248.20. We could have just said $33,000, but making it $33,248.20 makes it more believable.

What we're going to do in the follow-up marketing is what we call "taking the cream off the top." So we put this upsell offer out there to the people who already are distributors; that is, people who gave us the $39 for the distributorship. We're going to take all the immediate revenue that comes in from the people who say, "Man, this is a great deal! Here's my $495. Take it!" Then, we're going to go to the people who didn't send in their $495 right away with a series of sequential mailings that proves the value of our offer. It breaks it all down, it shows them where we came up with that figure of $33,248.20, and it speaks to their skepticism. A lot of people will still think it's a number we just pulled out of our heads, that there's no logical reason why that number is even real. They still don't believe it... so we're going to show them. We're going to break it down. Each one of these websites has a value of $649. Plus, we're going to give the distributor three years of hosting on top of that. Here's our normal price for hosting. When you add it all up, it's $33,248.20.

These days, people don't just trust you; you have to win

that trust. Part of the way you do that is by making your case for your product or service: by showing people why you're not just leading them on, why it's real, and why you can do what you said that you were going to do. This backs up your claim: it's an honest value of $33,248.20. When you add it up, people say, "Okay, yeah, it really *is* worth that."

Here's a true story. In August of 2002, we had a huge seminar with four or five hundred people. On the third day of that event — a Sunday morning — we made our customers a special offer, and then went through a two-hour presentation that proved to them that we were going to give them $484,000 worth of free websites. The offer was simple; they just had to pay the hosting. We were going to build these websites for them, and then they had to help us by letting us run a series of these tests to get them ready for the marketplace. Software companies do this all the time — it's called beta testing. Those were the only two conditions: they paid the hosting, and let us use their sites for beta testing. We spent two hours showing them exactly what they were going to receive. We made a great presentation, and when the presentation was over, people literally stampeded the stage. We made them a compelling offer, and they stampeded us trying to get it. One guy was injured in the process — he either broke his thumb, or thought he had.

I was frightened! I was thinking, "Crap! Get them away from me!" Now, I've heard stories before about how the crowd can sometimes respond in a way that's just overwhelming, but this was the first time I'd witnessed it. People went crazy! We made them an irresistible offer; we did our best to prove to them that it was real, that it was true, and that it was something that, in the end, they just could not say no to — and they responded! I think this is a wonderful illustration of the power of Direct-Response Marketing, and of stacking an irresistible offer. We did a couple of million dollars worth of business right then and there, because we gave them a great offer. And that's really what I'm talking about. You absolutely have to give people good value in exchange for their money. In order to compete out there in the marketplace with all these very aggressive marketers, you've got to make your offer stand out above theirs.

Here's a good example. I have a colleague named Dr. Gallant who provides an amazing value to his clients. The items he sells them are, taken altogether, worth about $100,000. But he offers it all to them as 105 courses for $97 — a total of $10,185, assuming they buy all those courses. For ten grand, they can get a $100,000 worth of stuff! That's an irresistible offer — because he proves that it really *is* worth $100,000. That's the challenge you've got to meet and overcome.

**Step Five**

Finally, you need to end with a reminder of the promise, a summary of your offer, and a strong call for action. You've got to summarize it — especially if you're doing long-form sales letters, which are the ones you use if you're really trying to sell high-ticket items. Take the letter for our recession-proof system that I've been talking so much about in this book. It only asks for $495, but it's a 20-page letter. We're taking 20 pages to prove our claims, to make it real, to show them proof, to establish its uniqueness, to go through this whole thing. Twenty full pages! Now some people would say, "My God, do you need 20 pages to sell something for $500?" I believe that in our market, to our customers, more is better — and you *do* need that kind of thing. You need to make all your claims, however many pages it takes. You need to do a thorough job of selling, and then to summarize it all in the end.

When I think about this need for a strong call for action, I'm reminded of the HBO series "Hard Knocks." This year it's about pro football. In a documentary on the Dallas Cowboys,

Jerry Jones — the colorful, very charismatic owner of the Cowboys — was addressing the team and he said, "People have said I've been a very successful salesman, and there are three things that I've learned about sales in all my years in business. Number one is, you ask for the money. Number two is, you ask for the money. And number three is, you ask for the money." He's hit the nail on the head with that statement. When it comes down to your call to action, that's exactly what you're doing. You're asking your prospects for the money. You've built a good, solid case, sure — but if you don't take that last step and ask for the money, you're sunk. Sadly, a lot of people are afraid to ask for the money.

I've already mentioned Zig Ziglar's brother, Judd Ziglar, who wrote a book called *Timid Salespeople Raise Skinny Kids.* As he points out, even if you're a good salesperson, if you can't ask for the money at the end of your pitch, then you're going to lose a lot of sales — maybe even most of the sales that could be yours. So you've got to be aggressive with it. If you're offering products and services that truly do offer value, don't hesitate to ask for the money. Make that call to action. Those hundred reports that you have — what is their worth? A couple of thousand dollars apiece? Is that the value you've established for them? Are they *worth* a couple thousand dollars apiece? Sure they are, if people can use and benefit from what you're offering. So as long as you're providing real value that does exactly what you say it's going to do if they use it, then you have every right to ask for the money. It's your responsibility, in fact.

That's the mindset you have to get into. You need to be aggressive when asking for the money. Otherwise, you're always going to be losing sales, all the while wondering, "Man, am I too pushy here? Am I really too pushy? Should I be less aggressive? Should I back off a little bit?" No way! Because if you really believe in what you're doing and you really believe it can help people, and that they need it and can benefit from it, then just get out there and do everything short of physical violence to sell your product. Do whatever you have to do to try to make the sale. If it's really going to benefit people, if they can really be empowered by it, then you *owe* it to them to do that.

## Speaking of Summaries...

That's the basis of the five-step formula. What I would recommend here is that you do what I was suggesting earlier: Get on the other side of the cash register, and start studying other Direct-Response marketers immediately. Don't just look at general marketing stuff; study the copy of direct-response marketers who are doing a really good job with it, and you'll see the same formulas repeated over and over again. That's the key to your developing the skills and ability to do them yourself — by first understanding, in as many ways as possible, how other people are using these strategies on a daily basis.

# CHAPTER EIGHT:

# Apply Aggressive Marketing Techniques

Ruthless copywriting is what happens when someone feels so strongly that their products and services will be of such extreme value to the people buying them that they believe those people would be crazy not to buy. So they do whatever it takes to get the biggest number of people to buy their products and services. Again, I'm using the term "ruthless" as a stronger sibling of "aggressive." Your copywriting has to be aggressive and confident to succeed for you.

Never forget that copywriting is a form of marketing. You're writing copy that's part of a marketing campaign. You're morally obliged — to yourself, your employees, your family, and your customers — to get seriously aggressive when you're marketing. You have to aggressively go after those customers and prospects that you *know* need what you have to sell. Ruthless copywriting is all about a certain frame of mind that you have to adopt — one where you're relentlessly going after business in your marketplace. Whatever you sell, whatever your products and services are, if you feel confident enough in their value, if you know that your products and services offer your prospects the benefits that they want, and then it's your *duty* to do all you can to get as much business as you can from them. You're helping them even as you're helping yourself. Ruthless copywriting is a necessary strategy for getting as many of them as possible to do business with you, because you feel confident in your products and services.

Let's consider two hypothetical marketers: one who's a ruthless copywriter, and one who isn't. Let's say a gentleman in California has a great product. He's done all the research, spent a fortune on development, and has a product he knows millions of people desperately want and need. If there's any such thing as a perfect product, this is it. In fact, whenever he shows his product to anyone, they joke about his surefire winner and talk about how he couldn't possibly lose with this product. Everything's perfect about it — this product would practically sell itself.

He decides he needs to do something to sell this product, so he sits down and quickly writes up a one-page flyer, showing a picture of the product and listing a few points about it — what it's called, how much it costs, its specs. At the bottom of the flier, he tells people where they can buy it. And so, since he knows he has a winner, he doesn't bother testing. He just quickly mails his flyer to a list of people he thinks would be interested in the product — and he's sorely disappointed when he gets only one order. Worse, it's from his Aunt Tilly, who promised she'd buy his product as long as he'd come visit her next summer.

This is a perfect illustration of a guy who just doesn't get ruthless copywriting strategies. He thought he had a surefire winner, and he really did have a good product — but he didn't do any real marketing. He thought the product would sell itself. He thought that he didn't need to aggressively market — that he could just tell people about his product and didn't really have to do any real hard work to sell it.

On the other side of the coin is another marketer, say in Texas, who has a different product that serves the same marketplace. He's not entirely confident that he has the perfect product, though he knows he has a good product. He's proud of it, and thinks that the marketplace would want it, because it solves certain problems in the marketplace. He suspects that there will be a good demand for it. He also feels confident that he has good copywriting skills and could sell it to the marketplace if he tries — so he spends a good, solid week writing down all the main benefits of his product, all the main reasons why his prospects would want to buy it. Then, after that, he writes a four-page sales letter that teases people about his product, and asks them to send for a Special Report to get all the information. That's a type of lead generation system.

After he writes that four-page letter, he talks to his mailing list broker and asks them for 5,000 of the best-matched names they can rent him. Then he has his mailing house mail 5,000 copies of that sales letter out. While those 5,000 pieces of mail are in the mail, he writes what we call the back-end letter — the Special Report that tells the respondents all about his product.

About a week later, the leads start flowing in. It looks like he has a winner, but he won't know for sure for quite some time yet. So he finishes writing the main sales letter that will sell the product, and he puts together an entire back-end package that will go out to all the leads. A certain percentage of the 5,000 people he initially mailed to raised their hands and said they were interested, and wanted more information about the product. Recognizing that today's salad is tomorrow's garbage, he quickly mails the back-end sales letter *the same day* that the people requested his information. So he quickly followed up with them, and it wasn't too long before his orders started flowing in.

But he's not done yet. That was just the first step. While he's waiting for the orders to come in, he's busy writing a series of follow-up sales letters that he'll mail to all the people who requested his Special Report but didn't buy. Over the course of the next six weeks, he mails letters and postcards to remind them of the reasons why they *should* buy, and why they would find value in buying his product. He's relentless, because he knows that a) they requested information from him and are interested in his product, and b) it really would provide all the benefits they want and need. He's convinced of this.

After all that's said and done, he finds out that he's made a nice profit. So he quickly picks up his telephone, calls his printer, and gets all the pieces ordered again. He calls his list broker and orders a bunch more names and addresses to mail to, and then he rolls out the mailing campaign on a weekly basis after that and makes millions of dollars over the next several months.

To me, these two stories perfectly illustrate the difference between someone who's a non-ruthless copywriter and marketer versus someone who is. The man in California thought he had a really good product; and maybe it was, but he didn't have any kind of real marketing campaign. It was small and wasn't aggressive at all. He sent out one piddling little flier that told about the product, because he felt like it could sell itself. He thought all he had to do was tell people what it was and where to buy it. That's too passive. That's being apathetic toward the marketing process. It's saying, "Hey, I've got a good product and the people want it. They know where to find it."

On the other hand, there was the guy in Texas. With him, you had someone who wasn't quite as confident about his product; he didn't feel like he had a sure winner. But he felt confident in his copywriting ability and in his ability to sell it to a marketplace, because he knew that it provided value. So he systematically created a marketing campaign from start to finish that found the right people who wanted it. He wrote a lead-generation piece, something that would get people to raise their hands and say they were interested in it. Next, he followed up with those people aggressively to convert the biggest percentage of those leads into sales. That's the definition of a good ruthless copywriting system! It's all about what you do to find people who want your product or to develop products that people want, and then developing a marketing system to aggressively go after those people and convert the largest possible percentage of those leads into sales.

The problem in a lot of industries and local businesses is that people are good at what they do... but they're not good at marketing. That's one of the reasons we teach what we teach at M.O.R.E., Inc. Take a plumber, for example. He knows how to plumb, how to handle pipes. He's good at it. Maybe he's the best in town — but if he's not a good marketer, if he doesn't know how to aggressively go after all the plumbing business in his town, then it doesn't matter. He's not going to attract the business. You can have an average plumber making ten times as much money as the best plumber, because the average plumber understands good marketing. It's that way in a lot of businesses.

We have a good coffee shop in Newton, Kansas; we also have a local bookstore, a jewelry business, and several other retail businesses on our Main Street. I watch them do their marketing, and I can tell which ones kind of get it and which ones don't at all. Those who don't simply struggle, while the ones that at least halfway aggressively market make money. They're sending mailings to their customers, they're inviting people to come in for sales and that kind of thing, and so those businesses do better. They understand that in order to get people to give you their money for what you have to offer, you have to aggressively go after that business. You can't just assume that people are going to find you if they want to buy what you have to offer.

A good example of aggressive copywriting in action is one of my friend Chris Hollinger's ex-students. This young man

found out that college wasn't for him, so he left school and
started his own decorative concrete business. He's pretty good at
decorative concrete — but it turns out he's *really* good at
marketing. He really enjoys generating leads in particular.
Nowadays, he and his brother pretty much dominate the
decorative concrete industry in that part of Kansas City where
they want to work. What they do is generate prospects — people
interested in decorative concrete in their home or in their
business — and then cherry-pick the very best clients, the ones
who need big decorative concrete jobs with large profit margins.

They don't do the rest of the work themselves. They sell
those leads to their competitors, particularly people that they
trust to get the work done. They don't even have to push the
mud, and they still turn a tidy little profit from generating that
lead and getting sales material into those people's hands.
Basically, they have a sub-contractor come in and do the work. I
think that's such a great example of ruthless copywriting and
marketing. They concentrate on their copywriting in a market
that's growing by leaps and bounds, and they absolutely
dominate it.

Chris has had several conversations with his ex-student on
the subject, and the guy tells him, "You know, we're really just
learning as we go along. But the fact that we're out there doing
it is a step above what everyone else does!" His competitors —
the people he sells these leads to — are happy to pay fifty, sixty
dollars or even more per lead, depending on where that person is
in the sales process. If he just gives them something and says,
"Hey, go out here and here's the job. The guy is ready," then that
subcontractor is going to give him a cut. They've already
worked out how much they're going to make. And they don't
have to push an ounce of mud — which is great, because if
you've ever done concrete work, you know you never want to
do it again. This is a great example of how ruthless marketing

and copywriting can help your business. These guys are getting to the point where all they want to do is generate leads — they don't even have to touch the concrete at all.

This is further proof that you have to see things differently than your competition. You've got to think outside the box, to use a popular cliché. It's also a good example of how genius comes into play, where "genius" is the ability to see things that other people can't. There are all kinds of ways to make money in business. In fact, the choices are endless — and that's the one thing a lot of people just don't realize. We can only see past our own limitations, and sometimes what we don't see is the possibilities.

Chris's students are figuring it out as they go. Well, folks, I have a confession to make. This is something that, until now, only my closest friends and colleagues knew. I firmly believe that a lot of other people in the field are the same way, but they're just not willing to admit the truth. And that is this: even after more than 20 years of writing copy, I don't even know how I'm going to do it until I actually do it. I've done literally thousands of various ads, sales letters, and other projects, and more often than not I'm winging it, at least at first. That's even true of the recession-proofing project I'm working on now.

I'm not ashamed to admit this. You see, I'm not alone. There are lots of entrepreneurs and marketers out there who want to pretend. They want you to believe that they've got it all figured out, that they've got all the answers — and if you'll only shell out a certain amount of money to them, they're going to give it all to you. They tell you, "Don't worry. Just let me take care of everything. Go ahead and give me all the money and I'll solve all your problems. I've got all the answers." But they don't.

I'm convinced that no one in the marketing field has all the answers, or even a large percentage of them. And yet, I also know that there are a lot of experts — maybe ourselves included, sometimes — who like to pretend like we *do* have all the answers. The truth is, we're still figuring some things out ourselves. And while those other experts out there may have some of the answers, they're still figuring things out too.

Why have I made this astounding admission? Why is it important? Because I believe that there are a lot of people who get confused because they just don't know how to solve the problems they face, and they let it get in the way of their success. Well, I'm telling you that a lot of the time, I don't know how to solve the problems that I'm working on either — until I actually solve them! You have to get started and figure it out as you go. That's the point. You cross the bridges as you get to them.

My whole approach to writing copy is based on that reality. Let's look again at the copy that we're working on at the time of this writing — the sales letter for our new project "Recession-Proof Wealth." I'm going to take the lead role and write the initial first stage of copy, and then Chris Lakey and Chris Hollinger are going to help tweak it. We're going to rewrite it together as a group. Everybody's going to be working off the copy that I supply them. And — confession time — I don't know what I'm doing. I may have 20 years of experience, but I'm still working on it and figuring it out every day! Every day I get a little bit closer to the final product, but I'm figuring it out as I go. I'm still working on writing all the benefits, and the more I write the more I figure out. And the more I figure out, the more I write! On Day #4 I'm figuring out things that I didn't know on Day #3, and Day #7 I'm figuring out things I didn't know on Day #6. Give me another five days on this project, and it's going to all start coming together and flowing like hot lava. So when I give it to the guys, hopefully they're going to say, "Damn, that T.J. is a great writer! God, he's great! He's amazing!"

The truth is, a lot of those ideas they're reading are things that came on Day #6, Day #10, Day #12 — when the ideas were flowing freely, *after* I'd gone through a tremendous amount of confusion and frustration. Hopefully this serves as a good example for you, because you're surely experiencing the same kinds of frustrations, too. People get frustrated and they say, "Oh my God, I don't know how I'm going to do it," so they don't even get started and they don't even *try* to figure it out as they go. That's a huge mistake! Don't buy into the idea that there's some group of people — myself included — that has all the answers from the start and can bang out a sales letter without a moment's hesitation. We do have *some* answers; there's no question about that, or you wouldn't be reading this book, and I wouldn't be holding three-day seminars like the one this book's based on. I couldn't do any of that if I didn't have good, solid, concrete, *proven* things that have made money for us that I want to share with you. But we're *still* figuring things out as we go along, especially with new products. You have to be willing to go through some confusion, some frustration, to get there.

It used to be that with every new project I took on, I was looking for "the answer." But there's no real answer; there's just the solution that you find as you go through the process, the solution that leads you to the end. It's a never-ending process. Sure, you have an idea of what you want to accomplish with a particular project or a new opportunity, but you don't know how you're going to get there. As I've done this over and over, it's gotten easier for me to find the answers or to say, "Okay, who do I need to talk to? Where do I need to look to find this element of what I want to do?" There are no set-in-stone answers; it's a fluid process of always discovering new things.

When I was first starting, I'd write some stuff down and think it was actually the best I could do. And then I'd go back and look at it again and think, "Oh, man, that's just crap! It's not there yet." I didn't have the perspective then that I do now. I didn't realize that I'd have to spend a lot of time rewriting and editing and going back through my offers and ads. What happens is, I start wrapping my mind around the offer itself. And what I really want to do is start stacking together all those benefits and values for my customer, start showing them exactly why I've come up with the greatest product in the world for them. But sometimes my mind just doesn't grasp the big idea that I had initially. So I'll have to sit there and scratch my head, even though I have a place to start now, and try and get it all put together. Eventually, BING! the light bulb comes on, and I'm like, "Okay, I've got to get this all out of me," and I start really hammering it out, putting it together the best I can. I end up with a stack of yellow pads with a bunch of scribbles and notes on them — and then it's time to edit and rewrite. I'm not Beethoven or Mozart. I've got to hammer it out, and I've got to do the best that I can with what I have and, hopefully, that'll be good enough.

My colleagues and I *don't* have it all figured it out. It would be nice to say we did, but that would be a lie. Part of what makes successful copywriting and marketing so difficult to describe, and so difficult to teach, is because to a large extent it's based on instinct. Now, I'm a big NFL fan, although my team, the Chiefs, is pretty pathetic lately. They've been on a pretty bad streak. But when you hear the commentators talk about football players — especially younger players — you hear them talk about their "instinct" for the game, and how they're thinking too much. You see a young kid who's a rookie, and he overruns a play. If he's a defensive guy, he should have made the tackle; but he was thinking too much instead of just reacting. They talk about the transition that happens once a player goes from thinking too much to just going on adrenaline and instincts. They get to a point where they simply react. When a situation is happening on the field, their subconscious just takes over. They know what to do, and they do it — they react. A rookie who hasn't gotten to that point may think too much; he analyzes everything, and then tries to determine what he's supposed to do according to the Play Book. He ends up being a split second too late because he thinks instead of just doing.

As marketers, we all come to a place in our marketing journey where we don't have to think a whole lot. We react. We know the general marketing principles, and from there on it's all about winging it, reacting on the fly, adjusting dynamically, doing things the way we think they should be done, based on our experience and study. Maybe we don't have it all figured out, but we have the *basics* figured out, and we adjust from there.

You use what you know, and you test, and you try things. You access banked information, and you get to a point where you're running on instinct. It's just kind of there, and you don't have to think too much about it. Of course, you do think as you go and as you're working, and in the moment you remember what you know, and you're analyzing new information. Maybe you've seen something new that you want to test, and you pull it all together in a moment. So as you can see, it's not as if we experienced marketers have it all figured out; but we've built a foundation of knowledge, and we use that to build and inform our projects as we move forward. I suppose, like computers, our brains continue to store more information with each new test we run, with each new passing day as we analyze data coming back from new mailings we've sent, or new websites we're testing. We just keep feeding the mental computers. All of that data is there for us, so we pull it out in bits and pieces as we need it.

In the previous chapter, I went over my five-step blueprint to writing a sales letter that can quickly make you millions of dollars. Now, you can literally sit down and spend a day or so on each one of these elements as you're initially writing your sales letter, and that's certainly what I recommend. What often happens with me is that I'll get to, say, Step #5: close your argument by telling them why they must act now. Well, guess what? I don't have to reinvent the wheel here, even if I can't think of anything new, because I have a swipe file. What I can do is say, "Oh, I remember how Russ von Hoelscher or Chris Lakey did this in a sales letter," and I'll go over and rummage through a file. I'll find something and say, "Okay, that's it. This is how Russ did it on this particular offer. I can kind of just borrow some of his ideas here, mold them and make them my own."

As you become an astute student of marketing and copywriting, what will happen is that you'll pick up all these tricks. You'll learn new stuff from your colleagues and competitors. I encourage you to begin building your own swipe file. When you receive a sales piece in the mail, file it away so that you can go back to it and see how someone else handled certain points. The next thing you know, you'll have your own library of examples to draw inspiration from.

Eventually, you'll get to a point where you'll just look at something and say to yourself, "That's crap. I can do better than that." You'll have this library of ideas that are always swimming around in your head, and that's where the instinct comes from. You can also look at a problem if you get stuck and say to yourself, "Oh yeah, I know where I can get some help on that." The flipside of that is that it really helps to have someone read your stuff and help you edit it and give you a different perspective. Ask for their gut reaction, and you just might get a profitable discussion going.

There are two guys that really helped me a lot with this process. One is Russ von Hoelscher — this was in the very beginning. And Russ used to always say to me, when I would get all excited and call him up and blurt out this idea that was really making me happy, "That won't work." It used to really piss me off! I would get so mad at him. "What do you mean it won't work? How do you *know* it won't work?"

But he was doing me a favor, even when I wanted to crawl through those phone wires and strangle him. He was usually right — because he had 20 years of experience more than I did, and he saw things that I wasn't able to see. He'd already been where I wanted to go. That used to really make me angry, but guess what? Nowadays I do the same thing to people. I usually keep my mouth shut, because I'm a people-pleaser. I like to make people happy, so if I know something doesn't work I'll usually just shut up or I'll tell Chris Lakey, "That ain't going to work."

Dan Kennedy also helped me so much. I started working with him in 1993, and I'll never forget how he came out to the house and spent a couple of days working with us once. I had this sales letter that I'd spent two weeks working on. I did the best job I knew how to do. Well, when I showed it to Dan, he just looked at the sales letter for no longer than a minute. He flipped through it real quick and said, "I can do better," and threw it on the table. I just wanted to jump across that table and strangle him! I was so angry!

And yet, because I was so angry about it, it caused me to think. How would I have reacted if he would have just said, "Oh, T.J., that was a great sales letter. Yeah, I really loved it"? Well, I wouldn't really have thought through what might have been wrong with it. But he told me the truth, and the truth does hurt sometimes. We all know it, and that's why so few people tell the truth consistently. They don't want to hurt anybody. They want to sugar-coat everything. They want to put a nice positive spin on everything.

So I called him up a couple weeks later and I said, "Dan, is *this* why you said that?" and he said, "Yeah, that's one of the biggest reasons." The bottom line is, I didn't have enough proof in the letter. I was making a big mistake that I used to make all the time — one that I try not to make anymore. It's what I talked about in the last chapter, and few chapters before that: you have to realize just how absolutely, positively skeptical people are. Just because you're sold on the idea doesn't mean that they're going to be. If you come at it with that perspective before you get started, your sales material is going to be much more powerful. It's going to be much stronger. It's going to do a much more thorough job of convincing people.

You've got to show them proof. You've got to come at it with the belief and the understanding and the awareness that they don't believe you, they don't trust you, they're always holding back. You have to address their skepticism more than anything else.

# Chapter Nine:

# Learn the Ten Commandments of Marketing, PART I

In the next two chapters, I'll outline what I call the Ten Commandments of Marketing. Internalize these, use them every day in conjunction with I've already told you, and once again you'll find that you don't have to be the world's best copywriter to make money. You just have to continually use good strategies. That's what these Ten Commandments of Marketing are, and almost all of your competitors are breaking each one every day. This is to your favor, if you're the one following the rules! Some of this is going to sound like common sense — and yet, as Mark Twain said in the 1800s, "Common sense is a very uncommon thing." I'd say it's even more uncommon today.

## The First Commandment

Give people what they want. It's just that simple. Again, this seems like common sense, and yet so many marketers forget it. They fall in love with whatever it is that they're promoting, and they think the whole world is going to naturally be in love with it, too. Instead, they should be asking, "What are people buying right now? What are the things that excite them right now? What are the things that cause them to spend the maximum amount of money on related products and services? What are those common denominators? What are the benefits that people want the most? Who are the competitors in this marketplace that are doing the best jobs?"

Let's look at M.O.R.E., Inc. I'm proud to say that we're probably one of the top 10 companies in the opportunity market, by almost anybody's standard. We've earned our position in the marketplace. If asked, I think most people in the field would say, "M.O.R.E., Inc.? Definitely, you guys are Top 10." We think we're even better, but that's our sense of pride showing.

Why worry about who's the best in your market? Because you need to copy the very best things that they're doing. Not literally, of course — that would be plagiarism, and it's illegal — but you should use them as models for your own initiatives. If you're in the opportunity market, look at what we're doing and get some ideas from us. If you're going to be serving this market, you should definitely do what we're doing, because we've been doing it a long time and we work very, very hard at trying to be the best in the business. Within any market, there are leading competitors — people who are out there really trying to do the best job. Year after year, they're performing well in the market. It's good to copy what they're doing. Really focus on what is it about the products and services they sell that causes them to be one of the leading companies in the market year after year. Then ask yourself, "What are they doing to give their customers what they want?" That's the big question. Answer that, and then determine how you can create your own products and services that are similar to theirs, while building in some distinctions.

Often, the market itself will tell you what's hot. Occasionally you might hear someone say, "Hey, we've got this product, and we have absolutely no competition!" That sounds nice, until you consider why they have no competition. It's because there's no *money* there. You want the money to dictate where you're going with your offerings. Chris Hollinger recently went through a process of trying to determine what his prospects really wanted. He started by looking at what was selling in this economy, and then got on the phone and started interviewing some of the people who had responded to his ad but hadn't purchased. He asked them, "What is it that you want? What kind of home-based business do you want? What kind of product do you want to offer? What kind of money do you have to spend?" Then he took his notes from all those interviews and told himself, "Okay: to the best of my ability, I'm going to create exactly what they told me they wanted." So one way that you can find out what your prospects want is to *just ask*. Too often, marketers try to come up with all these clever, unique ideas on how to determine what the market wants, when the easiest thing to do is just to ask them. In Chris's case, the jury's still out. He's got some test pieces out there that are working; but his whole goal was to give his prospects exactly what they told him they wanted. We'll see if it works.

I see too many businesses that are very rigid in their thinking. Their idea of marketing is to say, "This is what we have. This is the way we do it. If the customers don't want it that way... well, then, we'll find the ones who do!" This isn't very smart, because it could lead to problems with sales. When a company is inflexible, they miss out on what the prospects really want — which changes constantly. The public might want something quite a bit right now; it might be superhot right this minute, but six months or a year from now they don't want it anymore. The market can be fickle that way.

This principle is important because it's all about the prospect, all about the marketplace you're serving. In business, too many people approach the subject completely backwards: they come up with a product, then try to figure out who wants to buy it. The better way to do it is to find a marketplace, and then figure out what that marketplace wants the most... and *then* develop products and services that give them that.

The opportunity market, the one I've been working in for the past 20 years, is made up of millions of people who want to find a way to make money from home. Everything we do at M.O.R.E., Inc. is oriented around serving that marketplace, by providing them with products and services that help them make money from home. Nothing we do goes the other way; we *never* start by developing a product and then try to figure out who to sell it to. Everything we do is built around knowing the marketplace, and then developing products and services for that marketplace.

It's all a matter of giving people what they want. A century ago, Henry Ford said about his market, "They can have any color Model T they want, as long as it's black." He was trying to give them what *he* wanted — and that's the wrong way to do it. You want to give people what *they* want, and the way you do that is by knowing your marketplace intimately. That's why I always talk about selling to a marketplace that you're a member of. You have firsthand expertise of how the people in that marketplace think, what their hot buttons are, what they respond to, what they care most about. You can develop products and services based on your own understanding of the marketplace.

That marketplace might be one that serves a hobby you're interested in. Look at golfing: the golfing marketplace is huge, and it generates a lot of profit for some marketers. Golfers buy like crazy; they're never satisfied with their game. I know that because Chris Lakey's a golfer, and I know how he thinks. He tells me that he sees all the people he golfs with get frustrated with the same things over and over again. There's a multi-million dollar marketplace that consists of people buying golf-related products and services. So if you're an avid golfer, you could get into in the golfing business — say, by selling information products or real golf tools to help people become better golfers. Based on your own knowledge of the marketplace, you'd have a good idea of what those people were looking for, wouldn't you?

It all starts with giving people what they want... so it all starts with the customer, not the product. That ties in well with the Second Commandment — but before we go there, let me just say this: a "want" is an emotional desire. And emotions know no logic. You can especially see that in the most extreme examples, so I would encourage you to think about the most extreme examples of why people do things, both good and bad, and realize that we're dealing with matters of the heart, not the head. We sell to people's emotions, not to their brains.

In a general sense, what most people want is to make more money, lose more weight, have more sex appeal. However, they don't want to pay the price to get the result. That's an emotional thing. We all know logically that the only way to get a specific result is by paying the price — monetarily, physically, emotionally. We know that *logically*. Emotionally, we all want the result for the smallest price possible. Again, emotions know no logic, and we sell to the heart of the emotions. You've got to remember that. Pay attention to the kinds of things that people are spending the most money on, and you'll see that there's an emotional element behind those things; and try to understand what that is. The best way to do that is to understand yourself. Look at your own life, pick some crazy thing you've done, and ask yourself, "Why in the world did I do that?" You did it because you were following your emotions rather than your logic.

## The Second Commandment

The Second Commandment of Marketing is simply this: It all starts with the market, not the product or service. So many marketers worry because they're lacking a product or service to sell; but really, what they should be doing is focusing on their chosen marketplace first. The marketplace is just a group of people who buy certain types of products or services, and they're reachable through specific media — specialty magazines, TV ads, email lists, or whatever.

The marketplace will tell you what it wants. Getting back to the golf example: What do golfers want? Well, basically, they all want to shave points off their score in the fastest, simplest, easiest way possible... and so they buy all kinds of goofy, outrageous gadgets so that they can show off to all their buddies and they can be the heroes out there on the links. There's a debate over whether you shave points off best by using a better driver or a better pitching wedge or a better putter; there are different schools of thought about which particular tool of the game is the most important. Some of them will say, "Hey, you've got to drive; and if you have this perfect driver you'll shave points, because you'll be driving farther," while some people say, "Drive for show, putt for go." If you want to make the most money on the tour, it's all about putting, they say; so if you want to shave strokes off your game, you do it at the putter — and so they sell people these fancy putters. Whatever your specific school of thought, in the end, it's all about lowering your score and impressing your friends — and finding a faster, simpler, easier, less painful way to get that result even quicker.

Those are matters of the heart; those are matters of emotions. With the Second Commandment, you're starting with the marketplace first, and really paying attention to the items that are most appealing. Think about that. One of the themes of this whole book is that you don't have to be that good at copywriting to make good money. If you're focused on the things that people really want, then you can be a mediocre copywriter and still get wealthy — because you're focused on those key areas that you know are red-hot.

I was looking at *Opportunity* magazine the morning I wrote this, and I discovered that there are a whole lot of people copying something that Chris Lakey and I started doing about five years ago. As far as I know, we were among the first to take this idea and really expand it, to try to do something with it on a major scale. What I'm talking about is the way we started building marketing systems around multi-level marketing companies. Nowadays, we see a lot of people copying those ideas, and this is a great example of what I've been telling you here. These people are putting into play the ideas we originated, ideas that are the most appealing to our marketplace.

You need to look for the most appealing items that other people are selling. If you focus only on trying to sell those items, you won't waste your time beating your head against the wall, trying to sell things that only excite or interest *you*. You'll be focused on what excites your marketplace, and how you can create something even better than what's out there right now. This really will help you understand your specific niche market and get you even deeper into that niche, because as I like to say, there's riches in niches.

So as a marketer, when you're looking to do anything, start with the market. Look at who that market comprises, and exactly what they're buying. Let the market tell you what direction you're going to go. Do that, and you're not going to be spinning your wheels with something nobody wants to buy. You're going into a market you know is full of eager, rabid buyers. You're just going to recreate the wheel a little better than your competitors are doing, and grab some of that market in the process.

This ties right in with what I was saying earlier about the First Commandment. First of all, it's all about understanding what people want, and then developing products and services that appeal to that specific marketplace. You start with their biggest desires; what does that marketplace want the most? Then you develop products and services that give it to them. That's one of the reasons I like information marketing. If you sell

widgets or anything else you have to manufacture, whether it's a
bottle of water or a dining room table, there are certain
limitations to how you can market that and how you can go
about creating products. But when you're an information
marketer, there are all kinds of ways to create information. It
could be as audio CDs, it could be as DVDs, it could be books,
it could be reports, it could be digital, or any number of other
delivery mechanisms and shapes that information takes.

Let's go back to the golf market. If I'm selling to the golf
market, I could write a book that contains tips and tricks for
shaving strokes off your game. I could produce a CD containing
the same information. I could decide today that I want a new
product and that I could sell it, and then I could go about
creating that product. I could have an information product where
I interviewed golfing pros. I could go all over interviewing the
pros at all the different golf clubs around my area for half an
hour each, and then I could create an information product where
they shared their best tricks and strategies. That would let me
quickly and easily put together a product I could sell.

Let's say I've developed a special putter that helps you putt
better. Well, I could sell that putter. But if I want to branch out
and sell other related products, I've got to create them. Do I
come up with a different kind of putter and sell that? If I do,
then I've got two competing putters. Or do I say, "Well, if I've
got a putter, maybe I need to also manufacture a driver," and
approach that side of the game? If I do, I've got to put all that
work into creating that new driver.

As an information marketer, you can quickly and easily
create products that target your marketplace. It gives you more
freedom to be in tune to what the marketplace wants, and to
adapt to it on the fly. We've created products that show you how
to create products in 48 hours or less. Information products are
fast and easy to create, and you can actually be out there selling

them as you're creating them. If I wanted to write a book today on a subject, I could compile it pretty quickly. Granted, it wouldn't necessarily be a really thick book, but I could write a 100 to 150 page book if I had the material. I could start selling that book immediately. If I wanted to create an audio program, I could interview the right people and create the program within a matter of days. Being in the information business gives you some freedom to be able to do this.

What I'm talking about here is developing products and services that give people specifically what they want. With information marketing, you can quickly and easily do that — regardless of the industry you're selling to.

**The Third Commandment**

The Third Commandment of Marketing is to make sure the products and services you offer for sale have the largest profit margins possible. Nothing that we know of has a larger profit margin than information products. That's part of their very nature. And the amount of money that you charge for information products has little to do with the amount of money it costs you to produce them. The real value is in what you're delivering to people. A good example of this would be painters who sell their works for hundreds of thousands of dollars. My wife Eileen is a painter; I think her paintings are very good. Sure, I'm very biased, but people have bought them for a few hundred dollars. The point is, the canvas she paints on is the same as the canvas that those top painters paint on. Her paintings may sell for a few hundred dollars, while a Thomas Kinkade painting, for example, might sell for hundreds of thousands. But here's the thing: The basic resources used to create those paintings, the canvases and paints, are more or less identical.

Information products are the same way. The papers or CDs they're presented on are inexpensive, and the costs don't change significantly from one product to another. It's the results they deliver that enable you to charge huge sums of money for them, in spite of the fact that, technically, it didn't cost you that much to create them. Software is the same way. There are so many high-profit products out there that cost very little to produce. You should focus on this fact, if only for one reason: *everything costs you more than you think it's going to.* That is the God-honest truth. And if you don't watch it, you could break yourself. In order to be an aggressive marketer, you have to spend a lot of money. Well, that money you spend has to come from somewhere, so you need to be focused on products that have high profit margins in order to acquire the extra money that you need to out-market your competitors. Do that, and you're going to be able to be more aggressive with your advertising.

One of the secrets to making the largest amount of profit possible is by "stair-stepping" your customers. I've mentioned this before. Look at the Recession-Proof Wealth promotion we're working on now. First, we're selling them something for $39. As soon as they get the $39 item, we send the letter that sells the $495 item. So we go from $39 to $495, and then we focus on selling products and services for thousands of dollars to that smaller group of people that first gave us $39, then $495. Now we're focused on spending the money to try to move them even further. We could always try to sell the $495 product first — but that wouldn't really work, would it? You can't just take somebody from cold to hot that fast. That would be like a young man who meets a beautiful, attractive woman and instantly asks her to marry him. If she's a good woman she's going to say no, even if she might want to or might consider it. Similarly, in our field you can't ask people to do too much too fast — so you have to stair-step people.

Here's an example from my friend Chris Hollinger. When he first started his business, he was preparing to sell websites to entrepreneurs around the country, and was giving a lot of thought to where his price point needed to be. Obviously, a website has a lot of design time invested in it, but there's not a lot of physical product, is there? At the beginning, coming from the Midwest and having just been a teacher and launching this new business, Chris couldn't fathom charging $1,297 for a website — mostly because there was no way he, personally, would spend that much on a website. And yet, when he discussed this with me, I told him, "Oh, hey, absolutely! You should charge $1,297 or maybe even more for your higher-end websites. And you could consider offering a middle-level website, and then an entry-level website." Chris was convinced that people would buy that entry-level $490 website before they'd buy the more expensive one — but the reality couldn't have been further from the truth. The vast majority of the sales that he made with that initial product offer were at the $1,297 level. People ate them up. They wanted the very best. And, of course, at $1,297 Chris knew how much time was involved in creating such a website — and it was surprisingly low. The profit margin in the majority of websites out there is just ridiculous because, especially now, there are so many different websites that can be used as templates. You just replicate them to a certain degree, and then add to and change them as necessary.

So let's say a local businessman in Wichita wants to buy a website, because he doesn't have the skills to build his own — even though there are a lot of good programs out there that would allow him to do that. He wants Chris to do it, and Chris is going to charge him for his time, his design fee, his overhead, whatever. Most of the time, the customer is willing to pay that. What really was an eye-opener for Chris were those higher-level sales. About 75 to 80 percent of his sales were the $1,297 level. It's really fun when you start getting orders for $1,297, $1,297, $1,297... and they keep coming in.

Six years later, it's still hard for Chris to determine a price for his products. That's a conversation he and I have had many times: will people really spend $999, $3,500, $5,000 for products? Well, yes, they will. As I mentioned earlier, people buy in an emotional vacuum. If you can build the value and the benefits in your sales copy to the point to where you can say, "This is why it's worth $5,000," and offer proof, then yes, they'll buy, if that's what they're looking for.

Of course, if you're going to charge $5,000 for something, you've really got to build that case up! You've got to have some serious, believable proof there: features, benefits, and value. And oftentimes, it might involve a stair-step type scenario. But if it's there, and it's convincing, people will buy it. Some people might claim that they don't have the money, but if they really want it, they'll *find* the money. It's almost a law of the universe: People will find the money for something they really want. If your copy's strong enough, they'll feel they really want what you're offering, and they'll find the money.

That's one reason it's always a good idea to have a bigger option or bigger package available. If at all possible, and generally it *is* possible, you should have A and B packages, or maybe A, B, and C packages — a good, a better, and a best. A silver and a gold. A basic and a premium; something like that. If you have just one package of products, split them into two. All you have to do is take some of them and make them available for the base price, and take the rest of them and make them only available with the upgrade. You can divide your content out to deliver it over a couple of different package options. So maybe Option A, your basic package, costs $397; and your premium package, Option B, includes all these additional products and services, features, and benefits and costs $997. If you have the ability, split it into three and offer an Option C that goes for $1,497 or $1,997. You'll find that just by having the more expensive option available, it does a couple of things.

Some people will always go for the most expensive option; they just do it. It's psychological. They want the best. Think about cars: when you buy a new car, you want all the options! So even though the base price is only $23,000, it's loaded up at about $35,000 — and almost everybody goes for the $35,000 option, because they want all the goodies on their new car. It's that way with most things. Sure, some people are cheapskates and always go for the cheap option, but some people always go for the most expensive. Having that package available increases your average ticket size.

Here's another thing it does. For the people who still opt for the lowest price, it makes that package more valuable in their minds, because they see that there are other things available out there that are even more expensive; this makes that lower price seem more affordable to them. If you have $397 on your order form and that's it, then they've got nothing to compare it to. But if you've got Package A, B, and C, and Package A is $397 while the others are even more expensive, it makes people feel a little better about that lower price. It can help get more people to go ahead and take it. So if you've got multiple products or services, divide them up into different packages. That can really help you make more sales *and* have a higher average ticket sale.

The great thing about information products is that their value is based on what's inside them, *not* what the product is made of. A single CD costs maybe a penny or two to manufacture. All a CD is is a piece of plastic that holds data. And yet, you could put content worth thousands of dollars on that single CD-Rom. If it's the right information, sold to the right person, they'll be happy to pay thousands of dollars for it. It all depends on what's on the CD. It's the same way with a book. Several years ago, a gentleman was selling a book no more than 50 pages long for a $1,000, and he sold it with a notice clearly stating that there were no refunds. It was just a little book about the size of a legal pad, not very thick at all. At M.O.R.E., Inc., we printed some up for a few of our friends and gave them away. I think that was the reason he said, "No refunds" — because he knew it would be easy to make a photocopy and return the original to him for a refund.

The point is, it's the information that's presented that's important, not what it's presented on or what format it's given to you in. Books sell all the time for $15, $20, $25. There's no reason that a book 100-200 pages long couldn't also sell for $1,000 if it contained the right information.

That's the great thing about information marketing. It's not the same as selling most products. There are certain abilities you need to sell what I call "mainstream" or physical products. If you have a product sitting on your desk, there are limitations on how much you can sell that product for. And it gets even harder to make bigger profits on a product that's available through other people. If your prospects can get your product at Wal-Mart, you're probably not going to be able to make much money on it, because Wal-Mart is selling them by the millions for a very small margin that you can't beat. In the Internet age, you have very little ability to sell your product for much more than what Wal-Mart is selling it for. If someone sees that you have it available for "X" dollars and they can go to Wal-Mart and get it for half that, then hey, they're probably going to buy it at Wal-Mart. That's reality.

With information products — especially proprietary ones, where you're the one developing them — you control the entire situation and all the content. You control the inventory, the supply, how many of them are available, and you can set the price. The price is based on whatever value the prospect perceives it as having. So you could sell information products for any price you want, as long as you can justify the price to a customer, they're willing to pay it, and they can see value in giving you the money you're asking in return for it. There's no limitation to that. People regularly sell information products for thousands of dollars, and sometimes even more — whereas very few physical products demand that kind of money, except vehicles and electronics like high definition televisions. The largest profit margins are usually made with information products.

There's an economic theory that says, "There's what's something is worth, and then there's what the market will bear." Add the ruthless copywriter to the mix, and it becomes, "There's what's something is worth, and then there's *what the copywriter can sell it for.*" A lot of business people out there are operating on the economic principles that there's what it's worth, there's supply, there's demand, and there's what the market will bear. But a copywriter can get the market to bear a much higher amount. I think our old *Dialing for Dollars* booklet is a fair example. The paper, the staples, the ink that went into that booklet cost, oh, forty cents; and in mass production, that cost went down even further. And yet, the First Edition sold for $12.95 — and later, we created other editions that were bigger and beefier that sold for up to $39. That's a pretty good markup. We parlayed the ideas in that booklet into millions of dollars.

And how did we manage that? By giving people what they wanted. *Dialing for Dollars* did that so well that we had thousands of people sending us checks and cash by FedEx (we didn't accept credit cards for the first eight years we were in business). They also wired their money to us by Western Union. In more than one case, they just jumped in their cars and drove from four or five states away just because the mail was too slow, and they had to get our product right away. *That's* how much it captured their imaginations. *That's* how well we hit on the giving people exactly what they wanted. We created the right product for the right market. That goes back to the First

Commandment.

Remember, it's the market that determines the price, not us. So many people just don't feel a particular product is worth a certain amount, so they don't try to sell it for more money. They don't understand that the market is willing to pay more money, so they lose out! The richest man that I've ever spent good, quality time with was George Douglas. At one point, he was making $1,000,000 a week in our market. We feel great when we have a million-dollar *month*, and he was generating a million dollars a week! He told us in a very commonsense, laid-back kind of way, because that's how he is, "Look, my average ticket price was $13,000. I always felt that the more money I charged, the more people wanted it — because everybody wants the best." And when they want the best, they're more than happy to pay for it.

Here's a phrase I want to share with you. It not my phrase, and it's a bit insulting, but it's worth thinking about: "Buyers are liars." You won't forget that, right? "Buyers are liars." The thing is, buyers always say they don't have the money for something. But what they're really saying is, "Get rid of the guilt... get away! Get out of here!" What we teach our sales reps is that every time a client says they don't have enough money, what they're really saying is, "You just haven't told me enough yet. I don't know enough yet. I'm not sold enough yet." It's a poor salesman who, as soon as he hears those words, "I can't afford it," says, "Oh, thank you sir." *Click*. They hang up. They're done; that's the end of the sales call right there! But remember this title, which was from a book by Zig Ziglar's brother Judd: *Timid Salespeople Raise Skinny Kids*. A timid salesperson gives up the first time someone says, "Oh, I don't have the money." But an aggressive salesperson will just stay after them, over and over again; so they won't just take no for an answer right away.

In order to maximize profitability, it's great to have all kinds of options for your customers, especially choices for those few willing to spend more money right away. There's always a small percentage of your customer base that's willing to spend big, big bucks with you. And if you don't have something to sell to them for big bucks, then you're losing out on money that could and should be yours. They're willing to spend that money; they want to spend it. They've got it. They trust you, they like what you're doing, they want more of the benefits you provide. If you have nothing to offer them, you're leaving money on the table. All you have to do is find or develop the products or services that sell for more money, and you'll have a small percentage of your customers that are willing to pay it. Even better, it'll raise the perceived value of the rest of the products you offer, even for the majority who won't pay the big bucks right away.

Our Platinum Plus Membership, a coaching program, sells for $17,885 a year. We've only got one Platinum Plus member right now; we've turned a few down, though, because if we feel we can't help a person or if we feel it's going to be too much of a strain on them financially, we don't take them on. So we've got one Platinum Plus member; and although normally the cost is going to be $17,885 a year, until we get 12 members we're grandfathering in our first members and letting them just stay aboard with us, year after year, for free after they pay that first fee. So we're doing something special for them. But the point I want to make is this: we started out two years ago with just two coaching programs; I believe it was Silver and Gold. But now we've got four coaching programs. The most expensive is the one I just told you about, at $17,885 a year. The cheapest one costs $495, plus $50 a month. So there's quite a bit of diversity between those two prices. Though just one person is taking advantage of that large $17,885 package right now, it does tend to elevate the value of our other packages. For example, it makes our $5,000 program seem a little less expensive. That's just perception, of course, but perception is reality in the marketing world. I'll just admit it straight out: one of the reasons we came up with the Platinum Plus package is because we wanted to make our $5,000 package seem cheaper. When you have the big package to compare to $5,000, you think, "Oh, come on, it's only $5,000." It really does alter people's perceptions — and that's not a bad reason to have the Platinum Plus, if for no other reason.

You don't want to just make something up, of course! If we had a Platinum Plus position but we never allowed anybody to be a Platinum Plus member, that would be wrong. That's not what I'm talking about. When we came up with Platinum Plus, we invented a new membership package that gave the buyer even more. It's a real package, even though we created it knowing that we'd have a hard time getting people to pay for it. After all, it's almost $18,000 a year! It's for a small, small group of people — and we've turned down more people than we've allowed in. But we do have one member, and we're working on getting a second one as I write this.

The point is, having that higher-priced package — that ultimate option — makes our other options look more affordable. Our main "sweet spot" package is our middle one — the Platinum $5,000 package. But it's only our sweet spot because we now have the bigger package to compare it with. If we didn't have the big one, then people would probably opt for the next one down — because for psychological reasons, people often opt for a middle-of-the-road package. Chris Lakey bought tires for his minivan a month ago or so, and I remember him telling me that when he asked, "What are all the tire options?" the guy at the tire counter said, "Well, there are five you can choose from. We've got the cheap options here. These have this warranty, and they cost this much. And the most expensive ones are over here on this end." And what did Chris do? He said, "I'm not a tire expert. Let's go with the one right in the middle!" and so he picked the middle-priced one. All the tire options probably would have served his van fine. They probably all would have been driven about the same number of miles.

Well, a lot of people do what Chris did: they go for the middle package. And so if we only had $500, $1,250, and $5,000 coaching packages, our average ticket would probably be in that middle range. By having an $18,000 package, it makes our $5,000 package look more affordable. More people opt for it, and that brings our average price up. So the higher you can get that high-end package, the higher your average ticket will usually be. Arrange things so you have several package options available, if you can. If your products and services lend themselves to it, divide them up. Split them into Packages A, B, and C. It will increase your average ticket.

Even if you don't have A, B, and C packages, what you can do is this. Let's say your sales letter has an offer in it, and your main price is $495. What you do is, you offer an upsell and say, "Right now you can get this…" and you just give it a little bit of mention in the sales copy, maybe on the last page of your sales letter: call it a "Last Minute Opportunity" or something like that. "For a limited time only, we also have this extra package. Normally it sells for $1,000, but you can have it TODAY with your $495 package for just $495 more. That's half price!" So then you have product for the regular price of $495, and then you have a check box that says, "Thank you for making me this extra-special offer. I'd also like to add this other product. Here is my total of $990." You get people to take that add-on sale, just like that. It's not really an A, B, C package; it's just another thing that you've added on as an option — and some people will take that option. It helps with your bottom line; your main sale is $495, but a certain percentage of your customers will go ahead and check that box. They'll send you $990, so it brings your average ticket price up.

The idea is that when people are hot for what you have, you

should try to make the upsell to them as fast as you can. That's when you should offer them more choices. Even if only 10% of the people check the box and spend that extra money, it raises your average ticket price, which increases your overall profitability. It's simple. It's easy. If you hadn't added the option to your order form, you would have lost money that could and should have been yours. All you have to do is add one or two little lines, and BOOM! All of a sudden you make 10-20% more money.

If I remember right, the first time we tried this, the upsell was about $1,500 — and the main product was just a few hundred dollars. It was a significant bump up, yet some people still opted for it — and so we increased our average ticket. At the very least, this process helps with your mailing costs. Direct mail is expensive; the more you can do things to bump your average ticket price up, the more you can help offset your mailing costs and get yourself into the black faster.

Let's look at our coaching programs again. We started a couple of years ago with just two of them; now we have four, which is probably where we'll stay. However, we're constantly taking the sales material for those four coaching programs and improving it. We're making it better. We're reworking it over and over again. As I've said before, people who aren't insiders don't realize that these sales letters they see others using were refined over a long period of time. Our Platinum package is undergoing revision right now, as I write this. I'll make more changes next week, and the week after that. In the case of our Platinum coaching program, I expect Chris Lakey will just put his foot down about three weeks from this writing, and he'll say, "Okay, T. J., we're done. This is it. We're finished."

When you're a copywriter, nothing's every really finished — but sometimes, you just have to abandon it. Most people don't realize this. They think copywriters have some innate ability that lets them put together this magnificent, heavy-hitting sales material the right way the first time. What they fail to realize is that a lot of times, they're working it and re-working it and re-working it — and that's what gives it its strength and its power, and causes more people to send more money when they read it.

Here's another strategy. If you're personalizing a sales letter, try personalizing the order form, too. If you do that, it makes it easier for someone to order, because all they have to do is enter their payment information — their name and address is already on the order form. The easier you make it for people, the more likely they are to not put it off. If they have to fill out a form... well, sometimes people are busy. Even if they like your product, if they have to stop and do something to order it, what will happen is this: they'll say, "I'll get to that later." So they set it aside — and never get back to it. Putting their name on the order form for them, personalizing it, is an excellent idea. If all they have to do is fill out their payment, it makes it easier for them to order. Similarly, if they're already excited about your offer and there's a check box that says, "Give me even more..." and it describes what it is and has a price, then a percentage of them are going to check the box because they want more of it.

It's easiest to get that upsell if it's related to the original product. We have an offer right now that we've been mailing for a short period of time that includes, for the base price, a manual — basically a three-ring binder. But if you check the upgrade box, you also get audio CDs and some other stuff. It's related; it's easy to make that jump, because you already got them excited about the first thing. It's more of the same, just in a different medium. The fact that the upsell is closely related to the original offer is a way to remove any barrier that people have to the order. If it's easy for people to check a box, if it's easy for people to send their order, they're more likely to do it.

And people do things out of habit. When we held the

original event this book is based on, we had about a hundred people who said that they were going to attend. Well, we didn't get that many. So why would a hundred people say that they wanted to attend, and then not show up? One of my employees, Jeff McMannis, told me, "Because you gave them an order form, so they filled it out and sent it in!"

There was a time, years ago, when I would have said to Jeff, "Man, that's such an overgeneralization! That's overly simplistic!" But those days are over; now, I'm inclined to believe *exactly* what Jeff said. People just do things out of habit; there's an order form there, so they send it in! We're all creatures of habit, and we buy for mostly unconscious reasons. The best example of that is where people are faced with a decision of good, better, and best, like I discussed earlier in the chapter. They've got three choices, and out of habit alone, they'll often gravitate to the middle one. Maybe they look at the price and know they can't afford the highest-priced one, so they go for the next one down. If you didn't have that higher priced package, there's no way they're going to move in for that middle spot.

Recently, Chris Hollinger had a gentleman call him up and say, "Hey, I just faxed you my order form. Did you get it? Huh? Did you get it?" Chris says, "Hold on, let me go check." So he went to the fax machine and yeah, there it was. Then the guy says, "You know what you need? You need an investor's position for, say, $12,000." When your customers get to that point, the sky's the limit!

That's another reason why you want to have additional products and services to offer someone who buys something from you once. This gentleman wanted to do more business with Chris, because he provided good value. If you can get out there with another related offer to them and say, "Hey, I know you bought this, so I think you also might enjoy this..." then you can make additional sales.

I buy a lot of stuff online these days from Amazon, and I use an electronics website called TigerDirect.com. Both are really good about sending an email that basically says, "People who bought this…" and "this" is whatever I just bought, "also have enjoyed this… and you might be interested, too." Amazon will do things like say "58% of the people who bought this also bought *this* item." What they're saying is, "Hey, do you want to be in the minority, or do you want to be part of the majority? Because most of the people who bought this also bought that, and you should probably add that to your shopping list too." Amazon makes it really easy — you can just click a button, they charge your credit card, and the product is on its way.

What you've sold your customers the first time should show you what they're interested in, so that should prove to you that you can sell them related things as well. So don't neglect getting back out there with a related offer to the people who bought something from you once, because oftentimes they'll buy other products and services that are similar. That should be the basis of your system for getting your customers to buy more. If you don't have a system for selling to your customers, you're at the mercy of their system of buying — and they don't have one. At best, most customers just say, "Do you have anything else?" and that's about the extent of it. The type of person Chris Hollinger encountered, the one who told him he should offer a specific new product, is truly rare.

We have a few customers at M.O.R.E., Inc. who have been with us for 20 years. We have even more customers who've been buying from us for 15 years, and an even larger group of customers who have been buying from us on a consistent basis for the last 10 years. The group of customers we've been selling to for five years is larger still. We have these customers identified as such in our system; we know exactly who they are, and we're constantly offering them more of the types of items we know they've bought from us before. People who aren't familiar with our market might say, "My goodness, why would somebody just keep buying such things?" Well, think about your own life; think about the products you like, and the types of things you've bought again and again. There's always that group of customers that's insatiable. They want what you have, and they just can't seem to get enough. The more they buy, the more they want to buy! It's as if the hunger increases. It's like feeding a fire. You just keep feeding it and it grows bigger and bigger. Their consumption leads to a desire for even more consumption, and they just can't be satiated.

As long as you're selling products and services that offer real value to these people, then you're going to keep bringing in the money. That's the key here. As long as you're providing good, solid value and delivering on your promises, then you'll sell people more and more. If you're not, and you don't have those offers, you're going to lose money that could and should be yours. It's on the table; people are willing to spend it. If you're not offering them something in exchange, you're just going to lose that money.

Anybody can go through a company and, in an attempt to increase profits, say, "Hey, let's cut here. Let's shave this. Let's fire him. Let's get rid of her. Let's X-out that department. Let's cut here. Let's cut there," and, yes, those are all things that can increase profits. But it takes a certain mindset to do that. Another mindset for increasing profits, one that may be easier to handle, is, "Hey, let's sell our customers more of this. Let's sell them more of that. Hey, we can sell them more and more and more of this other stuff!" What's really required when it comes to increasing profitability is a little bit of both of those mindsets: a bit of the frugal thing, and a lot of finding ways to do more business with people you already know. They like you, they trust you, and you already know they're buying from all your competitors — so they might give you more money!

Remember that phrase, "Buyers are liars"? God knows I
love my customers, and I'm not trying to put them down here;
I'm just trying to prove a point, that's all. We've had people tell
us, "Hey, I want a refund. I can't afford this. I'm hurting for
money." So we give them the refund — and then we find out they
took that money and gave it to one of our competitors right away!
People will never cease to amaze you. As marketers, you find out
the good things about people, but you also find out the not-so-
good things. You see, we're dealing in a world of emotions here.
Think about that. Logic plays a very small part in any of this, and
it's all kind of crazy — but kind of interesting, too. It's fun.
That's where the romance of business life comes from.

**The Fourth Commandment**

The Fourth Commandment of Marketing is to develop
marketing systems that identify the right prospect, and then
communicate the right message to them.

What is marketing? If you ask a hundred experts, they'll
give you a hundred slightly different answers. But here's
something I think they could all agree on: It's those things that
you do to attract the right customers to begin with, and it's the
things you do to re-sell them again and again. The first step is a
necessary part to get to the second step, which is where all the
profits lie. It's simple, if you use that definition; then you can
develop your marketing plans accordingly.

So if that's what marketing is — attracting and then re-
selling to customers again and again for the largest profit
possible — then a marketing system is simply something that
allows you to do that in a systemized way, so you don't even
have to think. You set it up once. It does take work to set it up
that one time; but from that point forward, you arrange for other

people to manage it for you. You don't have to do anything. You can be busy working on other things.

People often ask me, "How do you prioritize your customers?" We do it two basic ways, but the first way is the most important. Our customer list is divided by the amount of money that people spend. Let's look at it as a triangle; up at the very top is the smallest group of customers, those who spend the most money. At the bottom are the customers who spend the least money. That's the easiest way to do it. People who spend the largest amount of money are on the smallest list; we call those "Primo A" customers. And then we have B, C, and D. You have to spend, I believe, $49 bucks to get on our D list.

When you're talking about promoting the right products to the right group of customers, this kind of segmentation is crucial. But it's also important for other reasons. Here's an example. Whenever we have a new idea we're uncertain about, we test it to that small "Primo A" group of our very best customers first. That's pretty much an acid test for us. If the Primo customers don't respond like crazy, then we'd better abandon the idea and move on. If people who like you and trust you, people who've already spent a lot of money with you, don't want your product — then other people probably won't either.

So you develop your systems to help you handle things. The systems can be very easy to build, so don't let any perceived difficulties stop you. Let me explain an easy system; it's the one that we're working on right now. We've got a $39 initial offer. It's a one-ounce package, First Class, so it contains just the basic two-page sales letter, a large order form, a return envelope, and maybe a lift piece. All it does is ask for $39 — and if they'll send that to us, they get a free gift, a gift voucher for $495. It comes in a window envelope, so the first thing people see is the FREE $495 gift voucher that they get if they give us the $39. That's Step #1 of the system. Although this is an

offer that's going out to our established clients first, we expect
that it's also going to be used for new customer acquisition. So
once we get past the testing phase and prove it's successful, then
we'll use it to acquire new customers — people who have never
done business with us.

That's how it becomes systematized. Once we know the
promotion works and all the back-end related marketing upsell
materials are in place, then every single week we'll mail out as
many as 50,000 of those letters. I wrote it once. We're
committed to it. And if it works week after week, we're going to
send out as many as 50,000 of those Direct Mail packages every
week. The printer will just print them up, the mailing house will
mail them out, and we don't do anything except open up the
envelopes with the checks, money orders, and credit card
authorizations, and process the orders.

Then, we have the back-end sales letter, the second part of
the system. This is a letter that asks for an upsell. It can be of
any length, but let's say it's five pages long. If it's successful, if
we convert enough people to that next sale for $495, then it
becomes part of our system, too. On Day #1 we get the checks,
money orders, and credit card authorizations for $39; on Day #2,
or Day #1 if we're really operating fast, those who bought will
immediately be sent this package for the $495 upsell. Then, over
the next month, we'll create as many different follow-up letters
as we can for all those people who gave us $39 but didn't give
us the $495 right away. Then we're going to have a sequence of
maybe 10 to 12 different follow-up offers that, again, we'll
create just once. That's the point I want to make: that's the part
of it that makes it a system! We'll work hard to do it this one
time. We'll put together as many as 10 or 12 different follow-up
offers that keep saying, "Hey look, why didn't you upgrade?
Why didn't you upgrade?" and we'll continue to give them more
reasons why they *should* upgrade, and we won't let go of them.

Again, that's what salesmanship is all about. Stay on top of them! Keep telling them they need to upgrade. Keep making more convincing arguments.

Then, from that point forward, we'll start developing other upsells for the people that gave us the $495. We already know the things that we want to sell to them; it's important to know that from the beginning. This is part of our overall strategy; in this case, we have at least two things that we want to offer people. One is a $3,500 product we want to create with one of our joint venture partners called Global Resorts Network, and it's a great opportunity. We also have our Platinum Membership in the Direct-Response Network; that's a $5,000 sale. Those are the two ultimate sales that we *know* that we want to make to the largest number of people. But first we're starting by asking for the $39, for which they'll get a great opportunity. Part of the secret of upselling is this (and it *is* a secret, because most people have never figured it out): We're giving them so much value for their $39 that they're going to say, "Holy crap!", like Frank Barone used to in *Everybody Loves Raymond*. They'll go, "Holy crap! This is great!" and they'll be happy and excited. That's part of our goal. When they spend 39 bucks, we give them a *really* nice package, and they feel good about what they've just gotten — and now they're ready to move on. We've won their trust.

Only a fool starts out automatically trusting someone. Smart people are always holding back; you have to earn their trust. So, we're earning people's trust by first giving them a great package for $39. Then we go for an upsell that's directly related to what we sold them first. Now we've got a Master Distributorship opportunity that's so connected with what they bought that it's a natural upsell. It's a perfect extension. The goal is to convert the largest number of $39 buyers to the $495 sale. The idea is that we stair-step people. You can't just go from $39 to $3,900; there needs to be a more realistic progression. Each point along the way, you're earning more of their trust, showing them more and more that you're the kind of person they can depend on, and that they don't have to worry about losing their money or being taken advantage of.

If we do our jobs right, they'll spend $10,000 or more with us, because they'll get involved in all three of those big upsells that we have for them. They've got the money to spend. They're willing to spend it, and they *will* spend it with us if we do our jobs right. Sure, it may take us six weeks or eight weeks to put together all those steps and lay them out, but once it's done, it will work just like clockwork. It's like all those websites that have those auto-responders that marketers are familiar with, where they can set them up so that on Day 3 people are going to get this email, and on Day 10 they're going to get that email, and on Day 20 they're going to get this other email. Well, you can do the same thing with Direct Mail, too. It just takes a few people to work it and make sure that it happens right, somebody who's paying attention to the details. Once you get it going, once you prove that it's profitable, you can just sit back and create the next deal while the first deal keeps the money coming in. The system is really what you're building, and the copywriting is just all part of making that system work. Once the system is in place, it keeps cycling.

Some people, like my friend Chris Hollinger, might just use an outline on a dry erase board to document their system. It doesn't have to be terribly elaborate. Your system can be a list or flow chart that guides you through the process so you're not flying by the seat of your pants. It starts with just building an outline of the necessary marketing and sales steps, and it can look something like this: let's say it starts with a small space ad you could run in a publication that meets your criteria for the people you're going after. Interested people can call a 24-hour recorded hotline. So that's Step #1. The copywriting you've done has got them to the point to where they've picked up the phone and listened to that recorded message. If they're interested, then at the beep they leave you their information. What happens then? Boom... the mail package goes out, and it's a sales letter, an order form, and maybe a lift piece about you, to help them connect with you. Once you have a few sales, your outline takes it to the next step.

Some of the people who receive this first piece will order the product or service you're trying to sell them. Most won't. By not ordering, you assume those people said no. Of course, anything could have happened; your piece could have gotten chewed up by the dog, it could have got piled on, it could have gotten thrown into a desk drawer, or someone else's letter might have worked better. That's why you want your piece to be compelling — so when they get it, they act right away.

The sky is the limit on what you can do with your follow-up. Will it be a postcard? Will it be another letter? A CD? I might send a letter saying, "Hey, you didn't respond to my first offer, so I wanted to let you know about all this other stuff that wasn't in it." Or, it can be a simple email. Some of us, for example Chris Hollinger, like to use emails because they can be very inexpensive. There can be problems with email delivery, but at least it's another point of contact that you can put on your outline. Again, these are going out to that list of people who said no. They haven't responded yet, so now you want to try and drag them in so you can outline the features, the benefits, and the value of this particular offer, and have a specific call to action at the end of the offer.

Now, at M.O.R.E., Inc., I have an infrastructure. I have to make sure that they have an order form in their hands, or they can easily call in and order. That's all part of building the system. But bear in mind, as I'm putting this offer together, I'm building this system just once — and then it's a matter of the mailing house or our printer actually handling a lot of the day to day stuff. You need to concentrate on those things that make you the most money, and that's making sales with your copywriting.

I like to think that ours is a top-of-the line Direct-Response mailing system. It's systematized. It's just boom... boom... boom; and once we've proved the numbers are there, we can roll it out pretty big. You can, too. But you can also start rather small, and test carefully; and once you get some results and the margins are there — the *money* is there — then you can roll it out bigger and really start raking it in.

There are three things that stand out in this particular commandment. The first part is developing marketing systems. A system allows you to, well, systemize. You can boil things down to a step-by-step process, so you don't have to figure things out as you go. Earlier, I talked about the systems we have in place for when orders come in, for when packages are shipped out. We've got an Administrative Department that handles all of the incoming orders and everything associated with them. We've got systems in place so that every order gets processed in the fastest time possible. From there, we have systems in place with our Shipping Department to get things shipped out.

So orders flow in and out of our offices in a systematic way, using the systems we've put in place. We have systems in place for making sales, and we have a system in place for communicating with our printer so that he knows exactly what we need printed and exactly what it's supposed to look like. The system also includes working with a mailing house to make sure our mailings get out the door quickly and for the lowest price. That system works on the marketing side, to efficiently communicate our sales message to our clients. All of that is part of having systems in place, so that we get orders coming in the door and we get products going out the door. We have systems in place for customer service, for when people call and they need help; we have Internet support options, and people can email. We have systems in place for coaching, so people who purchase our coaching programs can get support and help from us.

We have systems in place for just about everything we do. There are even marketing systems in place for how we write sales letters. All of that is systematized to maximize productivity and get the biggest results. Those are the systems that we've put in place to help us run an efficient operation. We need to have rigorous systems in place because we have a large overhead: we have a building and a staff to pay for. If you're working by yourself, your systems can be slightly different, because they'll probably involve a lot of outsourcing.

The next part of the process is identifying the right prospect, so you have to develop marketing systems that do that. How? Well, obviously, I've talked at length about giving people what they want. You start by knowing who your prospect is, at least in a general sense. The opportunity market may consist of millions and millions of people, but not all those millions are going to be interested in what you have to offer at any given moment. You could have a particular offer that appeals only to a small percentage of them, so how do you identify the right prospect for each offer you have? You do that through lead generation. That's why we recommend two-step marketing — so you can identify the prospects. You would never do a mailing to every opportunity seeker out there, but if you did, you could safely bet that only a percentage of them would be interested in what you have to offer. That's part of your two-step marketing effort. Maybe you mail out a four-page teaser letter first; maybe you mail out a postcard. Maybe you're doing it online; in any case, you've identified them somehow, and you're emailing them. Whatever the delivery method, you attract them, get them to request more information from you. That's how you identify the right prospect.

The final thing is to communicate the right message to them. That means you've identified them, and you're talking to them about the things that they're interested in. You're writing to show them that you can give them just what they want. You're telling them that you can solve their biggest wants and needs. And you do that through your system, so it's really a three-part equation here. First of all, start with the system, then identify the right prospect for your product or service, and then communicate that message to them in the right way. Those three things work hand-in-hand.

We're only marketing to the buyers — those people who have already bought the kinds of products and services we sell. We communicate to those people as part of our new customer acquisition program. You can have a mailing house that does all of this for you, by the way; you don't have to have a large Shipping Department. You can have your mailing house take care of everything for you. You can put together 12 different direct mail packages that go out after a certain customer spends money with you, and then they can manage the entire process. For example, on Day #3 they can send out the first follow-up, and on Day #5 they can get the second follow-up out. You tell them which customers actually bought from you, and they mark them off the list so those people don't get the rest of the sequence. A good mailing house takes care of it all for you. They're spending their money on their equipment, they're spending their money on their infrastructure, they've got their representative who's in charge of knowing where every step needs to go in the process, and they can take care of it all. You can also find companies that do all the shipping for you, too. So don't think you have to have a large infrastructure to run these heavy sequences.

The point is that if you're not following up enough with people, you're losing money. You can *never* assume that just because people don't respond, that they're saying no to you. You just keep asking them and keep asking them, until the numbers tell you to stop; that is, until the overall profitability for that list of prospects becomes so low that it just doesn't make any sense anymore, because you're not converting any more sales.

There's one more point I want to make. Let's say you have a local company that sells only to businesses, and you're looking for long-term customers. You're selling a product or service where the customers just stay with you year after year. You would easily lock in all of the prospective buyers in your area. Let's say you're located in an area of a million people, but there are only a couple of hundred primary prospective buyers. As a matter of course, you'd know where those couple of hundred companies were. You would have them on a list, clearly identified: here are the prospective buyers in our area. Then you would hire a sales rep or two. Their job would just be to work the territory. They'd go around on a regular basis and knock on the same few hundred doors until the people at those companies said, "Get out of here! We never want to see you again!" And even if that happened, you, the company owner, would probably send another sales rep there. They'd just keep it up again and again, until finally the sales rep would say something like, "Look, we've been coming here for two years. You haven't bought anything; so either you place an order with us today, or this is the last you're going to see of me for a while." You can see that this is how it's done in a traditional model. That's how Fortune 500 and Fortune 1000 companies are built. They've got sales forces that go out there and cover those territories; they just keep showing up on a regular basis, and they keep asking people over and over again, "Are you ready to do something this time? Are you ready to buy something this time?" Ultimately, they try to weed out those people who are never going to buy.

It works the same way with all direct-response businesses.

The follow-up is where all the money is. Staying after them again and again is where you profit. You can do that in a systematized way just by putting those pieces together once, and keeping it running on automatic after that. Every direct mail package you produce or create, every follow-up email, every tele-seminar that you record once can work as a system for all those new prospects. It's like a funnel: You're taking in the new prospects at the top of the funnel, and then as they go through the system it's all laid out, organized and designed to take that large group of people and whittle them down to a smaller group. Your goal is then to get the largest number of those people possible to invest the most money in the other products and services that you offer.

Here's an analogy that illustrates the process. Recently, Chris Hollinger took his daughter to a place called the Kaufman Museum in Newton, Kansas, where they have an old-time corn de-cobber. You put the corn cob in there and crank the handle, and it starts spitting out all these dried corn kernels. That's what a system really is. You have the hopper there, the funnel, and a good solid marketing system that helps you keep the prospects pouring in at the top. The cranking of the handle is all those follow-up pieces and mechanisms that you send to your prospects. When you crank the handle, dollar bills start shooting out the end.

## The Fifth Commandment

The Fifth Commandment of Marketing is reaching and selling to your customers as fast as possible, for the largest possible profit. Now, a lot of what I'm going to talk about now is repetitive. You've seen it mentioned before — but as they say, repetition is the mother of all skill. So whenever you see these things again and again, you should know that they're the common denominators that you should focus on.

Again, the basic idea is that you're looking for a primary, targeted prospective buyer — somebody who has already purchased the same types of products and services that you provide. You want to upsell them as fast as possible, for the largest profit possible. But you still have to realize that you can't take somebody from A to Z without going through the intermediate steps. You can't just start off by asking them for many thousands of dollars; that usually doesn't happen until and unless you've established just how qualified they are, and until you've done a few things to earn their trust. Then you're looking for the most natural, logical upsell, one that's closely related to what you sold them initially. Let's take a look at our current promotion again. The first packages are going out today with a distributorship for $39. Later, we'll follow up with the Master Distributorship for $495, which is closely tied to what they got from us the first time; it's a natural, logical fit, and that's part of the secret to maximizing your profitability. It's easy for somebody to grasp the idea of upgrading a distributorship to a Master Distributorship.

If you're doing two-step marketing, that means you want to get to the sale as fast as possible. So you need to get that lead to request your information, and then you need to get your sales material into their hands as quick as you can, so that you can convert that person from a lead to a sale.

I've already talked about large profits and selling information, and being able to have a high-ticket sale with a large profit margin. But you also need to keep this in mind: You shouldn't try to do it on the cheap. Too many people try to cut corners on their marketing. I'm not saying that you shouldn't pay attention to the bottom line, because it's important. It's a factor in profitability — that is, how much money you spend in relation to how much money you make — so there's certainly something to be said about watching for that. But it shouldn't be your main focus. If you focus on doing it as cheap as possible, you probably won't be as effective as you could be. It's much more important to focus on bringing in the largest number of sales and doing everything it takes to do that. Generally, you're never going to out-spend yourself. You can spend more money than you have, of course, but in most cases you can't spend too much money to make a sale. Too many people try to shortcut that part of the process. As you try to sell your products and services as fast as possible, to as many people as possible, for the largest profit, keep in mind that we're not talking about spending as little money as possible.

What's truly important is being ready to reach and sell to those people as fast as possible. I've talked about people being heated up and ready to buy. You want to reach them right then, because there's a time frame involved. Systems help you do that. As soon as that prospect has identified himself as being interested in what you have, boom — you want to be right on them with your sales message to get them while they're hot. To do that, you have to spend money to make a sale. Back when Eileen ran the day-to-day operations of our business, this was something that we went around and around about, to the point where it caused friction in our business. Chris Hollinger tells me his wife is the same way. She's always got her finger on the budget button saying, "I don't know...", while he's saying, "No, no, no... we'll spend this much to make these sales. It'll be worth it because we'll gain these customers, and we'll re-sell them." That one point takes a lot of us quite some time to realize, but it's reality.

As a business person, you're going to have to address that at some point — how much money you're willing to spend to break that first sale or that next sale. Here's the key: knowing the lifetime value of a customer. How much are you willing to spend to make that first initial $39 sale, in this example? You've got a whole system in place to upgrade them from the $39, to the $495, to the $5,000 sale. If the numbers are working, and you're getting those closings and conversions at the higher levels, you can spend a lot of money on the front-end. I was in the business about eight years before I realized that every sale must be bought. By that time, we'd already generated millions of dollars in sales, but I'd just never puzzled it out.

A sale has to be bought. In other words, it's going to cost you "X" amount of money to make that sale, and you have to calculate that cost against the potential lifetime value of your customer. A lot of people have difficulty understanding this concept, especially when they're getting started. They don't *know* what the lifetime value of a customer is yet. But look at the situation closely. What's the total value by the end of the sequence you're planning to build? Let's just go back to the example I've been using. We start out with a $39 sale. We're mailing thousands of pieces on the front-end for new customer acquisitions, so we get enough people who give us that $39 initially. Then we've got the $495 upsell. We're going to spend some money on the sequence to try to convert the largest percentage of those people who've already bought to that $495 sale. Then we've got the third sale, which consists of one of three additional, more expensive items — or all three, if possible. So if you can't figure out the lifetime value of a customer, just figure out the value as that whole sequence plays out, and let the numbers tell you what to do. It's all about return on investment. It's about dollars spent versus dollars made, and not being afraid to spend some money in order to make some money.

Yet most marketers are trying to catch a whale by using a little, tiny minnow as bait, as the great marketer P.T. Barnum used to say. In this analogy, the whale would be those customers who spend thousands of dollars.Everybody's looking for those customers, because that's how we make all our profits. But they're using minnows for bait; and by that, I just mean they're trying to spend as little as possible to acquire those big customers. It's foolish thinking. Sure, every once in a while, you might get lucky. You should, instead, be willing to invest as much money as you can, at least initially.

Let me just give you an example of that to make the concept clear. If we ultimately prove this model that we're just getting started with, we'll end up with many thousands of dollars for the final back-end items we have. On that $495 intermediate upsell, we might be willing to give up every penny of that. Why not? If we do, it will let us spend more money in order to make that initial upsell. We'll be spending up to $495, maybe more, knowing that we're going to get the largest percentage of those people to convert to the $495 offer, so that now we can make them that additional offer, which is where *all* the profits are. That's an example of spending money to make money.

# CHAPTER TEN

# Learn the Ten Commandments of Marketing, PART II

In Chapter 9, I discussed the first five of what I call the Ten Commandments of Marketing, which I believe every copywriter has to study and internalize if they want to make any real money. In this chapter, I'll finish up the list.

**The Sixth Commandment of Marketing**

Our next Commandment is simply to re-sell to your clients as often as possible, in order to squeeze the largest amount of money out of them. That may sound ruthless, but that's what you're here for, isn't it? This is one basis of any ruthless, aggressive marketing or copywriting strategy. As long as you're delivering products and services that have real value, then you're doing people a service by doing more business with them.

There are only three ways to build a business: just three. First, you can bring in more new customers constantly. As a matter of course, a percentage of those people are going to do more business with you. By the way, that's how a lot of businesses handle things: They just keep trying to find new customers all the time. But the other two ways to build a business are where all the profits are. The second way is to increase the number of times you re-sell to those customers. So if you've got a thousand customers, and the average company you're competing with is only trying to re-sell to those people three times a year, while you're trying to re-sell them six times a year — then potentially you're doing twice the amount of business your competitors are, because you're going to the customers more often. Finally, the third way to build a business is to increase the size and profit margins of your transactions. In other words, you're trying to sell people more expensive items with bigger price points.

The real secret to overall profitability is to do all three of these things. First, you'll need a system in place for bringing in new customers — that's #1. Number 2: you're trying to re-sell to those customers more often, which is Step #6 on the 10 Commandments list here. That's what I'm talking about. But #3, you're also trying to increase the average transaction size, every single time you do more business with your customers.

This is where most business people blow it, because they ask themselves, "When is it too much?" The fact is, it's almost impossible to overdo it. For every marketer who's too aggressive and ends up going bankrupt (and we all know they're out there), there are God knows how many thousands of *other* marketers who are holding back too much, too often. They could and should be doing more to make additional sales. People *will* buy more. People in most markets are insatiable, though in some markets they're more insatiable than others. And for the most part, most companies are just not re-selling to their customers nearly as much as they could and should be.

I was talking to a fellow marketer recently, and one of the points he made is that he never sends a prospect anything unless it's got a call to action of some kind on it. Even if he's fulfilling something they've already bought, there's another offer in there. You need to consistently make those re-sells; consistently give them the opportunity to buy more. It took me eight years to learn that — which is why I'll keep trying to pound it into your head in this book! I want to cut your learning curve down. That's one reason why it's good to keep reading books like this, to go to seminars and just generally spend time studying and learning this material: It cuts your learning curve down dramatically.

The easiest sale you'll ever make is the one that you make to an existing customer, because they're already pre-sold on you and what you're doing. *That's* where all of the profitability is in your business: re-selling to the same people again and again. There are a lot of marketers who never learn this. All they ever do is try to acquire new customers. All they want to do is keep slamming in new people, new people, new people — and then they just move on. They don't service their existing customers. That's not even part of their system. All they're doing is bringing new people in, making that initial sale, and moving on, happy with the money they're making. And that's a mistake!

You should *never* pass on an opportunity to attempt to sell something to your customer. They've proven a few things by buying from you in the first place. For example, they've proven that they like you and trust you. They've decided that you were worthy of giving their money to, at least once. And they've proven that they're interested in the types of products and services you sell. Armed with that information, you can be confident in making them additional offers, because you know they're interested. You've already built some kind of a relationship with them.

One of the things to keep in mind with this principle is that you don't want to let too much time lapse between communicating with your customers. A mailing list is extremely valuable when it's used properly. But that list can also go stale; if you don't mail to it, then there's no bond with it, no relationship with it, and it *will* go bad. One of the ways that people get around this is by offering a newsletter. This ensures they're mailing to the list on a regular basis. If it's an email list, you can have an email newsletter that costs you nothing to send out. Even if it's not, this is a systematic way to stay in touch with your customers on a regular basis. A lot of people who have newsletters sell products in their newsletter. Maybe they have a spotlight on a particular product; sometimes they offer affiliate products they didn't even create. Sometimes they're just pointing you to a website where you can get information about someone else's product. Maybe they offer a product of the month. It all depends on the business model.

In any case, staying in touch with your customers is important, because if you don't communicate with them regularly, you'll lose them. They won't have a relationship with you, and so they'll become no different than a person you haven't sold to already. The value in your list is in the communication; your ability to re-sell to that list is often predicated on you having an ongoing relationship with the people on it. That bond can grow stronger with time, just like a friendship. The more you hang out with a friend, the stronger your friendship can become. The more you communicate with your customers, the more they do business with you. And the more that relationship is nourished, the stronger those business bonds can become. So it's important that you cultivate that relationship, and through that, start re-selling those customers over and over again — squeezing as much money out of them as possible.

Again, it sounds like a ruthless marketing strategy, which is really the point here. When I speak of squeezing the largest possible amount of money out of your customers, I'm talking about discretionary income, of course. Just about everybody has a certain amount of income they spend on things they don't need to sustain them. There's all the money they're spending at McDonald's twice a week, or going bowling on a Friday evening, or deciding to go play a round of golf or buy the latest electronic toy. All that extra money is going to be spent somewhere; we Americans put less than 2% of our income into savings. So you know we're blowing it somewhere, right?

The trick is to find the best ways to squeeze as much discretionary money out of your marketplace as possible, because you know they *are* going to be spending that money somewhere. If they don't spend it on you, they're probably going to spend it on your competitors, on other non-related products and services. As a marketer, you want to get them to choose to give the biggest percentage of that discretionary income to you, by offering good value and by keeping the lines of communication open. Again, most business people just aren't doing this nearly enough. That's why it's a real, competitive advantage for you to determine that you *are* going to do it — and certainly, I've strived to do that myself. There have been times when I probably haven't done it enough, either.

If you have a large, well-developed mailing list, all it takes to make a profit is for a small percentage of the customers on that list to buy from you. Let's say you're doing a mailing to your customer base every month. Depending on the price point, you could make that an excellent profit even if 95% of the customers *didn't* buy from you that month. That explains why we're able to "rain mail on your head," as Chris Lakey likes to put it. That's why people who have been with us a long time get a lot of mail from us. Sure, they can throw it away every time — and if a customer doesn't purchase something from us, we'll eventually take them off the list. But it'll take three or four years before we'll decide that we have to do that, for whatever reason. Meanwhile, we'll continue to send mailing after mailing to our entire group of customers — and if only a small percentage of them buy from us every month, we've made excellent money. I want you to think about that in terms of your business, because it's exciting.

Let me repeat again that when you're writing to existing

customers, you don't have to be as good a copywriter as you have to be to get them on your side in the first place. Now you're writing to people who trust you and like you, and they've shown that through their purchases. They've voted with their checkbooks. What they're really telling you every time that they spend money from you is, "I like what you guys are doing. I want more of what you sell." That's the language of spending money.

## The Seventh Commandment

The Seventh Commandment of Marketing is to create sales messages that build strong bonds with your customers. I'll tell you how we've done it — and again, I didn't figure this out all on my own. Now, I've got a friend who's just getting into this business, and he keeps grilling me over and over again. He wants to know, "When did you start figuring *this* out? When did you start figuring *that* out?" Well, we really didn't do it all on our own! For the first five years, we just copied some of the best companies that we had seen and done business with, and who we knew were good marketers. And we didn't reflect a lot on what we were doing; we were just out there doing it!

But hindsight being 20/20, our story has made us millions and millions of dollars. The quick version is that for years, I was struggling; I was on every single opportunity mailing list out there, and I kept sending away for program after program. I was buying one program after another, spending all the money that should have gone to pay bills — electric, rent, and water. I hated my job, and I knew there was a chance to make real money. All my friends and family said I was an idiot; they told me I was wasting my time, that I was a fool. My wife was the only one who believed in me.

We didn't give up. We finally found a couple of programs that worked, and started making $16,000 a month. That wasn't bad at all, but then Russ von Hoelscher started working with us.

We went from $16,000 a month to almost $100,000 a week within nine months. The best part of the story is that because we didn't give up — like all of our friends and family told us we should — we ended up making millions. That's why *you* shouldn't give up either. You have to keep believing in your dreams!

That rags-to-riches story has made us a fortune for the simple reason that people identify with it. Everybody identifies with the fact that we're just average Midwestern folks. We have no special knowledge, skills, or abilities; they just look at me and say, "My God, if that guy can make millions of dollars, what's my excuse? Why can't I do it? I ought to be able to make a hell of a lot more money than he's making!" And they're right! This inspires people, and it motivates them. Sometimes I wonder, at three in the morning, "God, am I going to be 70 years old and still telling that story?" Well, I imagine so, if I'm still in this market, selling to the same type of people. I imagine I'll be telling that story if I live to be a hundred. I'll be telling it a little differently then, I'm sure, but the story remains. It's absolutely true, and it's a story the market has identified with. It's a story that bonds us with our customers, because in large part, they've also been sending away for one program after another. They've experienced the same frustrations I've experienced, and so they connect with us at a deep emotional level.

In almost every sales letter that ever goes out now, we tell some version of that story, because it's our signature story. You need one, too. This is the thing that connects us with our market. If you'd told me 20 years ago that you could have relationships with tens of thousands of people, that would have sounded like the shallowest of concepts to me. My mind couldn't have grasped that idea. How in the *world* can you have a relationship with thousands of people? Well, if you think about it, these rock stars, actors, and other celebrities feel much the same. They have people that they feel they have a relationship with. Admittedly, some of those people are a little fanatical, but they *do* have those relationships with thousands of people. That's real. The same principles apply to business. You actually can have a relationship with thousands, tens of thousands, hundreds of thousands of people; real relationships where they feel connected to you, they feel like they know you, and they like you and identify with your story.

I've got all kinds of stories that I tell about me, my family, and my past. They're unique to me, and help to build a relationship with my customers — and that does lead to more money, because people are drawn in by stories. Once you've found those stories, you need to be practiced at the best way to tell them, the best way to draw people in — or they can come off as hokey, or stale, or unbelievable. The more you tell your story, the better you'll get at that. And that's one of the keys, actually, to building sales copy that gets attention and arouses interest, because it helps to draw your prospect in, to get them paying attention to your sales message and to start building that bond.

Ultimately, direct-response marketing is a form of relationship marketing. We build relationships with people through our marketing efforts — through the ads, the sales letters, and lift pieces — that we send out in the mail, post on websites, or mention in conference calls. It's all about building relationships. The entire industry of network marketing, for example, exploits existing relationships. Our industry usually builds those relationships completely from scratch. It starts with the initial sales generation piece, whether it's a mail piece or an ad in *USA Today* or some other publication. You get responses from people who don't know you at all. So while I've told my story for 20 years now, I know I'm likely to keep telling it for another 20 years. Why? Well, let's say that ten years from now, we get a brand new customer who's never done business with us. Well, guess what? That story is brand new to them. So even though we may get tired of telling our own story, to that new person, it's the first time they've heard it. We tell it because it's proven to work and to build relationships. And still it's inspiring because, again, it matches the market. It's just human nature to be drawn in to those stories. The unfortunate side of this particular strategy, of course, is the fact that some people just make up stories. They make them up so they can pull you in, and they're good at it.

Think about some of the catalogs and magazines you get in the mail, and the sales copy they use to sell the products in those catalogs; think of the storytelling methods that they use. They talk about how they found this product in the jungles of South America, and how when you rub it on your wound it instantly heals — things like that. True or not, it's a good story. Writing good stories is an effective way to get a sales message across, assuming you're telling the truth. Everybody can identify with a good story, and people feel *good* about hearing stories. Some stories have humor in them, and that's a good way to build relationships with customers. Put simply, one of the quickest ways to bond with someone is by telling them stories and finding common bonds with them.

This building of strong bonds with your customers happens over time, just as it does with friends. The longer the relationship has been cultivated, the stronger the connection is — the stronger the friendship. It's a lot easier to tear a friendship down in an instant than it is to build one up in an instant. So you have to build strong bonds by constantly communicating with customers, by doing things that relate to them, by telling stories. The nice thing about personal stories is that they change a little over time. Now, the historical aspect of a story stays the same; mine will almost always include the first time that Russ von Hoelscher contacted us and said that he could help us. It will always include talking about how Russ took us from $16,000 a month to as much as $100,000 a week in sales. That will always be there; that's the historical nature of the story.

But the *ongoing* nature is that my story's being written every day; so there will always be something new to add. When I tell my story five years from now, it may include things that happened to me this week, this month, this year. So your story evolves over time; and the more you tell it, the more you find ways to improve upon it. My business experience goes back over 20 years, so I have many aspects of my story that I could expound upon — but most would be pretty boring for most people, even though they might contain valuable truths. So I hand-select the stories that best illustrate the points I'm trying to make, the ones that best build the bonds I'm trying to build. Over time, you can perfect your story so that you're illustrating the highlights and downplaying the lowlights. You're telling the story to present the case you're trying to make to your customers, and that story evolves over time as you grow as a person, as your life unfolds, and as you gain experience in life.

One way to do this is with a newsletter. Your existing customers are along for the ride, and communicating with them through a newsletter is a great way to continue to build those bonds with them. You spend a few pages talking about whatever the newsletter is about, sure; but maybe the first page or two of every newsletter covers something interesting or funny that happened to you that month — something that will help build a connection with your customers, something they can identify with. You can continue the relationship with your existing customers, and they'll build on that story in their minds. They know your past. They know the story you already told them, and you continue to build on that story through the ongoing relationship. Someone who's new hears the story for the first time, and it contains all your life experiences that you want to share with them up to that point.

Building strong bonds with customers is vitally important, because people aren't going to buy something from you unless they trust you. So you have to build that bond in some way; you need to try to build a connection to your customer as fast as possible, and get that relationship going. From there, continue to develop it so you can have the relationship that's required for ongoing sales.

We have a lawyer named Shelly whom we've only used a half-dozen times. He has a law firm in New York City at the Empire State Building, and he charges about $500 an hour — which is one of the reasons we've only used him a few times! But the other reason is because he specializes in just one area of the law, involving certain regulatory agencies. He's got a solid reputation. Frankly, if you have problems and you need that type of lawyer, you'd be a fool to hire anybody else. Now, he came out to our house once and spent a couple of days with us, and I asked him, "Okay, Shelly, what's your secret?"

Shelly told me, "If I have to go to a certain city to meet with one of the regulatory agents I work with on behalf of my clients, I'll have my secretary dig up all the newspapers for that metropolitan area first. Let's say, just for example, that it's Atlanta, Georgia. Well, first I'll study every sport teams in Atlanta. I'll memorize the top players, I'll look at their schedules and how they're doing this year; and of course, I'll take note of other things going on around Atlanta. Then, when I get into the agent's office, I just kind of feel him out. We make some small talk until I find that one thing that interests him. I might see something in his office regarding one of those sports teams — the Atlanta Braves, maybe — so I'll say something like, "Hey, the Braves are having a pretty good season this year."

So the guy gets excited about the team, and then he and Shelly start chatting. Shelly knows everything about the Atlanta Braves, because he just spent the last five or six days studying

163

all the local teams. He knows the names of the superstars, the kinds of scores they've been achieving. They have a great, animated conversation about the Atlanta Braves — how does this season rate with last season? What are some of the biggest issues they're dealing with? And then, suddenly, their hour is almost up and Shelly says, "Oh, well, hey... we've got to take care of some of this business here. What about that case?" And the guy says, "Well, just give me the short version of it." And then they work out a favorable deal, they shake hands, and Shelly's out of there with what he wanted. During the hour-long meeting with that regulatory agent, they spent maybe 45 or 50 minutes talking about everything else that interested the regulatory agent!

When I heard that, I was dumbfounded. Shelly charges $500 an hour, so you'd think the secret of his success wouldn't be anything like that at all. Right? It ought to be something like the fact that he knows more about that one area of the law than anybody else. You'd think that since he's the established expert in that one area, he'd go in there and use all that knowledge, skill, and experience to overwhelm the regulatory guy. But it's not that at all — Shelly just makes friendly conversation about what the agent really wants to talk about! I just thought that was great — it's a perfect illustration that salesmanship is salesmanship is salesmanship! I don't care what it's about: If we're dealing with people, we're dealing with human emotions. So we need to look for common ground, things that build rapport. The fact that you can do that on a one-to-one basis is fairly easy for people to understand. But to think that you can also do that with thousands, tens of thousands, even hundreds of thousands of people... it's amazing. But it *does* work, and knowing that could make you millions of dollars.

Shelly's story just proves the power of building relationships — even if it happens within the confines of a structured meeting between a regulatory agent and an attorney. What really came to mind when I asked Shelly his secret was that old TV image where attorneys sit down on either side of a table and go at it. But in reality, one of the most successful guys in this legal niche goes in with an entirely different agenda. He spends a while chatting with the agent, then the next thing you know, boom — time's up, the agency guy is happy because they have a workable deal, and nobody's ticked off! There's a new, profitable relationship there, just because Shelly spent a few hours boning up on the city the agent calls home. If this doesn't illustrate the power of relationship-building in your business, then nothing will. It's just salesmanship; that's all it is.

## The Eighth Commandment

The Eighth Commandment of Marketing is to position yourself and your business so that you seem unique. That's a tough one for some people. At some level, we're *all* unique — we just don't always see it. Sometimes it takes other people to see it for us, and to help us see it. Early on, for example, Russ von Hoelscher got us to do seminars for our customers; in fact, this book is based on a seminar we did in October 2008. Now, I love doing seminars; one of the smartest things my wife ever did when she was CEO was to encourage me to expand that part of our business. It's really been a great thing — but, unlike most business professionals, I refuse to dress up. I don't enjoy it. And so Russ came up with this idea: "T. J., why don't you just start calling yourself the 'Blue Jeans Millionaire?' That'll set the stage right then and there that this is who you are. You're the Blue Jeans Millionaire. When people come to your seminars, instead of being upset because of the way you're dressed, you're just the Blue Jeans Millionaire; that's why you're wearing blue jeans and tennis shoes." What a great idea! It's unique, and it's part of my story. I think you should also find something that's unique about you, something that helps people understand who you are and helps dramatize certain things about you.

Whether it's right or wrong, good or bad, all great marketers are shameless self-promoters. You have to get comfortable with that — but it's a tough thing for a lot of us, since we're trained from childhood to blend in, not to stand out. Personally, I never learned that lesson well; but it's still been hard for me do some of the self-promotion I do. But I do it because I know I have to. As a marketer, you have to get to the point where you're not afraid to tell your story, where you're not afraid to tell people who you are. You're expressing yourself. You're finding those things that you feel make you unique.

I've watched Russ von Hoelscher do it. I've had a relationship with Russ for about 20 years, but every year I see Russ doing this more and more, and I think it's kind of cool and interesting. He gets more outspoken each year; he's not afraid to express his political ideas in his newsletter, and he's very forceful. He's no Democrat, and he's proud to tell you that! And if you really want to know how Russ feels about this liberal government thing, he'll tell you that, too. Does he upset some people? I'm sure he does. And I'm sure he wouldn't do it if most of his customers were Democrats — but they're not. I've seen him take a heavier stand in expressing his opinions about excessive government, and every year I see him just turn up the volume more and more.

I think that's a great thing. All marketers should do it. That's part of relationship building; you can't have a relationship with somebody unless you let them know who you are. So don't be afraid. Don't hold back. Always tell people more and more about who you are, but try to make it as interesting as possible. Let's take my colleague Chris Hollinger as an example. He's a former teacher turned entrepreneur; that's his unique position. He's the Professor of Profits — that's how he bills himself. You need to do things like that, because by and large no one else is going to toot your horn for you. You have to sell yourself! Oh, sure, you can get some good testimonials, but you still have to be that shameless self-promoter. It might run contrary to your personality, but it's something that adds to the bottom line of your business and helps you build your business.

Look at certain industries out there: pizza, for example. Yes, maybe some pizzas are better than others, and of course you have your own preferences. But pizza is basically pizza, isn't it? If you're a pizzeria owner, you have to find a unique selling position (USP) that you can work into the headlines of your advertisements to make you seem dramatically different from your competitors. Maybe it's how you provide the delivery of your pizza. Domino's Pizza used to have a guarantee: "Hot, Fresh Pizza Delivered in 30 Minutes or Less or It's FREE!" That was a very good USP. It built the whole company. You were getting hot, fresh pizza faster than all the other competitors, guaranteed! It's a way to make the brand seem different from the next one — even though both are basically crust, cheese, toppings and sauce. C'mon, there's not a big difference from one freshly made pizza to another.

But there's another marketing colleague of ours who has a client who sells pizzas for $50! And that lady's little pizza franchises are taking off since he took over her marketing. But a $50 pizza! When I first heard about it, I couldn't imagine anyone who'd pay that much for a pizza. But then I got to thinking about it and I asked myself, "I wonder what a $50 pizza tastes like?" I was curious! And now I'm trying to find a place where I can buy a $50 pizza just so I can satisfy my curiosity. Now, I imagine I can find someone to sell me one — but the thing is, I'd better not be let down. It had better be one damned good pizza, or they're not getting a re-sell out of me!

But this lady's still got a great idea going. She's positioned herself uniquely with her company. She's the high-end pizza provider, and she's going to find some people who are willing to spend fifty bucks for a pizza. Maybe they just want to impress their friends at their next party. Maybe they just have to have the very best of everything, or they're not happy. Whatever their motivations, some people will be willing to spend that money. That's just one way that this lady's pizza franchise is unique: Her pizzas cost $50. She just has to find enough people willing to pay that price, and she can thrive.

There are a lot of extreme food items like that — thousand-dollar hamburgers with all kinds of exotic ingredients, for example. One restaurant in New York City sells a chocolate sundae for $1,000, and for really special occasions they have one that sells for $25,000. You eat it out of a crystal goblet with a gem-encrusted gold spoon. There's a burger chain in the Dallas area that will sell you two burger-and-fry combos and a bottle of Dom Perignon champagne for $300. Quite a few restaurants are famous for a certain thing that's really expensive compared with what it would cost everywhere else. They do that to make themselves unique.

It's noteworthy that this commandment tells you to position yourself so that you *seem* unique. It doesn't say you have to *be* unique. So you don't have to be that creative, or that unique a person, to have a USP that makes you seem unique. You have to come across that way, do things that make you stand out. You've got to find some way to position yourself so that customers don't see you as a "me too" product. If they can get your product from everybody else, what's going to make them want to buy it from you? You can always try to be the cheapest, but that's usually not a good strategy. Almost everyone says they're the cheapest, and there's *always* somebody willing to undercut your price — no matter how badly it hurts them in the long run. So instead, are you going to be the most expensive? Well, that might not be a bad strategy, as long as you can justify it somehow. But in most cases, price isn't where you're going to be unique. Prices are all over the place. You've got to do something different, something that draws people to you, something that makes them want to seek *you* out instead of your competition. If you're advertising in the Yellow Pages, it's what makes them see your listing and say, "Yep, that's the one I'm going to call." If you're into Direct Mail and your offers are arriving at the same time as all this other mail from your competitors, what makes them open *your* envelope instead of your competitors'? What makes them choose to fill out your form and send it to you? That's what you're looking for: something that separates you out in the marketplace and makes people want to do business with you instead of your competition.

Sometimes you have to create that distinction, which all goes back to self-promotion. Take our good friend, Ted Ciuba, the world's foremost Internet Marketing Specialist. How do you know he is? Because he *says* so. There's no Foremost Internet Marketing Specialist Institute that anointed him! But, obviously, he's got a tremendous track record to back up that claim. That's his USP right there, his claim to fame.

**The Ninth Commandment**

The Ninth Commandment of Marketing: Create offensive marketing strategies that allow you to control the selling process. If you don't have a system for selling and re-selling to your customers, you're going to be at the mercy of their system for buying — which is sporadic and haphazard at best. So you always have to be looking for different strategies so you can control the sales process. I like the idea of controlling the sales process. Of course, there's some illusion with that; you can't control everything, but you *can* develop specific strategies that go out on a regular basis to try to re-sell to people. Offensive marketing simply means you're not waiting for people to come back and do business with you. Some people will, sure — but usually, you have to go to them.

We've got many customers who have been doing business with us for five, ten, or 15 years, or sometimes more, but here's the shocking part about our business: Any time we decide we want to fold the tent and be out of business, we can just stop mailing to our list — and the orders will stop coming in. Maybe I'd keep a couple of employees on to answer the phone and reply to the stragglers who might keep trying to buy from us, but otherwise I can let my employees go. I'm sure there might be a little bit of business coming in for a while; I'd hope so, after 20 years of doing business with the same people. I would hope that for a while, we would continue to get a lot of phone calls. I could probably keep about half of my employees for six months; then I'd have to let half of those people go. And within a year, it could just be one person and a telephone, and maybe one other person coming in part-time to ship stuff. The business would be gone.

In some ways it's sad, but that's just reality. There would be a certain amount of what we call "drag business" that would naturally come in over a period of time. But eventually, it's one person and a phone. It would probably be profitable for me to pay that person, because there'd be enough business coming in that it would justify the expense. But otherwise the whole business would just be gone. It's different in other businesses, of course, but I think this illustrates the point that if you're not out there and mailing to people on a regular basis, the orders won't come. We mail constantly, and sometimes it takes one or two people, or even three, just to open all the envelopes containing the cash, checks, money orders, and credit card authorizations that come in the mail every day.

But all of that would be gone if we stopped promoting.

Offensive marketing of this type is a direct opposite of the kind of passive marketing most traditional businesses do. With passive marketing, you're just sort of there. You've got a Main Street business and your doors are open, your sign kind of indicates what you sell, people know where you're located, and they can stop in if they choose. There's not any aggressive marketing at all. If they were using an offensive marketing strategy, those businesses would say: "It doesn't matter that people know where I am. I need to do something aggressive to go after their business. I need to run ads. I need to sponsor local events so that my name's out there. I need to be aggressively promoting my name and my business's name so that people know who I am, what I sell, and where to find me. I'm going to aggressively go after this marketplace and get as much money out of it as I possibly can." That's the difference between an offensive attack versus a passive one, where you're hoping that people will find you. I suppose it's a lot like a football team's offense and defense: both are important, but the offense is the part of the team that scores the points. In business, the offense is the part of your strategy that scores the cash.

Our friend and fellow marketer, Russ von Hoelscher, tells a really good story about an ex-printer in his area who was a friend of his. The guy's business was kind of slow and he was looking for advice, so Russ gave him some very tangible, quick advice about putting together some flyers and mailers and distributing them, along with some discount coupons. And the printer shot back something to the effect of, "People know what I do. If they want it, they'll come get it." That's a good example of passive marketing. He just said, "Here's my business. I do really good printing. People should come to *me* when they want their printing, because I'm the best." He wasn't being offensive at all, and now he's an *ex*-printer. He couldn't get enough business, even though I'm sure the guy did great work. But so what? Even if you do great work, if you can't get out there and toot your own horn and tell people that, they're not going to just come to you naturally by osmosis, just because you put your shingle out there on the door. You've got to give them a reason to come in and do business with you. That's what creating an

offensive marketing strategy does. It goes out there and drags
people to you.

## The Tenth Commandment

The Ninth and Tenth Commandments of Marketing could
be considered the same basic principle, because the Tenth just
clarifies the Ninth somewhat. What the Tenth Commandment
says is this: When you're making specific offers to your
customers on an ongoing basis, you're taking them by the hand
and compelling them to come to you instead of waiting for them
to somehow gravitate to you on their own.

The key point in this last Commandment is that you're
making them offers. Whatever business you're in, what you
really sell is offers — not products and services. Think about
that. This is something that took me years to figure out. An offer
is more than just a product or service. It's all of the other stuff
that goes with it — the free bonus gifts, the special price, the
extra secrets and tips. It's everything you're offering to give to
someone in exchange for the money you're asking for in return.

Those infomercials you see on TV do a great job with this.
They tell you, "You're going to get this, this, and this. But wait...
there's more! If you order now, you're going to also receive this
and this and this as a bonus, absolutely free! But wait... there's
still more!" and they just keep building it up. The idea is to
finally make you just say, "Holy crap! What am I waiting for?"
So you run to the phone or get on the Internet and order. That's
why you've got to think in terms of offers — and the more you
study great direct-response marketers, the more you'll see that's
what they're selling. They build their products and services
around all kinds of free bonuses and premium gifts, special
pricing, and special limited situations, reasons for people to take
action NOW. They give it the greatest appeal possible, so that
people are excited and they're compelled to do business.

It's all about the offer — not necessarily the product or service. You see, anybody can sell a product or service, and that's kind of flat. It's just not enough anymore. We've got a client who's always saying, "Is that all you can do? Can you do any better than that? Is that all you're going to do?" He's always coming up with those questions whenever someone makes a presentation at our seminars. He says it as a joke, but I like the way he says it — because that's how people think these days. They want more and more and more. People want great prices, there's no question about that. But what they really want is a great offer. Give this some serious thought, because, again, it took me years to figure it out. What people really want are items that are very expensive and very valuable for dirt-cheap prices. When you're creating an offer, that's the perception you're trying to clearly communicate: that what you have is worth a tremendous amount of money or, if it isn't, it can potentially provide tremendous benefits that are important to your prospective group.

If it's not money, then give them something else that's really important to them. Give them so much that when they're weighing out what you've got on the table, they're just overwhelmed and feel that they'd be a fool not to take you up on the offer. That's something that Chris Lakey and I did recently. We hosted a teleconference for some of our clients and we made them a special offer, but here was the deal: Today Only. After that, they had to pay full price. We laid it all out, we showed them all the benefits, we showed them everything we were going to give them, we added all these great incentives and proved the value, and then we said, "Now, here's the deal: today, you can get it for half price. Tomorrow, full price." And sure enough, 80 of the 130 people on the call ordered right away. We made them an offer that most of them just couldn't refuse.

Again, you're going to them and doing all this for them,

RUTHLESS COPYWRITING STRATEGIES

instead of waiting for them to somehow gravitate to you on their
own. You go on the offensive and get them to do business with
you, instead of waiting for them to find you. Sometimes it's
costly. Let's go back to those infomercials I mentioned earlier,
the ones that just keep building and building the offer. It's always
"But wait — there's more!" and you have to wonder how the
heck they can possibly give all that stuff for only $19.95. The
answer is simple: They can't. What they're doing is making you
such a compelling offer that it would be hard for you to say no.
They pile benefits on top of benefits; they throw in so much stuff
that it makes it hard to turn them down, so you pick up the phone
and call. At that point, they've bought you as a customer.

You're right to think that there's no way they could sell all
that stuff for just $19.95: They might have spent $50 to make
that sale. But when you call them, they instantly make you
another offer while you're on the phone. Then, even if you say
no that one time, when your product arrives, guess what?
There's another offer with it. They try to recoup the money they
just spent "buying" you as a customer as fast as possible by
making you additional offers. They have to! Even if they got all
those items they just sold you from Malaysia or China, their cost
is going to add up to more than what you're going to pay them.
And think about all the ads they run — the infomercials
themselves cost a lot of money. But they have a system in place
where they're immediately going to try to upsell you on
something else as soon as you contact them. All their profits
come on those back-end sales that happen when make that first
order. It's a gateway product. It gets you in the door and captures
you as a customer, even at a loss, so they can convert you on the
back-end. They know that's where they're going to make
money... and usually a lot of it.

You get that profitable repeat business by continuing to
make more offers. You can't ever simply assume that someone

will find you and do business with you. Sure, if you're a retail business on Main Street, some of the people who live in your town will stumble upon you, decide to stop in, and maybe buy something. But if you're selling on the Internet or by direct mail, there's no way someone's going to just stumble upon you easily. It's up to *you* to let people know you're there, to let them know exactly what you sell, and to present compelling offers that make them want to give you their money.

# CHAPTER ELEVEN:

# Use the PAS System

In this chapter, I'm going to reveal a copywriting formula that can make you more money than any other I personally know of. And best of all, it's amazingly simple and easy. It's called the PAS Formula, because there are only three steps involved: Problem, Agitate, and Solution.

When you read sales letters as a marketer, you'll see this formula used again and again. First they bring up the biggest problem that's solved by whatever it is they sell, then they get you agitated about it, and then they offer the solution. Let's use my friend Mike's marketing as an example; he's the guy who sells the soy candles. His marketing does a really good job of illustrating the PAS Formula, because it first brings up the problems with traditional candles. They're made of paraffin, and paraffin is this sludgy stuff that's left over from the oil refinery process. It's poisonous goo that they couldn't figure out what to do with, until somebody said, "Hey, let's bleach it and sell it to candle makers!" Well, it's bad for your health, and it's hurting your children, and it's just a *terrible* thing. You have to tell people that; that's the "P" part of the PAS Formula, the problem. In making that problem clear and telling them what it can do to their children, you're agitating them; that's the "A" in the PAS formula. You're personalizing the situation; you're making it real to them. And then, of course, you offer the solution — the

"S" part of the formula. In this case, it's All-American soy candles. Forget those candles made in Vietnam and Indonesia and Malaysia, the ones they pay people 20 cents a day to make. These candles are made in America from healthy agricultural products that benefit the farmers, and they're good for you — so just burn them like crazy! The PAS formula is very effective, which is why you'll see it used again and again.

All you have to do when you decide to use the PAS Formula is to try to identify 10 or 15 of the biggest problems that your product or service solves. Then you just write these little bits of copy, where first you talk about the problem, then you agitate it and make it real to that person, and then you introduce the solution. Instead of writing this huge sales letter, all you're writing is just a little bit of copy each on these 10, 15, or even 20 different points. Then you just link them all together, and you've got a sales letter! Your very best copy becomes part of your headline, and you build the whole thing around those problems, which you're making real to people. You're personalizing it, making them agitated, and then you're introducing the solution — which is the thing that we all really sell. We sell solutions and results. Well, people can't appreciate solutions and results until they know what the problem is — and that problem has to be real for them.

Marketers use the PAS formula to do everything they can to scare their prospects. It can happen in a TV commercial in 30 seconds. A big industry that uses this method extensively is the maternity industry. They use fear to sell their products. They insinuate or even outright tell you, "Your baby could be harmed if you're not using these certain kind of wipes that eliminate all the germs." And they'll even show you the little microbes growing on all these surfaces if you're not using their product. They grab your attention and captivate you with fear, or a problem that you have — even if you didn't know you had it until then. It goes back to understanding your market. What are

the wants, needs, desires, and *fears* of your market? This
particular strategy — Problem, Agitate, and Solution — is such
a powerful strategy because, again, it captivates. It grabs your
attention. You're using something that's very personal to them
— the fear of not being able to lose weight, the fear of a bad
candle, the fear of not having enough money, the fear of their
children suffering — to agitate then. This is a ruthless strategy,
obviously, because you're capitalizing on the human emotion of
fear. Metaphorically, you pull back that scab and pour salt on the
wound, and then you rub it in. You agitate that pain.

And *then* you get them to the point where the only way
they're going to relieve the pain is through the solution that you
can provide. You offer them the most compelling, concise
solution to the pain that *you*, as a marketer, helped to aggravate.
So many different industries use that. You can't go to the
grocery store without seeing a form of this strategy in play
somewhere. It works very well with information products, too
— especially with a bad economy.

Again, this is one of the truly great and simple strategies for
making money with advertising. There are just three steps:
Problem, Agitate, Solution. It's easy to build an ad or sales letter
around this concept — or you can build an entire campaign
around it. If you'll write the three words down and then spend a
few paragraphs talking about each one as it relates to your offer,
that's a good foundation for a postcard or classified ad — or it
could be the start of a sales letter. You start with the Problem.
You're making people aware of a problem you know they have,
because you've followed the other formulas I've been talking
about. You know your prospects inside and out, and you start
with them in mind. Until and unless you can convince people
that those cheap candles are ruining their home by getting all
this black soot all over the place, and they're stinking up their
houses and ruining their children's health and killing all the

house plants, you're not going to be able to Agitate them enough to make them want the Solution you're offering.

I've had water-purification system salesmen who've sat down in my living room and made their presentations, using the PAS formula. Those expensive vacuum cleaner guys do the same thing. They tell you, "We not only clean your carpets phenomenally well, but we clean the air your children are breathing — and that air is just filthy." They'll happily show you how filthy it is. There's a commercial on TV as I'm writing this that's very similar. They say, "If you had a mouse, you'd trap it." Then they show you this baby sitting on the floor, watching a mouse walk by. That's ruthless! "If you had bugs, you'd trap them," and they show roaches run by the baby. Well, they're selling a filter for your furnace that catches 98.9% of the germs in the system. And then they show these creepy-looking microscopic bugs that you normally can't see all around this beautiful baby. The baby has this look on his face like, "Oh crap, Mom, you've got to go buy this right now!"

The flipside of that is, how long have we, as a species, survived without this filtration system? I don't want to ruin the sales for these guys, but lots of people have been born and lived their entire lives on regular water and air. But this is marketing, selling a product. Okay, you get nice soft water, and you get nice clean air. Who doesn't want that? But they use that fear to sell their expensive water and air purification systems. And they *do* sell them. They know that if they can get in your house and make this presentation, they're going to close enough sales to keep that money rolling in.

And it works! Problem — Agitate — Solve. For the most part, people won't even realize that you're using this formula. The average prospective buyer who buys unconsciously in an emotional vacuum is never going to be able to see that you're using *any* formula, assuming you're doing your job right.

## CHAPTER TWELVE:

# Internalize These Nine Secrets to Success

In this chapter, I'm going to blow the lid off what I firmly believe is the single greatest copywriting method ever, something hardly anybody talks about — even though all the world's best copywriters use it. Once you're armed with the nine secrets to this method, you'll have the ability to write the same type of powerful ad copy that the world's best copywriters write. Here's how it works.

**Secret #1:** Instead of just thinking about the problems that your product or service solves, as you would with the PAS System, start thinking about all of the problems and frustrations of your average prospective buyer. What are their biggest fears? What are their biggest frustrations? What are the things that make them the angriest and most confused? You're looking for all kinds of those types of situations. Make a list of them. Don't think about it too much; just write those things down as fast as you can. Speed is important. The idea is to write as much as you can as quickly as you can.

When you can't write another word, you're ready to go to **Step #2,** which is writing down all of the ways that your product or service or company can solve each problem. Again, you're writing as fast as you can; you're putting as much copy on the page as possible. You're not worried about spelling or grammar at this point; you're doing what I call a massive brain dump, putting it all out there until you can't write another word. Then, **Step #3:** Edit it all out and all down and, if necessary, connect your problems and solutions with agitations.

The first three steps, this extended PAS System, are the basis of this secret method. You create your lists of problems, and write just a small amount — as much as you can in a limited time — about each one of those things on your list. And then you boil it all down. This is the simplest and easiest way to write powerful ads and sales letters, because it lets you focus on the problems your prospects and customers face, along with the solutions you're offering. You never have to write that much at one time, really. Get it all down, and in the editing process you can smooth it all out and reformat it. No one has to know that you wrote it a little at a time; that can be disguised in the editing process. It's like a quilt. Each little bit of copy you write might represent a small patch; but in the end you sew them all together to form a big patchwork quilt.

That's one way to write a 20-page sales letter, like the one we're using for our Recession-Proof Wealth System. When you look at it, you might say, "My God, I could *never* write a 20-page sales letter!" But when you think about doing it in small blocks, it's not so bad. You're making lists, you're focusing on your prospects and the things you know are bothering them the most, you're thinking about the problems your product or service solves, and you're trying to agitate it all and make it real. Then you're finding a way, in the editing process, to boil it down and make it all fit. To me, editing is the fun part, because it's relaxed and calm, and I can do it with my wife right there on the couch while I'm spending good, quality time with her. She doesn't mind; she just doesn't want me talking on the phone all night, or being down in the basement working. She wants me right there with her, so I've got my little laptop computer and

I'm editing as we watch TV.

The writing is the intense part. That's the part that really does take work; that's the part where you have to find that time of day or night when you're feeling the most energy, when you're able to do your best and clearest thinking, and you're able to get it all down on paper or computer screen. When I type it on a computer, I often don't worry about paragraph breaks. I don't worry about any punctuation. I don't worry about spelling. In fact, the faster I type, the more misspelled words I have. I don't worry about *anything*. Sometimes I'll just close my eyes and type, and when I open my eyes I'll realize it's in all caps or something. That's all right — I'm just dumping it all out. And then, in the editing part, I stitch together all those little bits of copy and smooth it out and reformat it. It's a simple and straightforward process — and yet in all the books I've read, all the seminars I've been to, and all the audio presentations I've listened to, *nobody* has ever taught that. But I've found that it really helps a lot.

Even a big project isn't so tough when you break it down into small, discrete segments. Chris Hollinger tells me that when he was a teacher and had a big project with the students, he'd always break it down into little parts so that the whole didn't look so overwhelming. You can do that here. Keep in mind that you want to identify some pain, you want to agitate that pain, you want to solve that pain; but then you're going to go through the steps to break up the entire project into smaller projects. Start making notes. Start making lists. Let it brew up in the cranium for a while, and then start connecting the dots a little at a time to create some solid copywriting. By going through those steps alone, you'll end up with some compelling copy. Once you've done it, do it again. Do it seven times, and you're going to start building a lot of muscle memory and internalizing it, to the point where it'll start coming out in an easier, more innate form.

This is a great little system that you can put together to help guide you, so you're not sitting there saying, "Oh my God, I should have probably 20 to 30 pages here." Well, 20 pages can fly by pretty quickly once you start putting it all together. Now, I'm not saying that 20 pages is what you should shoot for. You're shooting for whatever makes your message most compelling in the end — however many pages that is, whether it's eight pages, 12 pages, 20 pages, or a hundred pages. I'm talking about salesmanship, after all. If you had a salesperson working for you, you wouldn't tell them to just stop after five minutes; you'd tell them take however long it took to make the sale. If that's five minutes, do it in five minutes. If it takes 35 minutes, fine. If it takes five hours, fine; get the sale! You want to put as much selling power in all of your sales material as possible, since you never know what's going to work best.

Again, when you're writing, just put it all out there. Don't worry about anything except focusing in on the prospective buyer you're trying to sell to, and keep in mind what Neil Young once said: "If you think, you stink." You just do it! Just get it all out — Steps 1 and 2 — and then iron out the kinks in the re-writing process, Step #3. I can't imagine not having a computer to do the editing part of it, because I usually end up with huge amounts of copy, written as fast as I can with no regard as to punctuation or spelling, and then shuffle it around as necessary, cutting and pasting as I go. I keep all of it in a separate file from the edited version, in case I edit too far and want to restore something. Do that, and you never have to worry, "Am I going to cut into it too deeply and not have something I need later?"

**Secret #4** comes from an interview with the late Gene Swartz that I read a few years before he died. Gene was a great copywriter; he made millions with the sales letters he wrote for himself and his clients. He's arguably one of the best direct-response copywriters who's ever lived. During the course of this interview, there was one sentence that really stuck out, and that's what this secret is. They asked Gene, "How long does it take for you to write one of those million-dollar sales letters?" And Gene said, "It takes about six hours." Then he went on to say that he does his research, sometimes, for weeks or even months in advance before he sits down to write the letter. In other words, he did his homework — and how! He wasn't just pulling all this stuff out of thin air. The real secret here, according to this interview, was that although it only took him six hours on average to write one of these Direct Mail letters, he broke it up into a three-day period where he only worked on it for two hours every day — and then he'd stop.

The fact that you can do your copywriting in small steps and then tie it all together is a secret that I never learned in all of the copywriting seminars, programs, and books that I've spent money on. I had to piece it together myself — which is why I'm making a big deal of it here. I think it serves you best to clearly explain that this, in fact, is how it's done — not just by me, but a lot of other marketers and copywriters I know. I'm not sure why more people aren't sharing that, except that in the case of most freelance copywriters, it's in their best interest that they don't tell. You see, what they want to do is charge you thousands of dollars to write those sales letters for you — and they want you to believe that they have some special ability or talent, or they're so much better at it than you are, that they're able to just sit down and crank it out. I strongly expect, however, that they write it in pieces the way I'm describing here.

Whatever the case, I have to point out that some of those freelancers are doing horrible work. I know what they charge their clients, and I've looked at a lot of sales letters with a trained eye. Some of them are just plain terrible. It's clear that those freelancers have never sold anything in their whole lives using direct-response marketing — except for their copywriting services. That's their only real experience, so a lot of their work is simply not very effective. You'd be better off avoiding it, and learning to write your own copy. Even if a sales letter takes you a month to create, you're going to put more time and effort into it, and you're going to care a lot more about it, than those freelancers. Instead, maybe you should pay those freelancers just to give you suggestions and pointers on how you can make your writing better. That's something like what our friend Russ von Hoelscher really specializes in.

I want to put a plug in for Russ again. Russ can take any sales letter and show you how to make it better. He'll say, "Change this. Change that. Make this better. Take that out. Improve this," and there you have it: The best of both worlds. You have somebody who's very experienced, who shows you how you can improve what you yourself have written. You're the one who's carrying the ball. You're the one putting the most work and time and effort into it. What you end up with is a letter that's very powerful for a small fraction of the price that a copywriter would charge to do it from scratch.

Gene Swartz's hidden secret makes sense. It's an excellent idea to break your work up into small, easily achieved portions. Lucky for me, I was already doing that when I read Gary's interview — I just hadn't formalized it. When we first started this business, I realized there was a lot about copywriting that I didn't know; so I would give myself an artificial deadline just to make sure that we got something out there. It usually didn't take me several months to accomplish, because I can get vapor-locked on something and keep working at it until it's done. Often I'd end up spreading things out like I'm talking about here, simply because I'll make all these lists and write down my ideas on my yellow pads before trying to put them all together into a logical format that had been bubbling in my head for a while. And boom... they'd come out. It's just my process, and it happens to be like what Gary was talking about in the interview: a long period of pre-work, doing the research, and thinking about it before trying to write.

Even when you've got all that good stuff in hand and you sit down to put it together, don't try to do it all at once. If you've done the work ahead of time and you've got all that support material, the actual writing just kind of flows out of you, because you've been working it over for so long. But you still don't want to piece together a huge letter all at once. Sure, I've done that, where I sit down for hours and write like crazy. But if I'm lucky, the phone rings or something takes me away — and it's probably a good thing, because I *didn't* sit there for hours and pound it all out. I came back to it, sat down, and maybe got to accomplish something while a little fresher than I might have been if I'd tried that part after working for several hours. It makes each element more compelling and more powerful.

As I've said before, sometimes your best ideas come on the third or fourth or fifth day of working on a project, and then those ideas become the central theme of the whole promotion. They go right up to the front of the page. You have understand that the whole secret of getting people to read a 20-page letter is get them to read the first page, and turn. Once they get past the first page, you've got a greater chance of getting them to read all of it. The most important page is always page one. It starts with the headline. The purpose of the headline is to get them to read the first sentence. The purpose of the first sentence is to get them to read the second sentence — and on and on.

I've talked about making a list of the problems that the customers or prospect has, and how your product or service or opportunity solves those problems, before you ever start writing. But another thing I'll do is write headline after headline and bullet after bullet; even if it sounds a little nonsensical or stupid at the time, I'll write it all down. It's a good warm-up, if nothing else. Later I'll go back and it'll jar my memory, and then later, deeper into the project, I might come up with a headline that I want to put at the very top that will replace what I had there the first or second day.

**Secret #5:** how a goofy little guy from Orlando, Florida gave me the single greatest copywriting secret I've ever discovered. I paid this guy $8,000 cash and only got this one secret, but it's been worth millions to me. And now I can't wait to give it to you! Of course, you'll have to get out your credit card first...

Just kidding, of course! However, this secret really did cost me $8,000. I picked this guy up at the airport in Wichita, Kansas, in 1994, and about halfway home to Goessel I wanted to stop the car, turn around, and take him right back to the airport. I came *real* close. But I didn't do it, and I'm glad — because in the end, he gave me a secret that helped me make millions. He's a famous copywriter, an interesting guy — and he told me something that completely went against what I'd learned before. You see, a lot of copywriting formulas tell you to do the enclosures first. Those enclosures might include the order form, the outer envelope copy, any of the lift pieces or additional material. They tell you that once you've done those, *then* you do your sales letter. But he taught me that this was all wrong — and I listened to his idea and thought about it. Ever since then I've done what he said.

The sales letter comes first. Let's look at my Recession-Proof Wealth letter. This 20-page letter took me more than 10 days to write it, just a little bit every day. But it wasn't until last night (as of this writing) that I started working on the order form. And what did I do? I took patches out of the letter that I knew were the strongest, a paragraph here, a paragraph there. I put it together in about three pages, and then I started boiling it down, until the order form was essentially the best of the best of what's in the letter.

I'm grateful that I learned this from that guy from Orlando. It's the only thing he really taught me of any real value, but it was good. It cost me $8,000 — and now you won't have to pay $8,000 for it. I hope you'll pay attention to it, too, because the order form is more than just an ordering device. A lot of habitual direct-response marketing buyers won't even read the sales letter. They'll maybe look at the headline, then go straight to the order form. They just want to know, "how much is this going to cost?" That's the most important thing to them at that stage of the game, because they don't know anything else. So your order form has to be *more* than an order form. It needs to be a sales-making form as well. When you boil down the best parts of your offer and put them there, you're giving them a summarization of your entire offer. Our experience is that people have to be able to read the order form and "get it." That's worked great for us.

Not only do we get our order form copy from the sales letter, that's where we also get our enclosure copy — the copy for the lift pieces, the outer envelope teaser copy that we use or, sometimes, a little flyer that goes with it. It all just grows out of the sales letter itself. This is also where I get some of my best headline ideas. Instead of just writing down a whole bunch of headlines, I look for ideas that were written while I was hot, while I was excited, while the words were just flowing out of me and I was focused on giving the prospective buyer as many benefits as I could.

Chris Hollinger tells me that this particular strategy helped him early in his business. Because he was coming into it brand new from the world of teaching, he hadn't given order forms that much thought. But he soon realized that they're very important, if only for the fact that I mentioned before: when some people get your materials, they go straight to the order form and apply. So you need to have things on your form that give them the information they need, or information that catches their attention so that maybe they'll go back and read the whole letter. Maybe the order form itself is compelling enough for them to say, "Okay, I'm just going to fill it out and go!" And that's fine.

If you start with the enclosures and the order form first, you're boxed in — you're limited with what you're going to be able to do in your sales copy. Similarly, don't think that just because you've done a good job on your sales letter and your other materials, you can just have a basic order form. You have to realize that the kind of buyers we're looking for are the kind of buyers that everybody else is looking for, too — and so they get a lot of mail from other people. They're usually people who have bought a lot of things in the past and because of that, they're trained to go directly for the order form and look for the prices. That's all they care about, initially.

I have a friend who has a traditional business — one that you'll find in the Yellow Pages. People call him up all the time and ask, "How much does it cost?" He doesn't understand this; I've tried to explain it to him, but he still doesn't get it. He doesn't understand that they just don't know enough yet to ask better questions than that. That's the only question that they *know*; it's not really the only thing they care about, which is what he thinks. So he'll pick up the phone and it'll be a new customer, and they'll say, "How much does it cost?" If he's having a bad day, he'll say, "If all you care about is cost, then forget it! Go somewhere else!" Click — he hangs up the phone! That's just the dumbest thing in the world to do!

Price is *not* the only thing new customers care about; it's just the only thing that they know to ask about. My friend is assuming that they're looking for the lowest price — and that's a mistake. Instead of throwing away all that business, he should say, "Well, before I tell you about the cost, let me tell you about a few of the things that make me and what I do unique," and that

INTERNALIZE THESE NINE SECRETS TO SUCCESS 

type of thing. Once he talks about the benefits he provides and why he's different than the rest of the competition, then he needs to talk about why he charges premium prices. That's part of the reason he gets mad — because he *does* charge premium prices, and he expects people to understand why without him telling them why.

**Secret #6** is something we've already covered a bit. Basically, it's that you have to write when your brain is on fire. I like to joke that I make sure I'm always excited at 5:37 in the morning. Basically, the idea is that you have to find that time of the day when you're most alive, whatever "alive" means to you. To me, it just means when my brain works the best, when I'm most creative. And I'll make a confession to you guys. Lately, in order to ramp up my creativity, I've gone back to doing something I did when I was a teenager: I'm writing poetry. Now, when I was a teenager I wrote a lot of poems, and I'm not ashamed to admit it. I just wish I hadn't thrown them all away when I got older! But recently I started to do it again, mostly as a creative pursuit, but also as a way of warming my brain up in the morning. I've got a couple of poets that I really like; my favorite is Charles Bukowski.

The reasoning behind my confession here is two-fold, insofar as it relates to copywriting. First of all, until recently, I hadn't written any poetry for about 30 years. When I was a teenager, I wrote poems to give them to girls — and they liked it! I noticed that right away when I was a young guy. Then I stopped for some reason, and went 30 years without it. Recently I started reading some of Charles Bukowski's books, and decided to try writing poems again as a warm-up, just to get writing in the morning. That's the hardest thing sometimes — just getting the first words out onto the paper or computer screen. Now I wake up, drink some coffee, and start writing. Almost all my poems sound exactly like Charles Bukowski's

191

right now, because I'm modeling after him. I'm reading all his books as I'm doing it. But eventually, if I stick with it and keep doing it, I'll develop my own style. I'll start writing like me instead of him.

We all have models we use, which is another reason I confessed about my poetry. You learn by doing, by studying what other people do, and then developing your own style. It's like muscle movement, in a sense — just like the way my drum teacher tried to teach me that drum pattern, which I never did learn. But through the process of trying to learn it, I developed my own drum pattern, and it's muscle memory now. Even if I go years without playing the drums, I can sit down and play that pattern I memorized.

The same thing is true when it comes to writing copy. There's a language of sales letters, of writing ad copy, that you pick up by learning and reading what other people are doing and seeing how they do it. Eventually, you learn it yourself.

**Secret #7** is to give yourself plenty of time. The sales letter that I'm working on with Keli as of this writing is something we've been working now for six or seven weeks straight. Before that, Chris Lakey and I worked on it for a while. Before that, we gave it to another freelance copywriter who actually did a bunch of work, some of which we're having to re-do. But she came up with some unique ideas, things we would never have come up with had she not been involved in the process. By the time that letter is finished, it will be one of the most powerful sales letters in the history of our company. But why will it be that way? Because of all the work and time that went into it. That's the real secret of Secret #7: Don't be afraid to spend a lot of time on your sales copy. Even if you spend three months on a letter, if it makes you a million dollars, won't that be worth it? I think that's pretty good pay; at least it is in my books! You just have to do a little bit every day. Just make that time; block it out, and discipline yourself to do it. Do your writing whenever it works best for you — maybe in the mornings, before the phone starts ringing. Try to have fun with it; mix things up if you think it'll help. Chris Hollinger drinks coffee some mornings at a local restaurant where a lot of retired gentlemen sit there at the counter with him. These guys are retired from a lot of your more typical professions — brick-and-mortar businesses and the aircraft industry, because where he lives, in Wichita, there are a lot of retired aircraft guys — and they don't understand what Chris does at all. He'll tell them a little headline that he wrote, and someone will say, "Oh, that's crap! What are you doing here?" That may be annoying, but it does offer Chris a different perspective. Try whatever works for you, but definitely *do* schedule some time for your writing on a regular basis, and do things to make it fun.

**Secret #8** I've already talked about, at least partly. You've got to be willing to boil your writing down to the best of the best. I've told you that a lot of sales letters are written in patches that are then joined together to create one big finished product. Another great truth is that a lot of sales letters then get drastically reduced in the editing process. In fact, some of the best sales letters that we've ever done at the company were those where I wrote 30 or 40 pages and then I gave it to Chris Lakey — and Chris just went and whacked it. He took entire paragraphs out, cut entire pages sometimes. He cut and cut, looking for little bits he could remove, and kept boiling it down. It's like cooking a gravy, where you keep heating it and mixing it and condensing it. So the final sales letter from that 30 to 40 pages I gave him might end up being 24 pages — or less. But that copy was the best of the best of the *best*. This ability to take a large amount of copy and then boil it down is a must. While you're writing it, there's no editing it whatsoever; you just let it flow, and then later, boil it all down — and what you end up with is really good stuff. People who don't know that you did this will look at you and say, "Man, what a great writer!" They won't realize that every other paragraph was cut out of it, and that you may have rewritten it all multiple times.

Again, it's just like a gravy, or a sauce. It started out as a whole bunch of stock at one time, but you reduced it down — and the flavor got more intense and robust. You start out with all this copy, all this stuff that just came out of your head, and ended with a laser-focused selling instrument. People don't realize that — they don't see that in yesterday's version, my sales letter was muddied up, filled with cross-outs and additions. I do that week after week with these jobs, and it just keeps going back and forth until I'm happy. When people see the finished product, it all looks nice and smooth and it all flows together. Part of the reason that happens is the editing. It's all in the rewriting.

**Secret #9,** our marketing strategy, took us from $300 to $10 million in less than five years. Step #1: We maintain a front-end marketing system that automatically attracts a steady stream of new customers, and an associated back-end system that then re-sells more products and services to those people. As Step #2, we take a generous portion of the money that comes in every day and put it back into *more* of the things that made it for us in the first place. With this approach, you're constantly rotating your money back into more marketing — constantly. And then, for Step #3, we schedule a weekly meeting where we analyze the numbers and we look at what's working and what's not. Even if you don't have any staff members, you can still find that time to track your numbers, analyze things, and schedule new mailings. That's what we do at our weekly meetings every Wednesday afternoon. We're constantly scheduling new mailings and pushing ourselves to do more. If we don't, nothing ever gets done.

Two quick stories. Number one, I have a former friend who, about 20 years ago, I got all excited about the direct-response marketing business. So he went out there and started running some ads and making some money. In fact, he was making more money than he had in his entire life. But he took that money and put it all into a nice office, computer equipment and fax machines. Every dime immediately went into infrastructure — and then he had no money left over to advertise. Six months later he was out of business. Whereas, what we've always tried to do is take a percentage of the money and always let it roll back into more marketing. But that's something he didn't want to hear.

My next story: I go to a couple seminars every year with marketing people from all over the world, and I keep running into this guy from Sweden. He goes by the name of Pack. I like the guy. I've known him now for five or six years, and I keep seeing him at these seminars, and I want to help him. So every year we spend time together, and I ask him how his business is doing, and I see if I can give him some advice. Well, his business is pretty much exactly the way it was when I first met him. Nothing has changed at all, except that every year I get more frustrated with him and I try to do everything short of just grabbing him by the neck and shaking him to get him to listen — because he's a smart guy. He has all the brain power that's necessary. He's got a hunger for the business. He keeps coming to these marketing seminars because he's really interested in all this stuff.

A couple of years ago in Chicago, I was in the course of trying to preach at him, saying things like, "Why aren't you doing this? Why aren't you doing that?" Now, he knows all the stuff he should be doing, he's just not motivated to do any of it. While I was getting frustrated and trying to tell him these things, he suddenly said, "But where do you get your incredible amount of drive?" That was the wrong thing to say at that time, because I was really angry at him — he was at exactly the same place he'd been the year before and the year before that. I said, "I'll tell you where I get my drive. I've got over 20 full-time employees and I pay them well. If you pay peanuts you'll get monkeys for employees, and I pay my people well; they're not monkeys. They're high-caliber people. They don't work for cheap." And I said, "I've got a lot of bills, I've got a lot of problems, and I've got a lot of pressures — a lot of responsibility. *That's* where I get my drive!"

It's like that little bumper sticker we've all seen: "I owe, I owe, it's off to work I go!" Well, that's part of where I get my drive from. I've got a lot of responsibilities, a lot of obligations, and a lot of bills to pay, just like everybody else. Some people make fun of the fact that I have a lot of infrastructure and granted, there are lot of days when I'm in complete agreement with them. But at the same time, it does keep me focused and driven.

How does that fit with Secret #9? The point is that you need an effective framework to work within, and sometimes the things that people run from are the best things you could apply to your business. The problems, responsibilities, obligations, and commitments you face can be good things. For me, those commitments include my 20 full-time employees, and a number of vendors, like my printer and mailing house, where I'm the #1 customer. Secret #9 can give you a framework to work within, one that really keeps you focused on the things that you need to be focused on: your front-end, your back-end, your mailing, your accounting.

It takes some time to get this system in place, especially when you're learning so many new things, and it's easy to get discouraged. And yes, there are definitely days when it may seem easier to go back to what you were doing once — but you know what? The money's too good for that. We've all had days when we've made more money in half an hour that we once

made all week or all month doing what we did before. Chris
Hollinger brags that he's literally closed sales on the phone
while he was outside bouncing on his trampoline in the middle
of the afternoon. Sure, there are some difficulties inherent in the
business — but having said that, how many businesses are there
where you get to make money while you jump on a trampoline?
How often can you make money while sitting on the beach or
fishing, or whatever floats your boat?

That doesn't mean you don't have to exercise discipline. I
remember once when Chris Hollinger and I were sitting here at
M.O.R.E., Inc., just talking, when I said to him, "So, what are
doing on your front-end for lead generation?" Chris had just
gotten his first big promotion out there and was enjoying the
fruits of his labor, and I was bugging him with, "Okay, now how
much of this do you plan to put back in?" Chris replied, "Well, I
was going to buy a four-wheeler." But that was a bad idea at the
moment, and that's just the way it goes sometimes. Knowing
you're going to put so much back in to your next marketing
campaign to keep that system going is an important part of
maintaining the business. At the beginning, Chris wasn't thinking
that it's all about systems, marketing systems that he can create,
implement, set up, monitor, and then just let them work. Now
that's all he thinks about some days. It's an all-important point
for an entrepreneur. You just start one of these systems working,
and then you start looking for ways to get another one going. It's
a learning process, every single day — one that lets you put
money in your bank accounts at the same time.

# Chapter Thirteen:

# Keep Your Eyes on the Prize

By now, you've probably realized that being an effective marketer takes work, dedication, and a willingness to learn a lot of new things. It's not easy, but don't let that get you down. Along the way, you need to keep your eye focused on the prize — the exciting things about the business, like the potential to make millions of dollars, and having the time and freedom to do what you want. The more you're able to do that, the more you'll be willing to pay the price necessary to develop and practice these skills I'm teaching you about, and to learn whatever it takes to get where you want to go.

## The Two-Step (Not the Texas One)

I've told you repeatedly that you don't have to be the best copywriter ever to make good money, you just need to use the right strategies. But let me make this abundantly clear: It *does* take work. I realize that work is a four-letter word for a lot of people. Let's face it: Many of us are looking to get rich with no work at all on our parts. In fact, we had a program that was quite successful for a number of years called "The No-Work Wealth Maker." I know that sounds cynical, but it's what people want! We sold a lot of copies of that one, because we offered to do the work for them. But in order to achieve the biggest results consistently, you have to be the one to carry the ball. I hope I've made that clear so far. This is a creative, fun kind of thing. It's challenging and stimulating. To me, that's part of the joy of life. In fact, that's one of the *biggest* joys of life — doing things that are creative and fun. This is the kind of business where there's a million ways you can win.

One of those ways to win, and one you really need to focus on, is two-step marketing. I've mentioned two-step marketing a number of times already, but I haven't stopped to really explore the topic. In this chapter, I'm going to remedy that. Two-step marketing is one of the foundations of any successful marketing campaign, especially ad-based and direct-mail campaigns, so you need to know why it's important and how to put it into play in your own campaigns.

How you handle two-step marketing depends on where you're planning to use it, and for how long. If your approach is a published ad, for example, how you angle it depends on the publication. A lot of opportunity magazines are monthlies, whereas something like the opportunity section in the Friday edition of *USA Today* is weekly. *USA Today* is a pretty good place to run a classified ad. The neat thing is, it's going to hit Friday and it'll be out there on the stands on Saturday and Sunday — so you'll immediately generate prospects.

I like 24-hour recorded messages, because they let you hit those prospects with a good, solid sales piece and follow-up. In 99% of the ads, there's an 800 number listed — for good reason. They no longer say, "Write to us," because so many people now carry their cell phones with them, and it's so much easier to get people to make a call. The challenge there is that it's also easier to get all the deadbeats to call. And by "deadbeats," I'm talking about people not in the market for what you're trying to sell — so they end up wasting your time and money. You have to look for ways to qualify people, and to ensure they're qualified; that's the true value of two-step marketing.

I was in Jacksonville, Florida, in 2002 for a marketing seminar, and I sat next to this guy who had kind of been my hero. His name is Rick Neiswonger, and at that time he was out of Las Vegas. He's a famous marketer, and I got to spend a couple of hours of good quality time with him. This one idea that Rick gave me made me a lot of money — and I probably haven't used it nearly as much as I should. Rick had a program that sold for $12,000. He told me that his whole strategy was that he ran his commercials on major networks. His most successful commercial ran during Larry King Live, and it got people to call a recorded message. That's all it did: it gave them a little teaser and got them to call the 800 number. He didn't want to waste his money on people who either didn't have $12,000 or who are going to be very difficult, so three different times during that brief message, he told people flat out, "The opportunity costs $12,000 — and if you don't have that kind of money, then this isn't for you." And I thought, what a great idea!

Immediately after that, I sent out a simple postcard offer, of a type that usually doesn't work for me. Now, postcard offers can work great in follow-up, but for the most part I can't use postcards in my business, because I have too much infrastructure. Yet this time I used Rick's idea, and I was able, for probably the first time in the history of our company, to use postcards effectively. In this case, I was selling a $4,000 package, and I used the postcard to have people call my 800 number and listen to a recorded message. Three or four different times during that recorded message I told people, "Look: I want you to know, right up front, that *this* is the kind of investment that's necessary. And if you don't have that, then I'm sorry, but this is just not for you. But if you *do* have that kind of money, you need to know that you can get all these secrets for $4,000. Don't worry, nobody is going to high-pressure you." And sure enough, we made it work.

The point is, there are many ways to keep your eyes on the prize. What you can accomplish is limited by your creativity and your knowledge, and by the strategies that you know that are theoretically possible. Luckily, marketers love sharing ideas. Over the years, you can subject yourself to more and more strategies, which give you more potential power. Remember, power is the ability to act. The more strategies you have at your disposal, the more knowledge you have, the more ability you'll have to do that.

When using the strategy of laying it on the line like I did with my $4,000 product, you don't have to be blunt about it; you can say it in a nice way. Use it as an advantage and say, "Look, if you're looking for a less expensive offer, that's fine. They're out there. But if you're looking for the *best* and you've got this amount of money, then here you are." Sometimes we don't even tell them the exact price; sometimes we just say, "The start-up costs are about the price you'd pay for a weekend in Vegas." We say things like that to people so that they know it's going to be kind of expensive. For example, "This opportunity costs about the same as a used car." Of course, we've had people who said, "Great, I can get a used car for $500!" Well, yeah — but not a very good one!

## Look Around Occasionally

I'm the first to tell you that you have to be careful with any opportunity — and while you should always keep your eyes on the prize, you also have to look around occasionally so you don't stumble. Here's an example of such a stumble, one that plays a riff off that two-step marketing idea I already discussed. Once upon a time, Eileen and I bought a company from Russ von Hoelscher and a fellow named George Stern called "Profit Ideas." George wanted out of the business, so he told Russ to find a buyer — and we were right there. As part of the company, we got this full-page ad that they'd run for a number of years.

We acquired "Profit Ideas" after we'd been in business for three or four years; we'd already experienced a little success, and I'll admit it, I was cocky and arrogant. I thought I knew more than I really did.

In that full-page ad, Russ and George asked for one dollar for information, and one dollar for shipping and handling. And I thought, "Let's get rid of that dollar thing, because then more people will respond!" And I was right! On the short-term it looked like I knew more than Russ did. I was patting myself on the back, all inflated with my own stupid sense of self-importance. Sure enough, we got double the amount of leads — but we just couldn't get the conversions. It didn't work. And had I listened to Russ, he would have told me (as he did later), "You know, that asking for one dollar... that's nothing. Everybody has a dollar. Everybody." A dollar's not that big a deal; you really can't buy much with it. And yet, just asking for that dollar was enough to make people feel a bit more qualified. They remembered us, then. I think that's a lot of the success of two-step marketing: People remember that they've qualified themselves. They remembered sending the dollar in, whereas if they'd just picked up the phone and called that 800 number, they might have forgotten. The dollar made the difference. Yeah, they raised their hand... but they remembered it, too; whereas the ones who just called and left their names and information blew us off. There has to be a mechanism there so that the dollar is exchanged. It's another step, another hoop they jump through in the process of qualifying themselves, of raising their hands higher and letting you know they're serious.

## Different Strategies Work for Different People

There are all kinds of ways to do things in this business, all with their weaknesses and strengths. Some might work for you even when they don't work for me. We learn what does and doesn't work by testing, and the numbers tell you if you should continue or not. In the aforementioned case, not asking for a dollar for the information failed to work for us. Here's another good example, associated with our *Dialing for Dollars* program. Now, this is a marketing system based on voicemail that still works today; people are still using the basic system 20 years later. But just as a way of showing you that there's many different ways to work even an effective system like this, let's take a look at Jay Peterson, our distributer out of Provo, Utah.

When Jay was still working with us, we were bringing in about $2,000,000 a year using the system — and he was making about $5,000,000. I knew that for certain, because until he cut us out, all his wholesale orders were coming through us. He was doing almost three times more business than we were by using the "COD Method." You called an answering machine and listened to a message, and you were told to leave your name and address, and Jay would ship you the product by COD — Cash On Delivery.

Well, the bad thing about COD is that people would call the number, they would listen to the COD message, and then they would say, "Yes, ship that $39 package to me by COD," and leave their name and address. But when the package came and the postman asked for the money, most of them would say, "No, thank you. Changed my mind." In some cases, the postman just couldn't contact them. In any case, when push came to shove, as many as 60% of the recipients wouldn't write the check — and the package came back "Postage Due."

Those are the major problems inherent with the COD model. And yet, Jay was making it all work. He factored it all into his business plan. The 40-50% of the money that he was able to collect on was more than enough, for him. It's kind of like if you have a liquor store in a really bad neighborhood of Los Angeles or Miami, where every year you're probably going to get robbed an average of three or four times — and you're also going to lose money through shoplifting. You have to factor all that into your business; you charge three times more than the other liquor stores charge, so you build it into your business plan, and you still make money year after year.

Different marketing methods work for different people, because there's no single, perfect marketing model — and believe me, I'm still looking. I still fantasize about the perfect marketing model, where it's all upside, just good, good, good with no downside. That's all just a great big fantasy, because I know in my heart that reality will never live up to it. But you still need to keep trying out those different methods until something clicks with you — and you have to remember that good copywriting, words written while your eyes are firmly on the prize, is crucial.

## Words Really Can Make a Difference

Here's something I've been putting off telling you, because it's a bit off-color — but it does serve to illustrate something important. You see, I've never really cared that much for doctors. So when my friend, Steve (who's a great salesman), went and got a colonoscopy, I told him, "I'll never do that. I will never *ever* allow somebody to shove a camera up inside of me." And Steve said, "T.J., you've got to do it! Colon health is very important." I said, "I don't even want to think about my colon, and I don't want to think about the *health* of my colon." Then Steve told me, "T.J., you've got to do this. If you've got a problem and they catch it early enough, they can fix it; no problem at all. But if you've got a problem and you don't catch it fast enough, here's what's going to happen. They're going to put you on an operating table — and they're going to gut you like a fish! They're going to cut you open, and all your insides are going to be spread out on that operating table. They're going to have to cut into those insides and take out huge portions of your colon. And from that point forward, you're going to have to

205

carry one of those little poop bags with you everywhere you go. For the rest of your life you're going to have your poop bag, and it's just going to be a terrible, terrible thing."

Well, sign me up! From that point forward, I started caring about my health of my colon. I never cared about it before, but when Steve started talking about how they were going to gut me like a fish, well... I got this certain visual image. I used to fish when I was a kid, and I've cleaned them, so I know *exactly* what that means. Nowadays I eat so much roughage it's not even funny. I buy Benefiber in those giant containers that you can only buy on the Internet because they're so big. I still haven't let them shove the camera up me yet, but I now care very deeply about the health of my colon.

The reason I tell you that story is because the words somebody uses can make all the difference in the world. Now, I could die tomorrow; none of us really knows how much time we have. But because my friend used such descriptive words to get me to reconsider the health of my colon, he may have saved my life. I won't know for sure until I have that colonoscopy, but I do know that words really can make a difference. As Mark Twain famously said, "The difference between the right word and the wrong word is the difference between lightning and lightning bug." So I want to encourage you to think about the power of words, and think about how certain visual images that you can express to the people you care about can change their lives. Steve cared about me, so he helped me think about something that I never wanted to think about.

As marketers, we can do that in our sales material. We can say certain things in a certain way to get people to take the right action. Consider the Recession-Proof Wealth System I've talked about repeatedly in this book. With this program, we're really helping people. We're showing them secrets that they've never been exposed to before. As I write this copy, I'll have the help of five other experts; they're going to help me rewrite that copy and sharpen it like a razor's edge. We're going to try to make people think about things they don't normally think about — things like, what would happen if the world economy went to hell? What would happen if the worst possible situation developed? What would they do if they had to live through another Great Depression? You've seen pictures from the Depression. It was a sad, miserable time. And yet, there were people who did quite well for themselves, because they knew some of the things we're sharing with people on this Recession-Proof Wealth Program. We have the proven methods, and we're teaching people things that normally aren't taught in business school. We're showing them how to take their financial lives into their own hands and start making them better, instead of depending on the government to somehow provide for them.

So we really can change people's lives. We can! Back when we were selling our *Dialing for Dollars* program, we had customers who were making thousands of dollars a month for the first times in their lives, because they bought this program and made it work. Some people went on to make millions of dollars with the ideas we shared with them. I didn't know anything about writing copy back then, but the sales letter I wrote was so passionate and enthusiastic that the excitement came through to our readers.

There are a million copywriting techniques that you can master, and you can spend your whole life learning them if you like. But when you get down to it, marketing, and the copywriting that defines it, is as simple as good salesmanship. What my friend Steve was doing was trying to sell me on the idea of living a better life, without some of the health problems that less vigilant people have had to go through. With our salesmanship, we're trying to make a difference. We're trying to deliver value. As long as you're committed to delivering good value that really does help people, then all the ideas I've shared about squeezing the largest amount of money possible out of the mailing list, of going out and "attacking" people in an aggressive way — these ideas are valid.

Think of it like this: What's the last really good movie that you saw? And when was the last time that you heard someone else talking about it — maybe a friend or a family member, saying, "Well, I wonder what that's like?" Remember how your eyes got a little bigger and you were like, "Oh, it's a great movie!" Do you remember how you tried to explain it to them — but didn't want to give it away? So you said enthusiastically, "You've got to go see it!" That enthusiasm is what happens when you've been working on an offer for a while and you're all excited about it. That's the kind of enthusiasm that you want to come across in your writing. You want to grab people and say, "You've got to take a look at this opportunity here; it's absolutely fantastic!" That's what you're really trying to get across in your writing. If you really focus on that one thing, you can create a very powerful sales letter, because people respond to that kind of enthusiasm. It grabs people, and it's what you're really shooting for. Sure, there are all kinds of strategies that can guide you and help you with your copywriting, but they're useless if they're dry and boring and monotonous. Practice getting that enthusiasm in place. That comes from that first strategy I shared — write when you're fired up. I get that way early in the morning, when I've got some coffee in me. That's the best time of the day for me; I haven't been worn down by meetings and business and life. The morning is nice and fresh, and I'm all pumped up and ready to go... and that comes across in my writing.

I tend to be naturally enthusiastic, but it's something we all can develop more. And people *do* respond to enthusiasm. Case in point: my sister Ellen. Over at M.O.R.E., Inc., I have an extension that I never answer; but I've got a message that says, "Hi, this is T.J.! Thank you very much for calling," and I'm all enthusiastic and I'm saying, "Man, I'm sorry I missed your call. I hope you have a great day." So whenever Ellen gets depressed, she calls and listens to my extension — and it picks her up just a bit. See? Enthusiasm is a great thing. You can be a poor copywriter, but still hit the jackpot if you're enthusiastic and sincerely believe your offer helps people. I'm a perfect example. I didn't know what I was doing 20 years ago, when I did that first *Dialing for Dollars* sales letter — I was just excited about the idea, and I wrote about it, and it took off! One of my pet peeves is the fact that some freelancer copywriters charge way too much money, and don't deliver enough value for what they charge. They know all the secrets, tricks, and advanced strategies, but they lack the enthusiasm that a person who's in love with what they're doing can share with another person.

So I would encourage you to start paying attention to good writing versus bad writing. What makes good writing good? Usually, the writer's extremely opinionated about what he believes — this makes him enthusiastic, and forceful in the way that he clearly communicates exactly what he believes. A good writer doesn't try to go for the middle of the road to satisfy everybody. He has firm ideas about what he believes is right and is wrong, good and bad. A good writer is extremely clear about those ideas. When you read a good writer's copy, you can tell what he believes.

Writing is just a form of communication; that's all it is. But let's face it: English teachers ruin it for most people. The joy of writing is one of the greatest joys there is — and they ruin it because they make it so technical and difficult. They split it into its component parts, and make you memorize all these stupid little rules. Today, if you asked me what an adjective or an adverb is, if I thought about it long enough, I could tell you. But when I'm writing, I don't worry about all the bits and pieces, the structure of the sentences and paragraphs. I don't even know what a dangling participle is, and I couldn't care less. I know the English language only in relationship to copywriting, and that's what's important here. It's all about one person getting excited about something and then sharing their passion with somebody else. That'll sell better than a knowledge of all the dry details of the language.

I've mentioned that Russ von Hoelscher has become more opinionated in his writing lately. Maybe he did that consciously, maybe not; but it's something that helps him connect with more people, and so he profits from it. People don't identify with the gray areas of personalities; they're attracted to extremities. Those at the extremes are cut-and-dried, black or white. Wishy-washy people who don't know which way they're going don't sell very well. I realize that some of the best people in this world are the ones in the middle; but nobody will ever find out about it, because they're always so nice, polite, and quiet, and they get overlooked. They're not putting their ideas out there in a bold way.

When you see an ad or read a sales letter that excites you, you should study it, look at what they've done. But don't be intimidated. For years I was intimidated whenever I saw good copy; first it inspired me, but then it made me depressed because I was thinking, "Oh my God, I'll never be able to write like that!" But I didn't realize that oftentimes, those letters were written in patches and edited down severely. Maybe the original was 30 pages long — but what I saw was 12 pages, the best of the best. While you're writing, you have to think about the benefits for the person you're writing to, just as if you were going to sell them on a particular movie. You'd try to get them excited about certain things without revealing the plot, because curiosity is such a big factor in what we do. In order to get the rest of the story, we want our prospects to send us money. That's the only way that they can satisfy their curiosity, and it's always done with a money-back guarantee — so if they get the answers and they're not happy, they can always get their money back. We're not here to cheat or hurt people.

Look for copy that's alive. Look for copy that moves. Look for copy that makes you excited, and then try to figure out what it is about it that influenced you in those ways. Realize that we're all more alike than we are different, especially emotionally. Emotions, human nature — those are the things that never really change. In a world where everything is constantly in motion, where markets do change, certain things that get people excited one year may not quite get people excited the next year. Regardless of whether it's changing in good ways or bad, your market is always changing a little, based on numerous factors. But the one thing that never changes is that good ol' human nature. People are exactly like they always were: they're creatures of emotion, and those emotions run the gamut of good to bad, happy to sad.

To me, the secret of dealing with emotions is pretty simple: the right motions create the right emotions. I don't start out being all enthusiastic every morning, believe me. But by going through the right motions, the emotions do catch up with you. To put it another way — fake it till you make it!

# CHAPTER FOURTEEN:

# Switch on the Five Keys to Wealth

Next, I'm going to talk about another formula that will help you succeed: The Five Major Keys to Wealth. Remember, the premise of this whole book is that you don't have to be especially good at copywriting to make good money. If you choose the right strategies, you can be a so-so copywriter, an average marketer, and you can still do quite well for yourself. That's what these five keys are all about, so we'll go over them one at a time. These are the five things that every business you get involved with should have. If your business has one or two of these, you can probably make pretty good money; if it's got three or four, you can make more money. If it has all five, then you stand a good chance of doing quite well for yourself, regardless of your skills as a copywriter or marketer.

**The First Key**

The First Key to Wealth is that your product or service must *appear* to be new. Notice that I emphasized the word "appear." It must *appear* to be new. In the Book of Ecclesiastes in the Bible, they say there's nothing new under the sun — and, of course, we know that that's not true. New things *do* occur. But more often than not, what we've got to offer has been done before. Our task is to give it the appearance of being different and new — *but not too new.* Ironically, if it's too new people might actually be turned off by it. What they really want is something that appears new, but has familiar elements that are reassuring. They want to know there's something solid behind it.

So look for some new way of doing something old, but do something bold or daring to wake people up and get them to take notice. Let's go back to the same example I've been using all through this book: The current Recession-Proof Wealth promotion I'm working on. The way we're trying to get people's attention and wake them up is by telling them a story that we hope resonates in their minds. Now, this is a brand new promotion, completely untested, so we don't know how it's going to work; at this point, everything's speculative. But we're telling them that during the Great Depression of the 1930s, there was a small group of average people who, because they knew certain secrets, made above-average income. In some cases they made millions of dollars. And that now, our group of millionaire-making experts has discovered an all-new way that average people can use that same secret to make even more money today.

That's our hook, our angle. It's designed so that it just drives people crazy. It's only a $39 deal, so we're not asking for a lot of money upfront. What we're hoping is that it's what I call a little splinter of an idea — just like a splinter that gets in your finger. You know, it's nothing, just a little tiny thing, but man, it bothers the hell out of you! Until you get that little thing out, you're just going crazy! That's what we try to do with the hooks and angles; we come at them with something a little bit interesting. It's all designed to sound new, different, and unique, even though it isn't entirely; and that's the First Key. If your product or service doesn't measure up to the First Key, you need to either change it so that it does, or move on. If you can't find some unique angle to come at people that will wake them up, then you won't make any money. This is one of the two or three keys that any business needs to survive.

I think that when you're looking at potential opportunities or businesses, that hook is either going to be there or it's not. If it's there and if it's strong, you're going to see it immediately. You're going to say "I get it!" and the lightbulb will go on. The same is true for your customers. That's a very important factor that takes some of us a while to realize, but eventually it sinks in. Our current promotion has a special timeliness, given our current economy; the whole Depression Era angle grabs people's attention, and that's all you need. Because if you don't get it right from the start, you're done. Your offer goes into the prospect's trash, or it gets ignored or covered up, and it's gone.

I've talked about the evolution of the marketplace. Well, one of those factors derives from the increased competition, and the fact that there are so many sharp marketers out there now. Hopefully, we're playing a role in that ourselves! But be that as it may, there are a *lot* of sharp people out there. And the Internet makes it easier for them to succeed, frankly. The Internet has lowered the barriers of entry for people to get started in business. Therefore, there's an incredible number of competitors who can do quite well for themselves with zero overhead, because the Internet allows them to market very inexpensively and effectively.

But remember this: It's also getting harder to get through to people. They've been hit by so much advertising that they're immune to most of it — they barely notice it. Here's a real-world analogy to that. My best friend has a pest-control company. I was working within it for a while, helping her with the business, and I got to know her crew and methods quite well. Like, for instance, the fact that on their monthly accounts, they have to go in with a different kind of poison every month — because in just one 30-day period, bugs can build up an immunity to the poison that they shot the previous month. If you go back and shoot that same poison, you're out of luck; the immune bugs multiply and take over. This is why the bug killer you buy at the store doesn't really work. The bugs develop an immunity to it, and eventually you can shoot them all day long and it won't work, till they grow three feet tall and come for you in the night!

People aren't bugs, of course, but it's a fact that most people have developed a real immunity to advertising and marketing messages. We feel like we've heard it all, we've seen it all, and just don't believe anything anymore. We're just not buying it. Well, one of the biggest mistakes that marketers make is this: They think that just because they're in love with something, everybody else is going to love it, too. Nothing could be further from the truth. People are busy. Their lives are filled with more stress now than ever before. They've built shields around themselves — invisible shields, maybe, but nonetheless real. There's a resistance to sales messages. So you have to find some unique angle, and you've got to sharpen it so that it cuts through the clutter of all of the other messages they're receiving, and jabs in through their shields to get their attention.

**The Second Key**

The Second Key to Wealth is to offer a strong solution to some major problem in a pre-existing market. With our Recession-Proof Wealth System, we're going out there to people who are already interested in making money. We know that because, first of all, we're hitting our existing clients with this thing first — as we do with all new offers. We never just take a new offer and throw it out to people who have never done business with us. That would be foolish. We go to people who already like and trust us. These people have a history of buying from us and know we're a good company that delivers; and if they're not happy, they know they can get their money back. We've earned their trust. If they don't go crazy about it, then

216

forget it. We drop the idea right then and there. It's over.

Some of our friends who don't understand our business ask us, "Man, how come you guys come up with so much stuff all the time?" Well, one of the reasons is because our customers will continue to re-buy, so we do it to maximize profitability. We're foolish if we don't constantly create new products and services. They're willing to buy, so in many cases all we have to do is offer it to them and they'll buy from us. But we also do it because our customers are our testing ground, and not every idea makes it. We're looking for only the hottest ideas, those that will stand the greatest chance of making the most money, so we go to our best customers first. They're our "acid test." If they're not crazy about a product, nobody else will be, so we drop it. And we drop a *lot* of ideas.

We go out there to a pre-existing group of people that we know are interested in making money. As I've said, you have to find a lucrative marketplace where people are already spending a ton of money, and then create a product or service (or a product/service combination) that offers a solution that people desperately want. The solution that people desperately want with our Recession-Proof Wealth System is obvious. Now, as of this writing, this is all still untested; but our belief is that it offers a *real* solution, because our customers are already worried about the economy. They're stressed out; there's constantly more bad news. That's why we're launching this promotion: to help people who are worried about all that stuff the media's hyping up. That's part of another strategy: positioning yourself correctly to maximize what's already going on, making sure you're at the right place at the right time. All this is part of launching this promotion, because it's what the markets were telling us we needed to do. Because of the way the economy was going, we wanted to give our people a product that can really help them.

And because we know that it *will* help people, I can

promise you we're going to be extremely aggressive with this idea. What we've got is good. And when you've got something that you can be proud of, which can really help people, you should feel *obligated* to offer it to them in an aggressive way. This requires a certain mindset that you'll need to develop if you don't already have it. You have to believe that you're doing people a disservice if you don't do everything short of coming over to their house, taking the money out of their wallet, and leaving their house with your product there on their table.

Here's a point I'd like to add about the Second Key before I move on. Sometimes, you'll see the problem out there, but most people don't; so it's your job to take that problem and make sure people know about it. And then what are we doing? We're going back to that Problem, Agitate, and Solve system, aren't we? The problem may not be on their radar screen, but it's already affecting them. We're just taking a problem we know exists and making sure they *realize* it exists, so we can offer them a good, solid solution.

And you have to personalize it for them. Part of the way we're doing that with this Recession-Proof Wealth System is by telling a little story in our sales copy. We try to get them to imagine the worst possible thing happening, to actually put themselves in this position. And we tell them right up front, "Look, we don't know if this is going to happen or not," because I don't want that kind of responsibility, and we don't want to panic people. Of course, there *are* some marketers who don't care whether or not they're panicking people. An industry that's absolutely booming right now is the survivalist industry. Beans, rice, and ammunition have all gone up in sales. So have things like water purification systems, rainwater collectors, and all the other stuff you're going to need to live in your little survival hut once everything goes to hell in a hand basket. You're going to need beans, rice, and ammo. You're going to need freeze-dried coffee and freeze-dried food of all kinds. There are survival websites out there doing great business — as good as or better than what they did coming up on the Millennium. They thrive on fear.

We're not trying to do that; we're genuinely trying to be helpful. Our message is simple; we're telling people, "We don't know what will happen, but be prepared." We're not economists. We study what the economists say, though, and some of them are saying some pretty terrible things — so we use their words, not ours. We're saying, "Look, we're not the experts on the economy. Maybe these things will happen; maybe they won't. But you at least have to be prepared for them. If they do happen, the future belongs to those that are prepared." That's our message. And it's a message that helps us save our butts in case everything works out just fine and this doesn't end up being something major, like some say it will. We can then face our customers and say, "Look, we told you that we didn't know for sure." So we're trying to cover ourselves a little — but we're also trying to just come at them in an honest, forceful way.

This is an idea that's applicable to a lot of different situations, and it goes back to human nature. The old adage says that an ounce of prevention is worth a pound of cure. Okay, sure; but people are resistant to prevention. They don't want it... but they'll line up in droves to get that pound of cure! So as a marketer, what do you think is more profitable — selling that ounce of prevention, or that pound of cure? The answer's easy. That's what our recession-proof product gives people: their pound of cure. As far as the economy goes, the time for the ounce of prevention is over.

Our Recession-Proof Wealth System is actually designed to be preventative, but it's only a $39 ticket item. One of the secrets we're using is that the product is going to be packaged up in an expensive way, in a huge, colorful binder. For $39, what we really want to do is to shock people. When they see this big, beautiful thing they just bought for $39, they're thinking, "Wow, this is a $99 product!" Then we're selling a Master Distributorship opportunity, which is more of a "hard" offer versus a "soft" offer. That's our immediate upsell, which is how we're making all of our profits here. We're using that Second Key to provide a solution that people really want — which is to make more money, and to ease their fears.

**The Third Key**

The Third Key is something I've talked about before. You've got to do something bold to penetrate the hard layer of skepticism in the hearts and minds of your prospects. If your offering sounds too new or radical, you have to create a strong justification for why you can offer them something this incredible... or why this new breakthrough really does work. You can get people's attention, but not get their money, if they're still skeptical. They might pay attention, they may actually read what you write, but they're damn sure not going to give you their money. So what good is it to get peoples' attention if the end result is that nobody gives you any money? You have to realize that nobody believes anything you say. There's a part of them that's always in doubt, a part of them that's always skeptical, so you have to offer as much proof as you possibly can.

Let's go back to this Recession-Proof Wealth System. We're using all kinds of quotes from experts on this project. I'm getting all my staff members at M.O.R.E., Inc. to find me those quotes. The goal is to find some talking heads with alphabet-soup credentials who are saying these things, and to get their ideas out there as a way of saying to people, "Hey, don't listen to us. Listen to what these other people say." We're hoping that breaks through some of the skepticism and gets their attention.

You'll always face a specific question: "If this is so great,

why are you offering it to me?" In your copy, you've got to
address that one way or another. You do that with believable
stories. You'll see the technique used in sales letters, you see it on
infomercials, you see it on the websites of the guys selling all
those Internet-millionaire marketing secrets. People will ask,
"Okay, why is he giving them to me? Is he just a nice guy?"
Whether or not they consciously ask that, it's going to be in their
heads: "What's in it for you? If this is so great, why are you
sharing it with me? What's the catch? I think you're trying to rip
me off! Why should I trust you? Why should I believe anything
you're saying to me?" The Third Key addresses that. You've got
to give them the whole justification, so that it makes sense in their
heads... and in their hearts. Remember, we're dealing with
emotions here, so it has to make both logical *and* emotional sense.

We're all protecting ourselves constantly, to some degree or
another. Shame on the person who's not; they're going to get
taken advantage of every time! So in your sales copy you should
address those things — and we do. We say, "Why should you
believe anything I say? Well, listen to this." I often say in my
sales copy, "I don't blame you one bit for being skeptical. In
fact, it's good to be skeptical. You *should* be skeptical. If you're
not, somebody is going to take advantage of you. But just stay
open-minded for a minute and listen to this point." Or I'll say,
"Here's proof..."

That's one of the reasons we have such strong money-back
guarantees: to reassure people that our products and services are
so strong, so effective, that we'll go to all this trouble to give
them their money back if they're not happy. We're confident our
product will help them in every way we say it will. Look, if I
never had to offer a guarantee, why would I? If you don't offer a
guarantee, you don't have refund problems. It's not a sale until a
sale sticks — and by not offering a guarantee, we'd get fewer
refunds and fewer returns. We do it because we have to. We do it

because people are skeptical. They don't trust us. Any marketer who doesn't realize that from the word go is, quite simply, burying their head in the sand. They're suffering from the delusion that just because they know they're honest, everybody else will know they're honest. People just don't trust anymore; they don't trust politicians *or* their religious leaders, and for good reason. They don't trust entrepreneurs, especially. They don't trust salespeople.

I watched an infomercial recently, and to my surprise they didn't address this at all. They totally ignored that part of the equation. But they did know the market they were going after — so let me tell you about the two co-hosts of this infomercial. They were both extremely curvy women with tight island-type dresses on. So, who were they going after? They kept interviewing all these people who were having success with their secrets... just one after another, showing how much money you could make. But they never did address any skepticism. They just had women in bikinis and fast cars and claims that these secrets are making people lots of money. There was one guy who said he was on the verge of suicide before he found these secrets; he'd been in and out of two marriages, had several bankruptcies, and was taking long walks along cliff-lined beaches. And then he found these secrets, he's making all this money and, of course, this woman has her microphone in the guy's face...

But it worked! They weren't addressing skepticism; they were just overwhelming their target market with what got their attention. You could tell that this was their strategy. They knew their target market very well, and they knew how to reach that market in the most effective and convincing way. They were painting this picture of success in the eyeballs of a lot of men, and it got their attention. Obviously they're building up the curiosity, because they never tell you what the secrets are remotely about. They were keeping you interested along the way, but they never ever once tried to cut through any skepticism. They just overwhelmed you.

Maybe they've got an offer so strong and so convincing that they're hypnotizing people and making good money in spite of it. Maybe their numbers are good. But your numbers will *always* improve when you just go straight at it, and don't try to ignore people's natural skepticism. It's that elephant in the room; whether you acknowledge it or not, it's there! It's composed of the doubts your customers have, their concerns, their fears that they're going to give you their money and they're never going to see any return on it, and they're never going to achieve the promises that you made to them. Now, sure; this is one of those keys that you could ignore. But I think you'll always do better by just going at it straight on, rather than hiding from it!

**The Fourth Key**

The Fourth Key to Wealth is another that you can do without if you have to, but if you do have it, you're going to be in a greater position of strength. This key is residual income. The products or services you promote should have some kind of built-in residual income, money that can come to you after that initial sale. When I think of residual income, I usually think of services that have a monthly fee attached, services with a commission that automatically comes in every single month, because the service is sold on a monthly continuity basis. But there are other ways of making residual income, and one of the most significant ways is through upsells.

With our Recession-Proof Wealth System, for example, we have a $495 upsell that doesn't have a monthly residual attached to it. We purposely did it that way (at the advice of our salespeople) so we could make as many upsells as possible. But it's still residual income, in the sense that it's money that can

223

come in automatically after that first sell. That's what the upsell is designed to do; and we have several additional upsells after that initial upsell.

So many people get a great idea for selling some product or service, and it *is* great... and it's exciting, too. But then you want to say to them, "Well, what are you going to sell them after that?" If you don't have a good enough answer to that question, you need to go out and find one. You need to find an effective resell strategy. Remember, once a customer buys from you once and has a favorable experience, they're more likely to buy again from you. If they're happy with what they bought, they'll naturally do more and more business with you if you offer them the opportunity to do so. It makes sense, because people are afraid of getting cheated, of getting ripped off. So when they find somebody good, somebody that they can trust, somebody they know is honorable and credible, they would much rather do business with that person than with somebody new. Again, it sounds like common sense; and yet, if you ask a lot of erstwhile marketers, "What are you going to sell them after the first thing you sell them? What are you going to sell them after the second thing? What are you going to sell them after the third thing?" They'll have no answer. They just look at you like you're speaking a foreign language.

Chris Hollinger has an affiliate system out there that he's beta testing. Recently, one of his founding teammates called him up and said, "Chris, I love it! I absolutely love it! I'm all fired up. But I want to know... Is there any way you can put more of a residual income into it?" He wanted to make this offer even hotter by adding residual income, in addition to the multiple pay lines that this affiliate program has already. So Chris started kicking that idea around; he's gone back to his original copy, and he's investigating different routes that he can use to build in that residual income — not only just for him as a marketer, but for his teammates as well. The words "residual income" gets people's attention. They like that idea of doing something once and getting paid repeatedly for it. It's a principle of wealth-building that people just gravitate toward.

As an entrepreneur, I see opportunities to make money in a lot of different ways. Just looking around, I'll see an opportunity: "Hey, there's a niche, and I could probably do something to make money in that niche!" But when you start to think about what it really takes to have a sustainable business, you've got to think beyond the first sale. You've got to ask yourself, "What else am I going to do to bring in revenue once I sell my first item? How am I going to continue that relationship?" That's why you typically want to stick to one industry; you want to serve one marketplace, and you want to serve that marketplace well. It's easy to get on rabbit trails and chase all different kinds of opportunities, but you have to think long-term in each direction you go. You really should stay focused on one area, build a customer base, and then focus on serving that customer base.

We like residual income. We love to attach a monthly fee to just about everything we do. It's good, automatic revenue. We sell websites, so we have monthly hosting fees for people who host those sites with us. We have coaching programs where they're paying us monthly for ongoing coaching support. There are all kinds of things you can do to make sure you have automatic monthly income coming in. You could have a monthly newsletter for your subscribers to purchase. Some people have a subscription base that's quarterly, or every six months, or once a year, so there's a continuity there as well. It doesn't have to just be monthly, although monthly is good. It's nice to be able to bill people on the first of the month and know your overhead is covered. If you've got five or ten thousand dollars a month coming in automatically at the first of every month because of a continuity program or something similar, that helps a lot. Everything else you do that month is just additional revenue — icing on the cake. The residual income is automated. It continues month after month. It's completely out of your direct involvement, and that money just keeps coming in.

If you have a monthly income option built into your product, you can continue doing more and more business with people while growing your monthly subscription base. You can set this up by selling something that has an auto-renew feature, where you're automatically billing people for it on a monthly basis. Plus, re-selling to the people you already sold stuff to once builds your income. New customer acquisition is one revenue stream. You're buying customers, getting them in the door. Then you're getting monthly continuity from the fees you're charging people for whatever monthly service you have, as well as continuing to do more and more business with all those new people as you build that ongoing relationship. Those are three ways to continue making more money on an ongoing basis.

Now, I talk a lot about my best friend's pest-control business — but the truth is, it's probably one of the most boring on the planet. There's nothing exciting about shooting bug-killer all day... except for one thing. Here's what I mean: she bought the business in the winter of 2001. I was with her when she bought it; she wanted my opinions and advice, and so the first thing I said to the guy she bought it from was, "What in the world do you guys do in the winter? There are no bugs this time of year! How do you make any money?" What I didn't know then was that a lot of their business is sold on a monthly basis. So believe it or not, her pest-control drivers go up to those houses they service and they're in there shooting poison, even in the middle of the winter, when it's ice cold out. Their tactic is this: "Well, look, just because you can't see them doesn't mean that they're not out there laying eggs and lurking in the dark. They're still here! They're ready to come out in spring — so we'd better come here and shoot that poison." A lot of the business is sold on a monthly continuity basis, although some is quarterly and some of it's bi-monthly. That evens out her income stream, and it makes hers one of the most interesting businesses out there.

And by the way, those businesses have extremely high re-sell values, and they're extremely easy to sell. There are plenty of pest-control people who do just one basic thing: They go build a business, and then two years later they sell it for some high-dollar amount. And then they take off and do nothing much for a couple of years, vacationing till the money runs out... whereupon they build up another little pest control route, and then sell the contract to Terminex or Orkin (mostly Terminex). Then they kick their feet up and take off another year or two! The reason these companies have so much value is because their services are sold on a contractual basis, which provides ongoing residual income that just keeps rolling right in, month after month. I think that's exciting.

I have an associate who's done quite well for himself financially. I was on the phone with him one day talking about residual income and he all of a sudden he said, "Yeah, every time I look at a new business, if it doesn't have residual income in it I just won't do it." I asked him, "What did you just say?" He repeated, "I look at a lot of different deals, and if it doesn't have residual, I forget it." That reason alone is why I've included the Fourth Key to Wealth here. If you're considering a business and it doesn't have residual income — if you don't have a way of making money consistently after they buy from you the first time — then just look for something else that does, or look for a way to build it in. Look, your bills are coming in every month! They come in automatically, whether you do anything or not. So you've got to do something to try to get that money coming in automatically every month, too.

Another thing to keep in mind is that it's not too difficult to get your customers to purchase a continuity program of some kind. People are used to paying monthly for things. They pay for their cable bill, their cell phone bill, their home phone bill, their electric bill, their gas. The practice is ingrained in their minds. If you have a way to automatically bill them — for example, to automatically take your fee from their checking account or bill it to their credit card every month so they don't have to think about it — it's easy to keep the money coming in. As long as you're providing good value in exchange for that money, obviously they can't just say, "Your program costs $20 a month, and I'm not getting my money's worth!" As long as you're providing something of good value, and as long as you explain that to the clients, most people are more than happy to pay a reasonable monthly fee. Heck, you can eat at McDonald's once a week and spend $20 a month. People blow $20 a month on all kinds of things. So they're more than happy to spend $20 a month with you, assuming you can provide good value to them.

So adding a monthly fee to your product or service is an easy way to generate automatic revenue. Of course, there has to be a time limit on it. People won't pay the $20 forever. They go through changes; the seasons of their lives come and go. Maybe they move; maybe something changes with them economically; in any case, that monthly fee doesn't just go on forever. There's an end to it, and as you develop your business you'll find out how long most people will pay that fee. Maybe those people stay with you for an average of six to nine months; maybe they stay for an average of two years. It depends on your business model and your specific products and services. But most people will continue for quite some time, so that's a great thing to build into any business. If you just try hard enough, you'll come up with a way to build in continuity income.

And here's another thing: Always keep asking yourself,

SWITCH ON THE FIVE KEYS TO WEALTH 🖾

"What's next?" because people *will* spend more money, whether you offer them something or not. You'd better be aware of that. If you're not, you're losing money that could be yours — and it *will* be yours, if you just keep coming up with new stuff that's based on what they bought before.

**The Fifth Key**

Last, but certainly not least, is something I got from Dan Kennedy. He calls it the "slack adjustor." The reason he calls it the slack adjustor is because, as I've said before, *everything* always costs more than you think it will. The bills are always higher than you expect. So what you need to do is have at least one product, service, or product/service combination that's high-ticket, so all you have to do is sell one or two a month in order to cover all the bills and, most importantly, pay yourself some money. An alarming number of entrepreneurs get paid next to nothing, given the number of hours they're working, the kind of dedication that they're showing, and all of the responsibilities and burdens to which they're subjecting themselves. They're just not making enough money to make it worthwhile. But by having this slack adjustor, where just a few sales can put huge sums of money in your pocket, you can pay yourself and all your bills and make yourself a lot happier. It's a simple thing, but many people don't do it.

Here's an example. I have a wonderful friend, a very smart man who will remain unnamed here. Everybody I know loves him and believes in him. Now, he's got one thing that he really could improve: He's afraid to charge enough money for his products and services. But despite what he's afraid of, people *will* pay more money! That should be the determining factor of how much money you should charge for your products or services: whatever the market will bear. I've mentioned my colleague George Douglas, who used to make a million dollars a week. When he started out, his average ticket amount was maybe $7,000-8,000. By the time he retired in 2002 or 2003, his average ticket was $13,000 — and not because his offer changed. He just kept raising his price, because the market bore it. First of all, when he raised his price, the sales didn't go away. Secondly, he just matter-of-factly figured that the more money he charged, the better people felt about what they bought from him, because people do tend to equate premium dollar amounts with highest quality.

I've struggled with this problem over the years, and so have my close friends and colleagues — Chris Hollinger, for example. I know that over the past six years, Chris has definitely had problems with this. As I've mentioned, when he first started offering his premium website at $1,297, he told himself, "*No one is going to spend $1,297 for that website.*" I don't know if it was his Midwest upbringing or the fact that he's just a cheapskate that had him telling himself that! But you know what? That expensive, premium website was the one everybody wanted. And quite frankly, looking back on it, he probably could have charged $2,500 or more for that site. And even still, when he's looking at price points and what he's going to charge, his first gut reaction is always a lot lower than it could be. That's just the way he is — but when you do that, you're just leaving money on the table. As I've mentioned before, there's what something's worth, and there's what the market will bear — and there's what you can sell it for, depending on how good a copywriter and salesperson you are. That's the bottom line.

Chris has yet to pitch a $5,000 product in his business — but maybe he needs to have one as a slack adjuster. Oh, he's got automatic, built-in upgrades on his current offer, but he doesn't have a really big slack adjustor, and he should. (He's working on this, by the way). This is an important point that a lot of people don't think about, so I don't blame him. Most marketers think,

"Okay, I've got products and here are my prices. I'm pricing Product A... well, let's see, Product A is going to be $79.95. I also have Product B... and it has a price of $199. And Product C... well I've got that product and it happens to sell for $395. And Product D is my most expensive package at $695." They don't think about those products in relationship to one another. They don't think about them in any way at all, except "This is my product, and I decided to price it at this price point." So the slack adjustor concept is lost on most people, because they never think about their products in the proper way.

What you need to have is an expensive, premium-priced product or service that fits with your lower-priced products or services to help bridge the gap in your marketing. Direct-Response Marketing is highly expensive; it takes a lot of sales to make money, because of the costs of postage and the cost of working with a mailing house. Having a slack adjustor product allows you to bridge that gap and be in the profit that much faster.

Our newest promotion goes from a $39 sale to a $495 sale, and then up from there. The purpose is to keep moving people up toward that highest-priced point, hopefully quickly. If we can move them along, we cover our costs and get into the profits faster. Even if you have a back-end strategy after you make a sale, if at least some of your products aren't expensive, you're still just kind of plodding along, slowly making money. The cost to make each sale is expensive. Even if you're using Direct Mail, making a repeat sale to a customer, can be expensive. So having a higher-priced item allows you to make the profit, to get into the profits faster.

I'm not good at math, but simple math I can understand. For every ten $100 sales, you only need *one* $1,000 sale. So it takes more low-priced sales to make the same dollar amount as it does to sell one thing that's more expensive. In fact, we've had models in the past where we need just one order out of thousands of pieces of mail to get us into the black, because of the cost of the promotion. So the higher your selling point, the fewer sales you need to make a profit. That makes mathematical sense. A slack adjustor just helps you get into the profit faster. It allows you to bring up the slack of the cost of the mailing. Imagine the strength of that.

One of the cool things about direct-response marketing is there's so many different ways you can do things. If you're running a business with very little overhead, then you can use models to run your business that someone like myself — someone who has more than 20 full-time employees — can't do. I have a bigger nut to cover. My fixed costs are so high that I have to sell so much more every month than I would have if I didn't have my infrastructure, before I ever put a dollar of profit in my pocket. But one of the things that I can't even think about doing myself could be a great working model for you. At M.O.R.E., Inc., we've actually had promotions that produced profit, just not enough to cover our entire infrastructure. We had to abandon them as models, but they might work for you. And by that, I just mean this: We talk about stair-stepping, where first you go for $39, then for $390, and then you go for $3,900. We've had models where we go directly for those thousands of dollars right up front, or directly go for those hundreds of dollars right up front — and we've actually made profit at it, too. We just didn't make quite enough profit, so we had to abandon this model.

The point is, you have choices. You have different ways that you can do business, and premium-priced products and services are something that you need to have in your inventory. If you don't, you're doing yourself a disservice.

It's a good idea to put as many of these five Keys into play as you can. They may not all be possible in a particular situation, but if you just try to get as many of them as you can, you're going to put yourself in the best position to make the largest amount of money. By utilizing the right strategies, you don't have to be perfect at what you're doing, and you can *still* do quite well. If nothing else, I want you to finish this book realizing that — because it's one of best things I have to teach when it comes to inspiring you, motivating you, and getting you excited about all this. The more you think you need all these skills, the less inspired you'll be to just go out there and do it.

I'll give you a real example of that, without using a name. I remember the first time I met one of our Roundtable members. It was at one of our events; he came just to hear us speak — not as a customer, but because he was invited. I remember sitting in our meeting room, and him just asking question after question. He was hungry for information. He was taking notes and he would be like, "Oh, okay, that makes sense. Yeah, I understand that." Every time we had any kind of break, he would constantly be asking me about things: "How do you rent mailing lists? How many pieces do you test?" They were good questions, but they made me realize how little he knew. He was a rookie and he really wanted to know a lot about direct mail, but didn't have a lot of experience at that point, didn't really know much about how it worked.

He kept coming to events, doing the same thing over and over. But all of a sudden, he stopped asking as many questions — although he still does ask some to this day. I think it's his nature. He likes to chat and ask how things are going, and he's always analyzing what we're doing and how it's working. But suddenly I started seeing him out there in the mail making money, and doing very well. He just did it. He went out there and just started putting all this into practice, and I don't think he even really had much figured out by the time he got started. He decided that he would use some of the principles we were talking about, that he'd just get out there and start doing it. He learned as he went along, and he's still learning, I'm sure.

It's all about just getting out there and doing it. There's only so much you can accomplish by learning and reading and being a student. You have to take it to the next level, where you actually start putting everything into practice. These Five Keys will help you do it.

# CHAPTER FIFTEEN:

# Dominate Your Market

In this chapter, I'm going to give you three rock-solid reasons why you can quickly dominate your market, even if you have almost no money or are just getting started. This is possible simply because most of the people you'll compete against are very weak marketers. I don't say that in a judgmental way; it's just an observation. We're not any better than those people, we're just better marketers. If you look at the mistakes that other people are making and simply correct those mistakes, then you'll have an edge over them. It just makes sense.

When I sat down and tried to determine why most marketers are so weak and ineffective, why they're losing money that could and should be theirs, I came up with three reasons. All three are simple, so don't let the simplicity fool you!

The FIRST REASON is, most marketers just quit way too soon. Look, if there's one thing about me and my wife that separates us from a lot of people, it's that we're stubborn as hell. She's more stubborn than I am, but I'm pretty stubborn too. Maybe I'm not that smart, but I'm pretty tenacious. I'll keep sticking with something long past the time when most people — especially smarter people — would have given up. You see, I'm too stupid to give up, so I just hang in there. That's been one of my biggest sources of strength, believe me.

I see a lot of marketers who give up too soon. They're not trying to do enough to make enough sales to prospective buyers. Heck, I've done it too. In 1994, Dan Kennedy shot an infomercial for us. We flew out to Phoenix, we shot it, he produced it for us, and we tested it in 14 or 15 different cities. It was a 30-minute, two-step, lead-generation infomercial where people were asked to raise their hand and send for a special package of information. And it worked; we had no trouble generating leads. We've never had trouble generating leads. What we have trouble with is converting those leads to sales.

I was pretty new as a marketer at that point, and I had a lot to learn. I'd already been in the business six or seven years, but I was a very weak follow-up marketer. Nowadays people make jokes about the fact that we rain mail on their heads — that if they don't buy from us, they'll just keep getting more and more offers. Well, I wasn't like that back then. Back then, we'd send out maybe one or two offers. To use a metaphor, it was like falling in love with a beautiful woman that you knew was the right woman for you, and then giving up after you asked her to marry you twice and she turned you down both times. She's the love of your life; she's perfect for you, and you know it... but you just asked her a couple times, and gave up. Similarly, most people just give up way too soon with their marketing — and I've learned my lesson about that.

The SECOND REASON you can easily dominate your marketplace is that most marketers are just too worried about offending their prospects or customers. And so they're always trying to be perfect; every hair on their heads is in perfect shape, their teeth are perfectly white, they're dressed impeccably — and they just look so polished and phony. This is a mistake, because if you're always trying to please everybody, you'll end up pleasing very few. You should only try to please the people you're trying to do the most business with. Nobody else matters.

Even if you do offend some people, you can still earn their trust and respect, even if they don't like you. The older I get, the less I worry about what other people think of me. When I was Chris Lakey's age, I suffered from all kinds of terrible insecurities. I constantly worried about what people thought about me. Now that I'm almost 50 years old, I don't much care. I'm trying to be honest. I'm trying to be real. I'm trying to give people good value — but I really don't care about what people think about me anymore. That lets me say and do things that I feel strongly about. So while some of my customers might say, "God, what an obnoxious, egotistical SOB he is," or "I hate that guy," at least they know I'm keeping it real. At least they don't have to worry whether I'm feeding them a line of BS. They know that even though I might say things that are offensive or non-PC, at least I'm real; and they trust me. That's liberating when you used to suffer from terrible insecurities, and it gets you good customers. It gets you people who trust you.

NUMBER THREE is a big one. People simply don't realize that in most cases, there's still a great deal of money that's just lying on the table at the end of the deal. They just walk away from it, oblivious. It could be theirs; it should be theirs. And it would be, if they simply went after it more aggressively, and stayed after it until they got it. That's one of the things Dan Kennedy told us back in 1994, when we got all those leads from the infomercial. We could have made millions of dollars on that deal, if we'd tried hard enough. I realize that now. It didn't work because, like Dan said, we gave up on them too soon. We didn't follow-up on them as aggressively as we should have. We didn't stay after those leads. We didn't do everything possible to make the sale.

Nowadays we try not to make that mistake; we go after people aggressively. Again, if you've got products and services that can really offer the value that you say that they will, if you're delivering high-quality stuff, then you *should* go after the business aggressively — as long as you're dealing with qualified prospects who really want and need what you're offering. You've got to get past this "quit way too soon" thing quickly — and you *will* encounter it eventually in your own business. You'll throw something out there and generate some leads, and then try to convert them — and when they don't convert right away, you'll want to move on and try something different. But don't do it! You have to get it straight in your mind that you're not looking at success and failure. You only look at the results, period. Point blank. End of story. If you're not getting the results that you wanted, then you need to change something. So instead of giving up on the whole shebang, take a closer look at your leads. If they truly identify themselves as interested, if they're serious prospects, then they're worth closer scrutiny. Maybe they've even paid five, ten, or fifteen dollars to get a little package sent to them; if so, that's a pretty qualified lead. That's when you go back to your sales pieces — your marketing — and say, "Okay, what do I need to change here?"

Change something! Think about it, change it, and send it back out. Don't quit, and don't think you're a failure just because they didn't buy the first time. Marketing is an ongoing process of testing to see what's going to work. When you figure that out, when the numbers come together for you, that's when you roll it out even bigger. Then you have that money machine system I talked about in earlier chapters. You have the lead generation on this end that's converting sales, a system you can roll out to keep qualifying prospects and making offers to them and making initial sales. Don't look at it as success and failure, just results. Good results or bad results. The answer lies somewhere in your marketing, because a good marketing system will solve your sales problems.

Again, don't worry about offending your prospects or

customers. From the very beginning, you have to realize that you're not going to please everyone all the time. It's just not going to happen. There's going to be somebody out there who's going to be offended by what you say or how you say it, or who you are and what you've done. You can't get wrapped up or bogged down in the fact that some people don't like you. It's like that old Sawyer Brown song: "Some girls don't like boys like me — oh, but some girls do." Your marketing is meant to attract the right people while repelling the wrong ones. You don't want to do business with people who don't like you.

And, of course, NUMBER THREE is, again, something that most of us have to go through a learning curve on. You have to fight your natural tendency to give up too early, just because you want to move on to what's next. With the recent downturn in the economy, it's easy to get depressed about things like the fact that people don't have as much money as they did just a few months ago. But human nature being what it is, prospects are still going to have the same wants, needs, and desires. And even today, even with this economy, there's a lot of money lying on the table for marketers to go and get. So aggressively stay after it. If your results are poor in the beginning, go back and look at your market. Restudy the concepts and strategies that I've talked about here and say, "Okay, what can I do to make my promise bigger? What can I do to paint a better picture? What can I do to give them proof of why this opportunity is good?" Go back and change things, and then test them. Keep moving. Be aggressive.

I think, in general, that the problem with most business people, especially those with local businesses, is that they just don't understand marketing. But most people *do* know their businesses. If you're a plumber, you know your pipes. If you're a gardener, you know how to work in people's yards and take care of plants and trees. If you have a local shop where you sell jewelry, you know all about rings and necklaces and watches, and all the kinds of things you can buy in a jewelry store. Whatever business people are in, they're usually an expert at it. Specifically, I think of service industries, like people who come out to your house and fix things — electricians, carpenters and plumbers, etc.

Here's an example. Chris Lakey moved recently, and he now has a sprinkler system in his yard. It's the first time he's ever had a sprinkler system, and he had some problems, so he had a guy who knows sprinkler systems come out. There was a lot of work that needed done, and they guy spent a lot of time at Chris' house working on the sprinkler system. Many days he would be there when Chris left in the morning and he'd still be there working away when Chris would come home. Chris would spend a little bit of time out there with him, sometimes as much as half an hour. The guy liked to talk. So Chris would get home and ask the sprinkler guy what he'd been up to that day, and he'd tell Chris what he was up to — and Chris would talk to him about marketing.

Chris is like me — every time I have people out to the house to do stuff, I talk to them about marketing because I like marketing and I like to find out what people in the service businesses are doing to advertise. I think a lot of people are just like the sprinkler man. He has enough referral business to keep him busy, so he really doesn't advertise. I'm not even sure if he has a Yellow Pages ad. He was referred to Chris by somebody else, and that's how he gets a lot of his work — so I think that oftentimes, small service providers don't ever think about doing anything bigger or better than what they do. This guy knows sprinkler systems, but he doesn't know marketing at all — and a lot of people in local businesses suffer from that.

Maybe he doesn't want to get bigger; but if his schedule was busy, he could hire someone else to work for him, and he could be doing more jobs that way. He could expand. Maybe he could get out of the working business altogether, and manage a team of people who did the work for him. He could certainly go beyond the business that he has. I think that a lot of reason that local businesspeople don't do that is because they don't know marketing. So they focus on doing their business, but they don't ever focus on acquiring customers, serving the customers they have better, and trying to get more business from their customers.

The more you're aware of these three big mistakes, the more you'll see that the marketplace is filled with competitors that are easy to beat. In the boxing world they call them "tomato soup-can fighters." Number one, people quit way too soon. You've got to assume that they've figured out that they actually have to be marketing. But even when they know their marketing and know they need to acquire customers, most give up way too soon. Maybe they've got an ad out there, but don't even have any way of following up; they just hope that ad is enticing enough to get people into the store or get people to pick up the phone and call them. So you've got a situation where they don't understand that you need to follow-up at all. On the other hand, maybe someone *has* figured it out a little, and they've got an understanding of marketing and the fact that you need to follow-up with people. But they give up too soon anyway. Maybe they've got a sales letter that's generating leads; so those leads come in, and then what do they do with them? Well, they mail them their Special Report, and that's it. They wait around for the orders to come in. Maybe some orders do; but even if it's a great marketing campaign, they get a good percentage rate right away, and that's it. They're done. They give up too soon.

Your goal should be to continue following up with people until it's no longer profitable to do so. What does that that mean? Well, it depends on a lot of different variables, but you have to follow your marketing and let that dictate what you do. We've had situations where we've had follow-up campaigns that lasted eight weeks or more. Sometimes they've lasted through 20 to 30 follow-ups. At other times, we've had situations where the money stopped becoming profitable after about six follow-ups. So it's not that there's a standard uniform equation for figuring that out. You have to just look at the numbers. Track the numbers, track where all your orders are coming from, and how many orders you got from each follow-up. Then you can decide when to stop, based on the number of responses you get each time. Usually you get a diminishing return, so each time you mail a follow-up, you get fewer orders than the previous time. Those orders continue to dry up. You've got to figure that the longer you go on, the more likely you've gotten the main people who are going to buy.

Most of your orders are going to come in sooner rather than later. So, with each passing follow-up, the number of people that respond gets smaller and smaller. It may be that, even if follow-up #10 got you three orders, it costs too much to make those three sales and it's not worth doing it... so you stop. You can't just look at the fact that you had an order come in and say, "Well, okay, I got orders from that. It's good." You need to look at the cost and determine whether it still made you a profit. Once it stops making you a profit, that's where you cut it off. You have to determine that through testing, looking at the numbers and seeing what they tell you, and adjusting accordingly. It all depends on the offer you're making, your price point, and other factors. As I mentioned before, we've have had promotions in the past where we needed one sale to make a profit. It may be that your offer needs three or four sales to make a profit, so you have to judge how far you're willing to go to get those before it's no longer worth the effort.

Use a mix of different methods. If you're mailing postcards as a follow-up, they cost a lot less to get in the mail than a sales letter, and so you don't need as big a response to cover the cost of those postcards. Let's say you have a 10-piece follow-up sequence; you could have maybe five of them be postcards, and maybe one of them could be a voice call. There's software out there that lets you call customers automatically. You just load the list, record a message, and let the machine call them with a verbal reminder that they need to do business with you. If you're a local store, you could call folks to invite them to visit your store because you've got a sale on Saturday, and they need to be there at 9:00 A.M. Maybe the doors don't officially open until 10:00, but because they're a preferred customer, at 9:00 A.M. the doors are open for *them*. If they bring in this postcard you mailed them, they can save 10-20%.

One thing we've done before in some of our follow-ups is a re-mail of the main sales letter. We've also done summary sales letters. In one recent example, we had an offer that was originally a 64-page sales letter. I cut it down to 36 pages for the follow-up. I kept enough material in there that it still gave people all the information they needed to buy, but I cut all the extra stuff... all the filler, I guess you'd say. Instead of repeating the main points five times, I repeated them three times. We mailed some of the list a full version of the letter as a follow-up; the others got the summary letter. That's something you can do, too. You can also do fliers where you remind them of the main bullet points.

Getting back to the main principle here, most people simply quit way too soon. You should do all kinds of things to continue getting your offer in front of your marketplace, especially to a lead — someone who has requested information from you. You want to make sure you follow-up to them over and over again, until it no longer becomes profitable to do so. If you give up before it's no longer profitable, then you're obviously leaving money on the table.

Let's look, again, at the second thing that holds most markets back: They're too worried about offending their

RUTHLESS COPYWRITING STRATEGIES

prospects or customers. Well, if you're not offending someone, you're not doing your job. You've got to have a stance, an opinion, and if you do, then someone isn't going to like something you say. Otherwise you're pretty boring, at least from a marketing perspective. If your sales message isn't offending someone, it's probably not attracting someone either. It's too watered down. You need to aggressively promote your business, and that means some people won't like your message. Maybe "offending" is too strong a word, because maybe you're not offending anyone — but you're just not attracting them. And if you're not attracting them, you're repelling them.

There are two parts to any sales process: One part is attracting the right kind of people, and the other part is repelling the wrong kind of people. Your sales message should be doing a good job of both. If your offer isn't strong to attract the right kinds of people, then it won't be strong enough to repel anyone, either. If you look at it as a continuum, you've got "attracting" on one end, and you've got "repelling" on the other. The blander your sales message is, the closer together those two ends are. You want them to be polar opposites, something like a magnet. The stronger the magnet, the more something is attracted or repelled.

One more comment on the third problem with most marketers: They simply don't know that there's a great deal more money laying on the table that could be theirs, if they were to simply go after it more aggressively and stay after it until they got it. This requires an awareness of how to use the marketing strategies I'm teaching you here to the utmost. This idea ties together intimately with the other problems I've talked about in this chapter; if they didn't quit too soon, if they went after their marketplace more aggressively, and if they weren't worried so much about offending somebody with their marketing, then more businesspeople could be making more money. The money's there and it can be yours, if you're willing to aggressively promote your business.

I love the business and service guys who come knocking on the doors in my neighborhood; they get it, usually. You know, we get Jehovah's Witnesses, we get Church of Latter Day Saints reps, we get guys selling the replacement windows and the siding, we get tree trimmers. And then, of course, there are the water purification and vacuum cleaner salesmen. I end up talking to all of them. Some of them I won't let come in and do their pitch just because I've heard it already, but in general I do like to pay attention to their marketing and their sales pitches.

Chris Hollinger was telling me recently that a trimmer guy once came by his house with this yellow flier in his hand that had been copied about a thousand times and looked horrible. He was going door-to-door in the middle of the afternoon, and most people aren't like Chris or me; they're at work. So Chris saw him coming down the street, knocking on doors, leaving his flier, knocking on doors, leaving his flier. He wanted to trim some trees. Well, Chris happens to have this humongous oak tree that does need to be trimmed, and the tree trimmer guy saw that and saw that there were cars in the driveway. So Chris met him out front and talked to him a while, and he might end up trimming Chris' tree.

Anyway, Chris gave him some business advice — some hints on what he could do, instead of knocking on doors while people were at work. Chris said, "Why don't you take this flier, and instead of the picture of this nice tree that you have, why don't you have a picture of a branch that comes off the tree and crushes somebody's house?" The tree trimmer just says, "What?" Chris said, "Yeah, why don't you have a picture like that? And by the way, clean up your flier a little bit, make it look a little better. It's been copied too many times." The trimmer was kind of interested, and said, "Well, what do you do for a living?" Chris said, "This is what I do. I'm a marketing guy.

Take a picture of a big limb that went right through somebody's house, because they didn't trim their tree. Then put your main points there about why they need to keep their trees trimmed. And then, instead of knocking on every door in this neighborhood, why don't you mail it? Do that, and just sit back there and let your phone ring."

The tree trimmer thought it was a good idea, so now Chris is waiting to see if he's going to get something in the mail from this guy — a better piece than that yellow flier. Instead of showing a nice-looking tree, he needs something that says to the client, "You've got a problem there, don't you? A big limb that comes through your house... that's a major problem that could have been prevented, had you hired me." People don't want that to happen. They're going to think, "Yeah, well, maybe I should," especially when it's spring storm season, or they're worried about winter ice storms.

It sure beats knocking on doors. That's another thing that makes direct-response marketing a winner. He's got the material; he's got a flier. He could just make that flier better, get a more appropriate picture, and lay out his major points. People like those bulleted points on why they need to keep their trees trimmed. If he did that, he could probably quadruple his business. He knows his business; he made that clear when he was talking to Chris. He went down his list of why Chris needed to trim this tree. He could put that information into a nice format, mail it out to everyone in Chris' neighborhood, and stay busy right there for a long time. But he's not thinking like that. He's thinking like a tree trimmer.

So many businesspeople out there think like a tree trimmer, or a restaurant owner, or a plumber. They're not thinking like marketers. This fellow's a good example. He's working hard, walking the neighborhood — but at a bad time, because there's nobody home! He's wasting his time. Yeah, he's probably putting the fliers on people's doors; but they could be just as effective in their mailbox without having to go walk door-to-door. Of course, he needs to make the flier look better first. And here's another thing: when he's pounding the pavement, every time he talks to somebody, he has to verbally give that sales presentation, over and over — and hope that they don't slam the door on him before he can say all 10 points!

Of course, he's got a handful of reasons why people should have their trees trimmed. But he has to get them to agree to open the door before he can tell them all that, and he has to hope that they'll listen once they do. Some people will open the door, but then be immediately turned off by what he's offering. Other people might listen for a minute, but they don't get very far before they decide that they don't need it. But a flier with a picture of a tree limb going through your house or through your car window makes people stop and think, "What...?" and then they read about it. It does a better selling job.

He could show pictures of last year's ice storm, of what happened when other people had to deal with the consequences of too many limbs on their trees that weren't trimmed. He could talk about the liability problem if your tree goes into your neighbor's house instead of yours, which is even worse. I see all kinds of advantages to a little flier like that. You could put together a two, three, or four-page flier that did an even better job, with more pictures of recent hail storms or bad things that happen when you don't do a good job with your tree trimming. He could make a special offer, and then have a voice mailbox taking calls and letting people order from him while he's out working. Or he could even offer a coupon.

So there are plenty of things he could do, and it's the same thing with a lot of businesses. This tree trimmer idea is just one example; all kinds of service people make this mistake. They're out doing too much physical work to try to get their jobs, instead of letting advertising bring in that work for them. Think about it. If the tree trimmer had a flier he was mailing or a sales letter he dropped in the mail, the only people he'd be talking to would be those who wanted his service. Instead he's talking to a lot of people, trying to separate the wheat from the chaff. Who knows how many neighborhoods he has to walk through before he gets a sale? How much time is he spending out on the streets hustling business door-to-door that could be spent doing something else? He could spend an hour mailing fliers each day, and spend the rest of the day either A) doing the jobs trimming trees or B) doing other things when he doesn't have jobs lined up, and enjoying *not* walking around all the neighborhoods.

It's a frame of mind. He's probably never thought about using mail. He figures the way to do it is to go door to door, talking to people, hanging fliers on doors. So here Chris is, answering the door and talking to him about some new ways of doing business, something that he hasn't really thought about. And hopefully he'll use that strategy, and he'll realize how easy it is compared to the way he *was* doing things. Granted, his cost goes up a little because he's not walking door-to-door, he's actually dropping something in the mail. But if you're a local business, you can canvas a whole neighborhood with mail a lot easier. You could hit 500 houses, and that's only 500 pieces of mail. That's not much when you compare it to what we do. We mail as many as 50,000 pieces a week, so he could certainly mail 500 to 1,000 pieces of mail to homes in his area and get a lot of business. That way, he wouldn't leave money on the table that could easily be his.

CHAPTER SIXTEEN:

# Profit from this Three-Step Formula

In this chapter, I'm going to introduce you to a three-step marketing formula that never fails. There are less than 30 simple words in this three-step formula, and yet each one could be worth a million dollars or more to you over the lifetime of your business. It's so simple and easy a 12-year-old child can fully understand it. If you do these three things, you simply cannot fail. I've talked about some of these things before in other contexts; this formula just presents them in a slightly different way.

Here are the three steps you need to internalize:

1. Make sure you're communicating with the right people;

2. Make those people an irresistible offer;

3. Do something bold to create a strong sense of urgency.

Let me repeat: This formula simply can't fail if done right. Most of this revolves around mailing to people that you're communicating with on a regular basis. Know intimately who your target market is. We use direct mail, so we rent mailing lists of people who have purchased some kind of moneymaking program from somebody else. Occasionally we get someone who will send us an email or a letter asking to be removed from our mailing list, which is fine. If they don't want to hear from us, we don't want to mail to them. But occasionally we'll get someone who sends a "do not mail" request to us and they'll say something like, "I don't know how I ever got on your list to begin with. I don't know why you're sending me mail." And I always reply, "Well, the only way we would ever have mailed anything to you is if you had either inquired about a moneymaking opportunity from us, or bought something from somebody else." We're happy to not mail to you if you don't want us to anymore, but don't think we just picked you out of the phone book — because that would be stupid on our part.

You see, it doesn't do us any good to randomly pick people to try to sell our products and services to. The first step of the formula is communicating with the right people. So we only want to mail our offers to people that we *know* have a history of buying the types of products and services we sell. Whatever industry you're in, you don't want to waste time advertising to people who probably aren't interested in what you have to sell. You want to find the people who are most likely to buy what you have to sell, and those are the people you want to target.

Once you know that you're communicating with the right people, make them an irresistible offer, something they can't refuse! That's your second step. And then, do something bold to create a sense of urgency. Maybe you've got a deadline, where there's something happening right away so that people need to act *right now* for a certain reason. As of this writing, we have an offer for a conference call that's happening 10 days from now. The offer is that "coming up in 10 days, we've got a very special conference call that you need to be on. So we need to get your order right away — because if you don't order now, you're going to miss it." So there's only a 10-day window that we can take their order in; if they order outside of 10 days, too bad, they'll have missed the call. We're creating a sense of urgency to make sure that they respond right away.

An irresistible offer is just all the things you *do*. It's not your product; it's what you do that makes people want to buy. It's how you package it up. It's the "buy one, get one free" deal. It's the infomercial offer that says, "But wait, there's more!" If you order today, you're going to also get this, and you're going to get that, and we're going to throw in the kitchen sink." That's making you an irresistible offer to make you run to the phone and grab your credit card and call them to order NOW!

On the sales pitch for the conference call that I've mentioned, the headline is: "How to Be One of Only 250 People…" That's our hook — our irresistible, bold offer. It's scarcity. The offer is limited. That's one way to generate some urgency, because it implies that once those 250 slots are sold, that's it — so you'd better act now to ensure that you *are* one of these 250 people. In other offers, we've used bright red date stamps that basically say, "Reply by this date, or the deal is off!" You have to do anything you can do to get them to act, because the bottom line with direct-response marketing is *response*. Do anything you can do to get them to act sooner, and make them realize that if they don't do it sooner, then it's not going to happen. It's just not. Some of the sales material that I and my colleagues put out there early on didn't have a sense of urgency or offer a compelling reason to act, and those offers suffered.

But that's how marketing is, sometimes: Until you've been through it and learned it, you just never know what to expect. That's why I hope this book guides you well enough to avoid some of these mistakes. I honestly believe that if you use the strategies I'm sharing with you, apply them seriously to any business, you're going to do well. Why? Because nine out of ten marketers out there aren't applying any strategies at all. They just look at something and say, "Okay, that sounds good. Let's do it." Or, the Yellow Pages guy that sells them their ad says,

"Okay, yeah, that's a good ad. Sure. Let's put it in there." But the Yellow Pages guys typically aren't marketers. They're about selling ads, not helping your ad be more effective than the other guy he's going to talk to tomorrow — the one whose ad is going to be right next to yours.

So, unless they're getting it from some other source, most marketers aren't studying. They're not reading a lot of books. Some of them do, but the marketing that they do read tends to come out of the universities. Well, guess what? My close friend and colleague Chris Hollinger has a marketing degree from a university — and he says it didn't teach him *anything* about direct-response. Zero. It wasn't until he got into business for himself that Chris started finding how effective these things could be.

# CHAPTER SEVENTEEN

# Put These Nineteen Secrets into Play

Much of what I'm going to share with you in this chapter you've already heard in one form or another, but I want to repeat it all for emphasis. These are the 19 marketing secrets that have brought us more than $117,000,000 over the years. I'll go through each one and cover them as fast as I can, but this will still be a long chapter!

I don't want you to think that these are just off-the-cuff items I came up with out of the blue. This is a list I boiled down from something much larger. Many of you may be familiar with my five-CD set of 3,529 Ruthless Marketing secrets I did a few years ago. It's a work in progress — I'm trying to do a new volume every single year. Well, I do my best thinking toward the end of a project, as I'm wrapping up a new volume. That's where these 19 secrets came from. While I was wrapping up Volume 4, I did a lot of heavy thinking, trying to analyze all the things we've learned over the years. I asked myself, "What are the top strategies that did it for us?" These 19 were the answer.

FIRST UP is premium pricing. Charge more for your products, because you're after better customers who will buy additional stuff and cause fewer problems. Plus, it gives you the ability to make good money in spite of bad numbers. Now, like any business, we have our bad customers. But when I've looked

RUTHLESS COPYWRITING STRATEGIES

closely at the worst customers we have, it never ceases to amaze me that these people are almost invariably new customers who buy very little from us — and yet they cause us the most grief. And then we have all kinds of established customers who have been buying from us for years who are a joy and a pleasure to work with. If for no other reason, *that's* why you should have premium prices. People who spend more money with you are just better-quality people, at least from a marketing perspective, since they usually cause fewer problems. It's just a fact of business. Your biggest troublemakers are usually the people who spent the least. In fact, we occasionally get people who will complain about something, and then we find out they haven't even bought anything from us! Or maybe all they did was request some information from us, so we sent them something for free — and they're still complaining. Think about how ridiculous that is!

On the flipside of that are people you've established a relationship with, who are good clients; that is, they've spent more money. Maybe it's not even that you have a long-term relationship, it's just that one time they paid a lot of money for a premium-priced product. Those people tend to cause fewer customer-service nightmares. They're the ones who are happy you're doing business with them; the relationship is strong and solid, and there are no problems. Again, I wish I knew psychologically what causes that to happen, but it's a reality whether I can explain it or not. The people who spend the least typically cause the most problems. Of course, a lot of people who spend no money with you, or very little, *don't* cause problems. Not everybody is a problem waiting to happen. But if you look at your problems, you'll see a good portion of them come from people who spent the least money.

And then there's the concept of slack adjustors, which is an extreme form of premium pricing. That's the whole basis of this first strategy — even if your numbers are bad, because you're selling things for premium dollars, you don't have to worry about going out of business. You're making enough profit on those fewer transactions. So you absolutely, positively have to have that slack adjustor built in to your business, because it will mean higher profits in the end. And then you need to have the system in place to upgrade your customers to those higher-priced items. Don't think for a second, like Chris Hollinger did when he first started with that $1,297 website that he thought was way too expensive, that no one is going to go for it. They will. People will end up finding the money for the things they really want in life. If you have that premium-priced item that you can convince them it's in their best interest to buy, they'll find the money for it.

If you don't try this, you're leaving money on the table. If you're not offering customers premium priced items, you're losing money that could and should be yours, because they trust you and they want more of what they bought from you the first time —and they're willing to spend that money. All you have to do is make them the offer.

And remember, buyers are liars. It's true. They'll claim they can't afford something when they actually can. I actually caught myself doing this recently, when somebody was trying to sell me something for $25,000. This was somebody I have some respect for, but the first thing that came out of my mouth was, "I don't have the money." Well, I probably could have come up with the money... but I just didn't think it was worth it. And he wasn't selling hard enough anyway. Everybody has that reflex. It's that initial thing we come up with — and for most people, I believe it's wrong.

NUMBER TWO: sequential follow-up mailing campaigns. You've got to keep the pressure on. You have to be like the persistent man who asked the beautiful woman to marry him a hundred times, in a hundred slightly different ways, until she said,

RUTHLESS COPYWRITING STRATEGIES

"Yes!" Speaking of marriage: When my stepson got married, he told me that he wanted me to wear a tuxedo to his wedding. And I said, "Chris, I'll never do such a thing. When I die, you can put me in a tuxedo and then you can have an open casket and come see me in my tuxedo then." Well, that was about a year before his actual wedding. He just bugged me about it. Every single time we spoke, he came at me at least a hundred different ways, until finally, to make a long story short, I went and got a tuxedo. I have the pictures to prove it. And I'm glad I did, because I would have been the only one dressed down. He just kept at me. He wouldn't take "No!" for an answer. When I think of aggressive salespeople, I think of people that just keep coming at you. They want your business. They want you to do what they want you to do, and they just keep applying that pressure.

So keep the pressure on, and get creative about it. If I see that it's a good deal and they could use it for their business, I give my prospect examples of exactly how this particular advertising or marketing is going to work in or will promote their business, and I give them concrete, meaningful specifics about how to take it and use it in their business. Too many times it's easy to get lazy and not give people what they need; and we do it, too. We'll just mail the same letter over and over again as part of a follow-up campaign. And while that may be effective, perhaps a more effective approach is to change it up, be creative, approach them in different ways. I talked about this a bit earlier. Mail them a sales letter, mail them a postcard, call them, email them, fax them, do this, do that. Hit them with one kind of offer and then hit them with another kind of offer. Change it up. Make the envelope look different. We use shiny envelopes sometimes. We even have a mailing that goes in a wallet. It's paper, but it looks like a wallet; and when you open it, it has a flap in it like a wallet would and out pops something. You can put, for example, a hundred dollar bill in the wallet that's got a sales message on it.

Try being creative, while sticking to proven direct-response principles. Creativity, in that process, means you're not sending the same thing over and over again. You're doing sequenced follow-up mailings, but they're unique. Each one is different than the previous, and you never know which mailing will strike a nerve or catch someone in the right way. Maybe you mail them a letter and it hits them at a time where they're busy, and then the next time you send them a postcard. Well, a postcard is easy to read, so they just see the postcard, they pull it out of the mail, and think, "Oh yeah, I *do* need to contact them or visit their website." Or maybe you call them on the phone and they're busy. But then they get your letter in the mail and they sit down and read it. The key is to put constant pressure on them by continuously reminding them to do business with you.

The only time you stop following up is when it becomes unprofitable to continue mailing. You have to figure out when that is, but you continuously mail and re-mail to people over and over again until it stops being profitable. That's when you know it's time to stop. So follow-up, follow-up, and follow-up some more. Continuously keep your message in front of your clients, until they buy or until it becomes unprofitable to keep telling them they should. Remember, I talked earlier before about the fact that most people just give up way too soon. By continuing to follow-up, you *don't* give up. And every time that they don't buy, well, you're following up; it's wrong to assume that they don't want what you have. Because they could just have a million things going on that day, or their whole lives could be traumatic. You never know. Just to assume that they don't want it to begin with would be a wrong assumption, as long as they're qualified.

NUMBER THREE: The concepts we sell are these: fast, simple, and easy. Here's a quote from the late, great Gene Swartz, one of the best copywriters in history —he died about 20 years ago, and made God knows how many tens or hundreds of millions of dollars. His famous quote was, "What people really want is a miracle!" I used to have that hanging up on my wall so I could just see it all the time. That's an emotional thing, and we sell to emotions. People are looking for easy answers. They want things that are very simple, so you've got to dumb things down.

Now, I'm not trying to insult people or say that they're dumb. Quite the contrary: people have built up an elaborate immunity to advertising and marketing, and so what you have to do is make it simple and easy to digest. People don't pay much attention to marketing messages. They read them in an apathetic, passive kind of way. They know you're trying to sell something. They know you're trying to get their money — and they've got a resistance for that. They're trying to hang onto their money! They don't want to pull out that credit card. So it's a fight, a tug of war over their money. They're fighting to keep it; you're fighting to get it. So you do things to make your offer as simple as possible, with the most appeal. The benefits are all out there up front.

Chris Hollinger has a phrase on his wall that he says reminds him of this particular factor whatever he's doing about anything: KISS — Keep It Simple, Stupid. If you get it too complicated, you'll lose them. And here's another little thing on his wall that's always there: "A confused mind says no." And we're "yes" men, in the sense that what we do is get people to say "Yes! Yes! Yes!" But if the mind is confused, if your marketing or your offer includes things that are just too complicated... the mind says no. It doesn't matter how good a deal it is for them. If their mind is confused, you get a no. You don't get the yes; you don't get the money.

Fast, simple, and easy is really the motto of society these days. We want everything fast, simple, and easy. Think about how many fast-food restaurants there are on every corner. Now they've got credit cards where you don't actually have to give it to the clerk. You just stick it up to the reader, and the RFID chip in it reads your card and charges you. We have drive-thrus so we don't have to go in and get our food anymore. Banks have drive-up windows. There are ATMs so you can withdraw your money fast, simple, and easy. There are fundraisers where the money is automatically deducted from your checking account. These days, a lot of churches have automatic giving, where you just give them your credit card number or your bank account and they'll draft your tithe. Everything in life is set up now for fast, simple, and easy. We don't want to wait. We have microwave dinners — and even microwaves are too slow. We want everything that way. And so, as a marketer, it's your job to find out how you can give people things in a fast, simple, and easy way.

We have one product where we offer to do everything for the customer. That's another example of fast, simple, and easy. Our society has turned toward more of the "done-for-you" type services, as well. That's a part of what we do for our clients, and more and more industries have options now where they'll do things for you that you used to do for yourself. A lot of home improvement has gone that way. You don't even have to go to the hardware store and buy the materials yourself; you just have to tell them you want them to do it for you. Places like Home Depot and Lowe's have installation services, whereas you used to have to go find your own installer. Now you just go pick the stuff out, and they have their staff install it for you. So society, as a whole, is moving more and more toward fast, simple, and easy. If you can find a way to incorporate that into your marketing, that's great; you're giving people exactly what they want.

NUMBER FOUR is to drive the sales. I've already mentioned our 20-page sales letter, where the premium is $33,248.20. Now, I know that sounds unbelievable, and I take five pages to show people why we can actually do it, so we're not expecting anybody to actually believe it without proof. We want to get their attention, and we do — but then we've got five pages of copy that explains how we can give them a bonus that big. Bonuses and premiums help drive sales. We're calling this one "the world's greatest free bonus gift," so we've got a big, huge bold title. "The World's Greatest? You want the best, we've got it!" The right premium won't cost you money, if you choose it right. It will *make* you money.

This is one of the greatest sins of marketing. Everybody's constantly looking for ways to save money and pull back and do things in a more economical way, when really the only thing that they should care about is ROI: Return On Investment. That's it. What you spend versus what you make. Things like choosing the right premiums will cost you more money, but you'll make more money because more people will end up buying.

Those premiums force people who wouldn't ordinarily buy to go ahead and take action. Our big premium that I just mentioned is a good example of that. Obviously, it just sounds outrageous! Imagine $33,248.20 worth of bonuses. But then, it takes five pages to go ahead and explain exactly where that came from, and why we're able to do it. And so it's believable; it builds up that value. They're like, "Oh wow, I'm going to be able to get so much!" It's all a part of stacking that offer, stacking it so high and deep with the benefits, values, premiums, and free bonus gifts that they're thinking, "This is unbelievable! It's fantastic. I'm going to do it!" And then they get a "thud" factor. They get so much stuff that it helps to drive later sales.

Looking back at some of my earlier stuff, where I had no concept of offering premium gifts, I can see that my sales suffered because of it. Remember, all that matters, ultimately, is results. If you concentrate on your marketing systems, your sales problems will disappear. When I go back and look at some of those sales letters and why they didn't perform well, I might say, "Okay, there was no free bonus gift there. There wasn't a good enough explanation of the free bonus gift itself." There's so many more things that I could have done with some of those sales letters to make them better. And that's one of the meaningful specifics there — did you offer a premium at all?

Doing so helps drive sales and gets you the yes. Big, bold premiums are the key. If a premium is weak, it's not going to drive sales like you intend it to, so you've got to use premiums that stand up and make people pay attention to them. It's been proven that some people will buy a product just because of the premium. And premiums are everywhere. People know they're buying a package deal; it's not like they really think they're getting something for free when they buy your product. People know that they have to make a purchase to get the premium. But still, there's something psychological about getting a free gift with your purchase that makes them buy.

A lot of stuff is sold this way. You're in the mall and someone's trying to get you to sign up for a credit card. When you sign up for a credit card, you get a free T-shirt. Premiums are everywhere. Cell phone carriers use premiums to drive sales. "Come in today and pick up this great new phone. We'll not only give you the phone, but we'll also throw in a car charger, a home charger, or a Bluetooth headset. It's free when you come in and sign up for a new service."

The thing that you've got to do is to make sure your premium is a strong, bold one. If you're selling something for $100, don't be afraid to give away something that has a perceived value of $1,000. The bigger the perceived value, the more people will want what you're selling them. The thing you have to watch out for is to make sure you're premium is believable. You can't just say, "This premium has a $1,000 value!" If people don't believe it, they're not going to take what you're offering. It has to have the three B's — Big, Bold, and Believable. If you've got those three things, then any premium will increase your sales. It doesn't cost you money. Don't think about having to give it away; think about how many increased sales you'll get if you use that premium. If you're uncertain about it, the smart thing to do is test. Add the premium to half your list, and keep the premium out for the other half. Do that, and you'll be able to see and measure how much difference the premium makes. Ideally, you would run with or without a premium and you'd be able to see, "Well, without the premium this is the response I got; with the premium, I got this much of an increased response." You'd know exactly what level of increased business you received as a result of using that premium. That's the way to answer the question, "Am I spending too much?" Most people never do spend too much; they're more likely to suffer from the opposite, which is spending too little.

For too many marketers, the premium is an afterthought. Okay, they're going to do a sales letter. They're working on it; now they know they have to come up with a premium, so they just pick anything. Well, what they should do is find something that ties in with the promotion as much possible. With the Master Distributorship for our Recession-Proof Wealth System, the websites we give people are called Recession-Proof Websites. That's how we tied it in, and then we had to make it believable. Even on a whopping premium like this one, we had to take five pages just to explain to people why we could actually do something like this, because people are skeptical.

NUMBER FIVE: Total risk reversal. The average prospect would never admit it, but they're scared. They're afraid you're scamming them. They're afraid you're going to rip them off. They're afraid they won't do a thing with your product or service. We talk about how skeptical people are, but we don't talk about that fact. Most marketers don't even take that into account.

With total risk reversal, we try to stack all the benefits on the client's side of the table, so that all of the chips are on their side of the table, metaphorically speaking. All of the risk is on our shoulders, not theirs. We want to ease their fears, we want to take care of them, we want them to know that if they're not happy, we're not happy. Sometimes we even give them a free gift — and they can get their money back and still keep the free gift. We do all kinds of things to make them happy. It empowers them rather than us, but ultimately we're the ones who are empowered, because our sales increase when we use these tactics. Stacking all those chips on their side of the table and then throwing a big fat guarantee on top of it just speaks volumes. The idea is to get them to say yes. A lot of these sales letters are just stack, stack, stack and guarantee... and off you go and make a sale. They're formulaic, but they work.

Risk reversal is important. People are afraid you're scamming them, they don't believe you, they think that they won't be able to do it, they know how lazy and apathetic they are... All these things enter someone's mind when they're deciding whether to respond to an offer you have. It all goes back to Point #3: we sell fast, simple, and easy. The faster, the simpler, the easier you can make something, the more likely they are to see themselves doing it. If they can't see themselves doing whatever it is or benefiting from the product or service you have, then they won't buy. So you want to stack everything in their favor. Explain to them how easy it is for them to use or how easy it is to do. Be descriptive in your sales copy. Write a paragraph or two describing how they will easily use your product or how easy it will be for them to benefit from it, how fast it works, whatever. That helps convince them that it's going to be simple and that they won't have a learning curve, that everything will be figured out for them.

One way to eliminate the risk is by giving them a ton of free stuff that they get to keep even if they back out. It's the ultimate risk reversal to say, "Hey, you're going to get this gift that's worth $1,000 even if you send our product back. So the worst that happens is you end up ahead, because you got our free gift just for checking us out." Or you might say, "Take a 30-day risk-free trial of our coaching program and we'll give you all these products absolutely free. If after 30 days you decide you don't want to become a member, that's fine. We won't bill you, and you'll get to keep all the free gifts we gave you." You're making it so they win even if they decide they don't want to participate. *Everything is stacked in their favor.*

Using risk reversal in that way puts all the pressure on *you* and none on *them.* If they feel pressure, they're not going to respond. They'll hold back. If they feel like there's some reason why they maybe shouldn't make a decision, well, they won't. So put it all on you and not on them, by saying, "Hey, the risk is all on me. If I don't perform, you're going to get to keep this free gift and I'm out the money. So it's all on me to perform to your expectations. If I don't, then you're out nothing." That puts all the risk on you and takes all the risk away from them, which makes it more likely that they'll respond. Tell them, "You have everything to gain; nothing to lose. All the risk is on our shoulders, not yours. All the chips are stacked on your side of the table, not ours."

NUMBER SIX: Two-Step Marketing. It's the safest and most profitable way to build your business. Step One: Separate the smaller group of the best buyers from the rest by getting those people to take some initial action. Step Two: you focus on doing everything you can to sell to those people that initially responded to your first step. The strategy involves spending more money per person on the smaller group of people who were more qualified, who initially took that first step. All marketing is about selling and re-selling to customers, and two-step marketing is the safest, most profitable way to do that.

I'm involved in a business with two other guys, and we just did a mailing. Well, we didn't get the results we wanted from it. It was a small promotion; nothing big. We made all of our money back. We made a little profit, but nothing to get excited about. But I was talking to one of my partners some time ago, and I told him, "If we would have used two-step marketing, we would have definitely done better on that promotion." On the first step, we would have asked them to raise their hand and send for the information, and maybe offered them a nice little free gift to incentivize them for doing so. And then we would have had a smaller group to work with, and would have put them on a sequence and stayed after them and reminded them that *they* were the ones who initiated the whole thing by taking the first step. We would have made more money; and we'll probably still do that. Two-step marketing is always the best; it lets you go after the smaller group of better qualified prospects in a more aggressive way.

I'm convinced that if you could employ just one marketing strategy, two-step marketing would be your best bet. Really concentrate on generating qualified prospects and then making them good, solid offers. Then follow up. That one concept alone is really the heart and soul — the core — of the type of marketing that I do on a regular basis. Produce qualified leads, make quality offers to those leads, and apply these strategies as they fit into that process. Stay after them. Hammer, hammer, hammer!

Occasionally we do one-step marketing, but not very often. If you rent a mailing list and do a mailing to a large group of people without two-step marketing, all you end up with is a small group of buyers. Maybe you even made a small profit at it, but you can't mail to the rest of them again unless you re-rent the list. You did a one-time mailing to a list, and you got some sales, and that's it. You have whatever buyers you got from that mailing. But if you do two-step marketing, you can mail to that entire list with an invitation to get more information. And then you have a list of leads — people who requested information from you. You can then mail to those people all you want without renting the list over and over again. They're your customers now. Even though they just asked for information from you, they "belong" to you. They're your names. Then you mail to those people over and over, and you get a percentage of them to buy. You're probably going to end up with more sales in the end anyway, but you get those sales from a smaller group of people that you followed up to over and over again.

So you end up with two lists: a lead list and a buyers list. And while that leads list isn't as valuable as your buyer list, over time it can grow. Maybe it's a list that you can email periodic offers to. You can joint venture with other people and say, "Hey, I know these people are interested in making money," or, "I know they're interested in x, y, z products. They might be interested in your product," and together you can mail to that list. Also, you can rent that list.

NUMBER SEVEN is tele-seminars. We've been having tele-seminars since the early 1990s, and we've experimented with many different formats. We even had some live tele-seminars that lasted five and six hours! Tele-seminars give your customers the same basic advantages that they'd get from coming to a seminar, except that they can stay at home. They don't have to travel, which is especially appealing to people since 9-11. Here's another good thing about tele-seminars: you can record them and turn them into audio products later. In fact, last Thursday (as of this writing) we had a tele-seminar, and we had about 130 people on it when we were recording. Now, all we were initially going to do was record a "pitch" CD; but we knew that by inviting customers to listen in, we would do a better job. Because if it was just Chris and I, and there was no audience to present to, we wouldn't have the same energy; we wouldn't have the same passion, we wouldn't put it out there as much, and we wouldn't work as hard.

So we decided to let some of our customers attend this event. We had 130 on the call. We were promoting a $495 product, and after the call 70 or 80 of those people called in. So it was extremely profitable, and we did a much better job knowing that there were people on the line. We were performing more. We were putting that energy out there, so we produced a better "pitch" CD than we might have. This just goes to show that tele-seminars can be great tools for communicating with your customers. They're excellent for relationship-building.

When we talk about copywriting, we're primarily talking about print or on the Web. But one point I want to make clear to you is that the more you write in a physical way, where you're expressing again and again the benefits that you sell, when it comes time for you to verbally communicate with the customers, it's going to be so much more powerful, so much more effective, so much easier — because the writing process also helps with other forms of communication.

My colleague Chris Hollinger does a lot of tele-seminars with events for follow-up, or even to launch something brand new. It's very inexpensive to, say, do a voice blast and drive people to a tele-seminar. It's also a good way to test things. And the neat thing is, there are a lot of companies out there that offer inexpensive tele-seminar services that are easy to set up, easy to use, and easy to run. You can literally have a tele-seminar set up in a couple of minutes and scheduled to run. Then you have to promote it. Maybe you need to send out a postcard or two; but Chris has done this a lot lately with email lists, where people that have opted in or given him their email address. He'll go ahead and send them a quick email out and invite them to a seminar, for no other reason than that it gives them a little opportunity to get to know him and start building that relationship a little.

And he'll spend a lot of time on the tele-seminar itself, even if it's just him presenting. Now, we've all done that a lot, but I do recommend using somebody else, because two or more people can play well off each other. In any case, spend a great deal of time on tele-seminars just building a relationship, getting that warm-and-fuzzy feeling going with people who up until now have only seen your ad and received something in the mail from you. They don't know you from Adam, really. But you can invite them to a very low-cost tele-seminar, get them on there and spend some time talking about who you are, what you do, what you're all about. That improves profits, and goes a long way when it comes time to ask for the money.

There's a service called freeconferencecall.com that lets you host free conference calls. A conference call is just another term for a tele-seminar. Whatever you call it, it's a service where you can have people on the call with you. When you're done, it actually gives you a link so you can download the recording it just made of your call. It's absolutely free. They have other services they hope you'll buy, but you can use their conferencing services for free.

Tele-seminars are good for many things, and can serve several different purposes, depending on what your goal is. You can use them for product creation, where you're actually on the call with customers, recording product. We've done that many times. The customers are in "listen only" mode, usually. They don't talk, but they're listening as we record live. Having live people listening provides a little added energy, because you know that you can't mess up. You can't just hit the "stop" button and start over! We also use seminars as sales tools, where we have people listening in with the intent of making a sale. Or we use them for information purposes. Sometimes we've had tele-seminars for members only, where we'll share information and news with them as members.

The great thing about a tele-seminar is that you can put one together fast, any time you want to, with email blasting, with faxes, with phone calls, through voice blasting. You can let someone know that you have a conference call coming up, and have that call happen in as little as a few hours, and certainly within days. Chris Lakey sometimes gets emails from a gentleman who throws together conference calls in one day. He'll get an email in the morning that says, "Hey, I'm going to have a conference call tonight. Here's what we're going to talk about. Join us if you want to." Chris never has, because he's too busy and rarely does things like that in the evening, because that's his time with his family. But I'm sure the man has people on the call, or he wouldn't keep inviting him.

Conference call lines are easy to get these days; you could have a conference call line available to you virtually any time you want it. Some of them have toll-free numbers; some are toll numbers. You should find a way to incorporate tele-seminars into your business model for all the reasons I've already talked about: for information, to create products, to sell things to your customers. Plus, you can pre-record them so that they play as if they're live. You do them once, and then just like a radio show that keeps playing over and over again, you can repeat them. You set it up and just let it go. We've had the same tele-seminar run for a year or more on a weekly basis — every week, sometimes twice a week, and sometimes three times a week. People are coming to it as if it's live. We never tell them it's recorded, but we're not trying to hide the fact that it is. If somebody asked us, "Hey, is that a recording?" we'd say yes. But they assume it's live; and in fact it was recorded live to begin with. So it's a good way, again, to do that thing where you do something once and get paid for it again and again.

NUMBER EIGHT: The power of personalization. We use it

in two ways. The first way is more subjective, where we use our rags-to-riches story. That story is an important part of our relationship with our customers. We tell that story over and over. It's a very personal thing. We tell other parts about who we are, and just like our friend, Russ von Hoelscher, as we go along we continue to tell more and more. For example: For years I wouldn't tell my clients that I'm a recovering alcoholic/drug addict, because I felt they just wouldn't understand if I shared those parts of my life. But I started experimenting, very slowly, first just mentioning the alcohol, no drugs at all. They were okay with all that. By the way, I've been clean and sober now for 28 years, since 1981.

The more my clients reacted to that, the more I met other people who had the same story. But also, I started to see that it wasn't a problem. People were saying, "Well, okay." So then I started mentioning alcohol *and* drugs. When I was a kid I had a problem with both. I got help, I straightened my life out, and then I met my wife, and *then* we started the business. It was that sharing of my story, the sharing of who I am and certain aspects about my life, that I was always so terrified to do; but once I did it, I found that people were pretty positive about something that's normally pretty negative. The more you tell your personal story, the more it bonds people to you. So that's one aspect of personalization.

The other aspect where we spend a lot of extra money is on people. We've got a room over at M.O.R.E., Inc., that contains a huge machine that does all our personal letters. It's like a giant laser printer, and it will put out a sales letter that's up to a hundred pages long — and on every page it will put the customer's name up at the top. The machine can even put a colored cover on it, so eventually we're going to do custom manuals with the customer's name on every page.

People are more inclined to look at a letter with their name on it. That's why we spend extra money doing things to personalize those letters, to make them more special. Our system does a nice job, but you can do the same on a small scale from a home office. That's what Chris Hollinger's wife does in their operation; she uses software to customize the front page or the cover letter that goes with their mailings. There are things you can do on the outside of the envelopes, too. I've done some of it myself.

The more of this kind of personalization you do, the better the odds are that you'll get a better response. Why? Because people like to see their own names. That grabs their attention, and that's what it's all about. It's part of relationship building. Most people like their name, and they like when people call them by their name. When you're having a conversation with somebody, they say that's a sure way to build a relationship faster with them: to say their name. People like to hear their names said. Well, there's a similar effect when you're writing sales copy. Use their first name (or sometimes their last name) in the sales letter. Say "Dear John" instead of "Dear Friend," and then throw the name in throughout the copy. "By the way, John, did you also know this?" And, "One last thing, John. I wanted to remind you of this..." It makes people feel good, because they like being talked to by their given name. Now, you can overdo this. Some people get going and drop the name in every paragraph: John, John, John. And then they mention the name of their town... "For people just like you in Goessel, Kansas," and just overdo it totally, ruining a good idea.

NUMBER NINE: We're totally real with our customers and prospects, and more so all the time. We show pictures of ourselves, our community, our families; we've got thousands of pictures that we send out to people. We're in a market that's full of skepticism — as all markets are these days — and so we have to do things to combat that skepticism. That's how we get past some of the skepticism. Plus, we do a lot of audio products. This book is based on an audio product we recorded at a three-day event back in October 2008. It's going out to different groups of customers who weren't part of that event, and they'll hear us goofing up and saying stupid things; they'll hear our jokes and some of the crazy things we do sometimes. We won't edit any of that stuff out (as we've done in this book!). Again, it may turn some people off — but hopefully it will turn off the people who are wrong for us anyway. And even some of the people who aren't turned off will still say to themselves, "You know, I hate that guy. I can't stand him. He's a blowhard. He's an egotistical jerk. Those two Chrises aren't so bad, but that T.J. is just a jerk." But at least they'll know that I'm a *real* jerk! I'm just trying to be myself, and I think there needs to be more of that in marketing.

Don't be afraid to tell your story. Let people know who you are and what you're about and what you stand for, and how you're different from everybody else. You need to express your honesty and integrity from the get-go. You need to just be yourself. Don't try to put up some façade that's not real, because you'll just end up lying and lying and lying, and it'll turn to nothing. There'll be no substance there. You'll just be an empty vessel, and who wants that? Just be you, and don't be afraid to be you. I went through that with some of the things that I struggled with and didn't want to share, and found out that I'm better off sharing. You're better off just being human instead of the perfect marketer guy with the slick hair and the white teeth and the million-dollar diamond smile. It's better to be yourself and be totally real with folks. That way you don't have to worry about anything. It's a liberating experience; it really is.

Back when I was first running ads, I thought about running the type that showed me and Eileen standing in front of the fancy cars and fancy homes we didn't actually own. Hey, that's how everybody else did it! But Russ suggested that we just be ourselves. That approach would have been fake. But you do see that in a lot of business opportunity ads. Maybe some of them are real, but I think most of them want you to feel like they're successful because they're trying to show you *how* to be successful. So in their pictures, they've got this fancy sports car in their driveway, and they're in front of a big mansion wearing a really fancy suit — and everything looks like they have extreme wealth.

But when Eileen and I were getting started, we went the opposite direction and said, "Hey, we're just like you." I'm the Blue Jeans Millionaire! There's no difference between me and you, except that I've discovered a secret formula that's proven to make money with direct-response marketing. And now I want to teach that to you! So that's the angle that we took — and it's a real, sincere angle that people can identify with. That's what I mean by saying that just being real, being yourself, is important. It's unauthentic to try to put a façade up and pretend you're someone you're not. We're all kind of goofy. Nobody's perfect; we all have flaws, and we're all in this human race together. We all struggle with various things, so why try to pretend to be perfect when we know no one else is perfect? If you can just be real, be yourself, tell your story, then people can identify with that. And yes, you may turn some people off.

I've mentioned that Russ von Hoelscher has started to talk more about his political beliefs as he gets older — and I expect that there are some people — especially die-hard Democrats! — who said, "I'm not going to buy from that guy ever again because I don't agree with his politics." But other people have said, "Hey, I like what you're saying. Maybe I don't necessarily agree with you 100%, but I like that you're bold. I like that you're putting yourself out there, and I like that you're talking about it." Again, it goes back to what we talked about earlier, about offending some people and having other people drawn to you. You're going to offend some people if you speak; there's no way around that. If something comes out of your mouth, someone's probably not going to agree with it, and they're going to be upset. That happens, because we're a polarized society. There are enough people on both sides of the political fence that when you say anything political, you're going to make about half the people in the room upset. But by being sincere, people who you want to do business with you will be drawn to you. And, hopefully, the people that you don't want to do business with you will be repelled.

The right people will accept you for how you are. I spent a number of years being a people-pleaser. I'm still struggling with it. The bad thing about being a people-pleaser is that you're always worried about what other people are going to think about you. When you're a people-pleaser, the stress is outrageous. I don't have that anymore, for the most part, and thank God! It's so damned liberating to just be myself. I used to only want to tell people what I thought that they wanted to hear. I don't do it nearly as much as I used to.

NUMBER TEN: This is an aspect of our rags-to-riches story. Earlier in this book, I talked about the PAS Formula: Problem, Agitate, Solution. Well, here's another great copywriting formula. It's called "Before & After." You see it all the time. "Here's the way I was before. Here's what happened to me. Here's the way I am now... and now I'm going to show you how to do it, too." It's like the plot you see in most movies. Here's the character, and then something happens. He works through whatever happens, and there he is, a different man at the end. It's a formula that's used over and over again. Our rags-to-riches story bonds us with the customers. It's inspirational for them. You know, I got sick and tired of telling it about ten years ago, but I realized that I have to keep telling it to people, because it's part of the story that they connect with, and that's what we're trying to do — build relationships with people. So we keep telling our story over and over... even when we don't want to.

NUMBER ELEVEN: Audio recordings. Remember, the more you write, the more you can communicate in other ways and speak with real authority and force. The writing helps with the audio. The audio has been so good for us, because people can actually listen to us, rather than just read our words. That has helped us enormously. We've mailed out God knows how many hundreds of thousands of audio recordings; it started with cassette tapes, and now it's audio CDs. It lets our customers feel like they know us a whole lot better, in a more emotional way than they would ever feel if they just read our stuff. You know, the act of someone actually taking something that you've written, and sitting down with it for a period of time to read your words — it's kind of flattering. Reading is a very intimate thing. Audio takes that to next level: they're sitting there and listening to your voice. It's very intimate, because you're putting your ideas, your thoughts, your call to action between their ears, in their brain, and hopefully it's going to help you make a sale. These audio recordings also help you to connect and build that relationship with new customers, or maintain that relationship with current customers. The technology is such that it's easy to make and reproduce these things, and get them out there like you need to. Audio recordings help you to get that "yes" you're looking for.

Chris Lakey likes to compare audio recordings, and building relationships with your customers and getting them to know you and feel like they have a connection with you, with stalkers. Now, before you decide Chris is just one weird dude, let me explain! People who stalk Hollywood movie stars or musicians feel like they have some bond with them — even though they've never met them, and have no real connection to them. It's not real. It's based on the fact that the stalker *hears* them, that their audio gets inside the stalker's head. Take a musician, someone who's been in the music business for 10 or 15 years. They've produced a dozen CDs, and they've got a fan base in the millions. Well, a certain percentage of those people feel connected to them. Some people just like their music, but others get connected on a deep, emotional level.

I think it's the same thing with movies. You build a relationship with an actor or actress because you see them in movies and you like their work. And so you buy other films that have that actor in them, and you feel an emotional connection with them. It's a subconscious thing that you don't really think about. It just happens.

You can use audio recordings, as an entrepreneur, to do some of that same kind of thing. People will get to know you better. They'll feel a connection with you. They'll feel like they know you more than if you never use audio, if the only way you ever communicate with your customers is in print. By adding the audio dynamic, you build the connection, taking that relationship to a completely different level — a much deeper level — and that makes it easier to get through to people with your sales messages. They feel a connection to you, they're more inclined to read your copy, and they're more inclined to respond to your offers, because of that deep psychological connection. Using audio gets you a closer connection with your customers, and makes it easier to do more business with them. And again, don't be afraid to just be yourself. It takes a lot less energy and in the end, people will appreciate you more because they'll sense that you're real.

NUMBER TWELVE: Seminars. Seminars are tough for me, personally, but every time we have one, I thank my wife Eileen for getting us involved in them to begin with. She ran the company for the first 14 years, and she was always very supportive of doing seminars. Now, it's a lot of work to do these events. We make it look easy because we've got a staff of people who just get them done like clockwork. And certainly the smaller ones are easier, compared to the bigger ones where we have hundreds of people.

We had our first seminar on September 22, 1990 — and Eileen and I were so scared to face our customers that we wouldn't even get up to the podium just to say hello! We sat in back the whole time, while Russ ran the seminar for us. And all throughout the day, people kept coming back there anyway, if only because that's where the bathrooms were. And we were out in the hallway, so we met everybody; and then at lunch time we sat and ate lunch with everybody. All afternoon Russ had a hard time keeping people in the room because they were out in the hall talking to Eileen and me! By the end of the day, we went from being scared and insecure to really loving it!

We held 13 different seminars here in Goessel in 1992. From that point on, we've done hundreds of different seminars — which is kind of odd, if you really know me. The truth is, I'm kind of an introvert, even though I can express myself well in public. If you didn't know me better, you might think I'm a real extrovert. In reality, I'm a loner. That's just who I am. I'm not lonely; I'm a loner. I actually enjoy spending alone time with myself and with my wife, and having a small, quiet life. Recently, one of my seminar attendees said to me, "You've got 500 people in Goessel. How long have you been here?" And I said, "Well, we've been in the area for 20 years." He said, "You must know all 500 of them." I replied, "I know five people in Goessel. That's it. Five, not 500." I'm a loner. They all know of our company; they all know who we are. But I only know a handful of people here, and that's it.

So seminars haven't come natural to us. Loners like me tend to want to stay that way, and so I've had to put myself out there. But it's been a great experience to meet with our clients, to get to know them, to spend time with them. It's been one of the best things that's happened to our company, and I thank Eileen for every single seminar. There are so many people in the direct-response marketing business who never want to go face-to-face with their customers. They never want to meet them. They never want to spend time with them. They're attracted to this business initially because they want to do everything by mail or over the Internet; they want to hide behind a computer and hide in a P.O. box. But having seminars has been one of our greatest experiences, because it puts us right there, eyeball to eyeball, with our customers. And although it's a little scary, it's not as scary as it used to be. I used to throw up in the bathroom before the events. But it's been a positive thing. In fact, it's been a great thing! So I would encourage you to meet with your customers, talk with them, spend time with them, get to know them. There are some phenomenal things that can happen at seminars, sales-wise.

Chris Hollinger and his wife had their first seminar about a year and a half into their business. They were actually doing some training on a specific opportunity, on some of the materials that they had created, and they had probably about 30 to 40 people at that event down in Wichita. He tells me that it was a little scary! Well, your first time with anything *is* a little scary. It was a lot of work — just the logistics, and getting it all put together, and the anticipation, and then the actual seminar. It took three straight days of being out there talking, presenting, and teaching, and by the time Friday rolled around, Kim and Chris were relieved it was over.

But they've had people who attended that event five years ago who purchased something from them *last month*. Now Chris looks forward to his seminars. Like all of us who take this step, he's learned things, and it's helped him get out of his normal weekly and daily routine. Now he comes and presents at my workshops, like the one this book is based on! And he's learned by doing so; as he told me at this workshop, he got new ideas for one of his products and made some changes to his copy while he was here.

I also like the way seminars build the trust relationship with your customers. Even if they don't attend, the fact that you have a seminar means that they're able to have access to you. Even if you have an event that only a handful of people attend, by letting all of your customers know about it, they feel like they can trust you more because you have an event that they can go to. You're not hiding; you're making yourself accessible.

Seminars also offer a good revenue stream. Not only can you make money getting people into the room, but you can make money while they're there by offering them other products and services. So there's a chance for additional revenue there, as well. You can also launch new products and promotions when you have a live event. Consider the event this product, this book, is based on. We were recording audio the entire time, so it became an audio product that we could sell. Now it's a book, too. So while we were standing there teaching our customers in the workshop, we were also building our product library, so we could make this available to other people in the future.

It's hard to put on a three-day event. It wears you out. It makes you physically and emotionally exhausted. But it's also fun at the same time. We love doing it. And so, you can have an event that totally drains you and wipes you out, but is simultaneously fun and profitable. We used to have two-day events instead of three. We changed it to three partially because of selfish, self-centered reasons. It's that I get a natural high. The first day is a lot of work for me; but even so, by the end of it, I'm feeling good. I'm feeling a natural high. It's a drug-free, pressure release kind of buzz that I love, because it's a great experience! You're really trying to help people at the seminar, and you end up helping yourself in the process, too.

NUMBER THIRTEEN: Use food to warm the hearts of cold prospects and customers. I have to credit this one to Dan Kennedy. I once asked Dan, "What's the fastest, easiest, simplest way to take a cold prospect and turn them into a warm prospect?" And Dan said, simply, "Food." I realized he was right. I started remembering that in a lot of these direct sales organizations, food is involved. Maybe you've experienced this before, where they invite you to some hotel or a nice restaurant. They buy you a steak dinner, and after you eat the steak dinner they try to make a sale to you. In every city, every week, there's some direct-sales company that's doing that for small groups of people, where they feed them first and then ask for a purchase. After a meal, people are usually pretty happy. And now, of course, the whole concept of reciprocity kicks in; they just gave you a free meal, so you have to listen to them now. And then they pitch you. A lot of businesspeople do that: they take somebody out for a meal, and during the course of that meal they'll try to get you to do something or buy something or whatever.

So we started giving people all these popcorn bags. We went to a company in Wichita, and had them put our label on their popcorn — and then we started sending out God knows how many tens of thousands at a time. It's added up to a couple of hundred thousand bags of popcorn, just in the last six or seven years. It's lightweight, so it mails cheap. We don't have extra postage costs, customers like it, and it serves us overall for building relationships. It separates us from everybody else. That's one of the big things that marketing is supposed to do.

NUMBER FOURTEEN: consistent front-end marketing. This is critical — and it's one of those things that I scratch my head about, because I know marketers who should be doing this and they're not. We have a consistent plan for bringing in new customers every week of the year — no exceptions. Each week we invest a specific sum of money to attract new prospects and customers. We mail year-round, 52 weeks every year, and we're constantly bringing in new customers. We've got another plan for constantly re-selling to those people. You *have* to do it. It confuses me when I run into marketers who don't have a consistent, steady way to bring in new customers on a regular basis.

Our lead generation method is to consistently do mailings, but there are other lead generation techniques you can do online and offline. Other marketers I know do space ads, and have gotten good at finding ways they can do that. We gave them up long ago in favor of direct mail, but space ads served us well in the beginning. Learning to do this well is an ongoing process. For us, it's absolutely never-ending. It's a consistent system of mailing, mailing, mailing. If you're not bringing new folks in, pretty soon the flow dries up; there's no one going into the top of the funnel. A lot of people don't reinvest into that part of it; once they have a nice pool of customers, they decide not to go ahead and keep prospecting, keep bringing those people in and generating qualified leads. But it's something you have to do. Find something that works for *you* and then keep tweaking it.

There are two parts of your business, in general: the relationships you have and the business you do with your current customers, and then all the things you do to attract new customers. If you're not constantly attracting new customers, your existing customers will dry up. You can only keep doing business with your existing customers so many times before you lose some of them, for one reason or another. People get out of your marketplace, they change, they move, they die. If you're not continuously working to bring in more customers, you'll lose the customers you have and you won't be bringing in any new ones to replenish your customer base. So you've got to constantly be doing new customer acquisition, as well as doing things to re-sell to your current customers.

The key here is consistency. If you're sporadic with your

front-end marketing, yeah, you might bring in some new customers here and there, but you don't have any consistency. You want to be systematic about it. You want to do it *constantly*. We have weekly mailings. If you don't do direct mail — if you advertise in magazines or newspapers — then you should make it a goal to do it on a monthly basis, so that every single month you've got new ads running. If you're running classified ads in a newspaper, maybe it's weekly or monthly. Whatever you do, it needs to be systematic so that you have some kind of accountable plan where you know that on a regular basis you've got new mail going out, new ads running, whatever the case may be, to bring in new customers. You need to have a consistent front-end marketing plan so you're attracting new customers while continuing to build relationships with your existing customers.

There are some marketers out there that do it sporadically. They'll do it, make some money, and then they'll just kind of glide for a while. And then they do it some more; and that's fine, too. They've found a system that works for them and their lifestyle.

Another thing I'll say here is that you need to make sure it's trackable. If you've got multiple ads out there, make sure that you can track how many prospects came in from each ad, and how many you closed. If not, then you're not going to be able to identify exactly where the success came from, and you won't be easily able to duplicate it. You're never going to know how much money you're making or losing.

I've got a friend who markets things sporadically. He'll put something together, the money will come rolling in for a while, then he'll quit until he starts getting broke again, and then he'll work really hard and he'll put something together and the money will flow in like crazy. He just keeps repeating that process. He's always complaining about it, and yet he's the one who's doing this to himself. Inconsistent marketing produces inconsistent revenue. Consistent marketing produces consistent revenue. Period.

NUMBER FIFTEEN: I think I did a good job in an earlier chapter of talking about how we build very expensive follow-up mailing sequences to convert the largest possible percentage of leads. All you care about is how much money you spent versus how much money you made. And here's a copywriting secret that I don't think I've given you yet: all of your sequential follow-up mailings should be what I call "chips off the block." Consider the 20-page sales letter I've mentioned many times in this book, the one that promotes our Recession-Proof Wealth System. From that sales letter, we'll derive a number of follow-up letters. We'll just cut and paste parts of those letters. We'll write some new headlines. We'll add some new things to the beginning. We'll add some new stuff to the end. All these follow-ups that you send out to your customers — well, you just write the sales letter once, and then you're able to take little bits and pieces of it and re-do it. This is one of the areas where you can be very competitive — just by doing a better job of following up, staying with them, not quitting.

Let me re-emphasize this: you definitely don't have to re-invent the wheel for your follow-ups. You just take a chip off the old block. After you've done a lot of work creating that sales letter in the first place, it should all just pop together pretty quickly anyway with all the ideas that you've put into it. I don't think your sequences necessarily have to be very expensive, though they can be; but you do want to keep an eye on costs. You don't want to frivolously blow money. The idea here is that most people don't do nearly enough. We have very expensive follow-up sequences because we want to put a lot of money into converting sales. We know what our profit margins need to be, and we know, more or less, what we can spend to convert each sale. You have to spend money to bring money in; you can't have a cheap follow-up campaign. You can't skimp on your marketing. You need to spend money on your marketing campaigns, especially when you're doing follow-ups to new customer acquisition. You want to spend some money with an effective follow-up campaign to convert those leads to sales. It's very important to do that. If you go cheap, if you try to cut corners, you're probably not spending enough money. It's not necessarily that you have to go all out and try to break your budget, but it's that you need to be aware that you need to spend some money in order to make money and convert those leads to sales.

NUMBER SIXTEEN: We're constantly re-packaging all our old offers. We do a lot of recycling in our business, where we re-write sales letters that worked for us once. We find ways to give them a new facelift, give them a new headline, re-position things a bit. Sure, plagiarism is illegal, immoral, and unethical... but you can't plagiarize yourself. It's interesting that you can just keep finding ways to re-do things that worked for you before. You want to give people something new, but keep an eye on the market. It doesn't change that much. People still respond to the same kinds of things they responded to before.

Six or seven months ago, as of this writing, one of our good friends asked, "Man, how in the world do you guys keep coming up with so much stuff?" And I said, "We just keep re-writing the same sales letters over and over again." It was meant as a joke, but when I thought about it later, I realized it wasn't. That's how we do it!

The same things that make you money once can make you money again and again. You have to keep finding creative, new ways to re-package them. For example, a secret strategy that we use in our marketplace is that we sell a lot of blind offers — where we're writing about the benefits that we know our customers want without telling them precisely what we're offering. A lot of the language we use in our sales copy is blind.

We're not talking about specific products; we're talking about benefits our customers are going to receive when they use our products. We talk about how our products will help you make more money. In this case, it doesn't matter what the specific offer is. All our offers are built to help our customers make money! So we can take a typical sales letter and change it up a little — give it a facelift — and that same letter (or big parts of it) can work for a different offer. Again, we're not necessarily talking about a specific product, but about the benefits we provide to our marketplace.

I suppose if you were in a retail business where you had a specific product you were trying to sell, it would require a little more creativity. But in our marketplace we're selling business opportunities and information products, all of which deliver the same types of promises and benefits to our clients. That allows you to interchange the parts and mix it up without having to do a lot of rewriting. And speaking of interchangeable parts, a lot of my sales letters — including, by the way, my 20-page Recession-Proof Wealth letter — uses them. I've never heard anybody confess this before, but I will. I strongly suspect other copywriters are doing the same exact thing. Sometimes I'll write a 24-page sales letter and, the truth is, I may have gone back and used parts of four or five or six or seven different letters. I cut a couple paragraphs out of this one, and a few out of that one, and mix them together. Why create something when you can just re-create? Recreating is so much easier. It's fast, it's easy, it's simple, and as long as it works, that's the only thing that really matters. It's a benefit that you can all have, although first you have to have the letters written to begin with.

NUMBER SEVENTEEN: blind offers, or semi-blind offers. That's one type of offer that works in our market. People love to be teased and taunted. They love the idea that there are secrets, and if they can only find them, it will turn everything around for them. They love the idea that all the super-rich got their wealth because they had some secret short-cut method, and that once attained it will become their magic key to the wealth and power that they crave. A blind offer, if done right, can make people almost thank you to take their money. They go ape crazy. They can't wait to get the secrets. Many people FedEx their orders; some even wire the money to you just so they can have what you're offering now. You'll always know something is hot when you start getting FedEx orders. You'll know that you tapped a group chord. It's the curiosity factor that makes blind offers so effective. People are so curious that they just can't wait to find out what the secrets are going to be — so we try not to tell them too much. We try to tease them a little, and it does increase our sales dramatically.

I think that a lot of marketers in more traditional businesses could and should be using more curiosity. I was part of Dan Kennedy's Platinum Group for more than five years, and there were all these other marketers who were part of the group who weren't involved in the same opportunity market. They all sold things in a very straightforward way. And yes, that might be okay after you've gotten the customers to raise their hands. But in order to get more people to raise their hand and initially respond, there is *nothing* that works like curiosity. They could have all been finding ways to use it in their business, but they just couldn't see it. We saw it in our market early on, simply because that's the way everybody does it in the opportunity market. It's not like we were some kind of geniuses or something; we were just copying the way everybody else was doing it. Curiosity in the opportunity market is very, very common... but it could and should be used in other markets, too.

Here's an example: The infomercial I mentioned several chapters back, where the two women with the microphones kept hinting and hinting about those secrets they were offering. They didn't show a shred of proof; it was all about the secrets, the secrets, the secrets. They were using the curiosity factor I'm talking about here in combination with a blind offer. They never would tell you what the secrets were, but they kept telling you how much money you could make by using them. They kept showing all these testimonials. The idea is that you'd get to the point where you were so curious about what those secrets were that you were compelled to buy the product, regardless of who was pitching it and how.

Blind offers are interesting because they allow you to focus more on the prospect. If you're selling a widget, you do everything you can to describe it; you try to make sure that the customer knows everything about it; you do everything you can to make sure that they have a full idea in their mind of what this product is. But if you're selling blind, you don't reveal what the product is. This allows you to focus more on the prospect, because all you're doing is talking about the benefits that the customer will get when they buy your product. You don't ever tell them what the product is. You just talk about the benefits. You offer bullet points that describe how they're going to feel when they use your product, some of the results they're going to get, what it's going to do for them. So it's more prospect-driven rather than product-driven, and that's what makes a blind offer so powerful — because it's all about the prospect, not the product.

The prospect likes to be curious. People are like that. That's one of the best things when you're a kid: At Christmas time you couldn't wait to open your packages. You couldn't wait to see what was in there. That's part of the specialness that we look back on fondly when we're adults. And even though we *are* adults, emotionally, at some level, we're still like children. People like to be curious, so you're making it fun for them by harnessing that power of anticipation. Remember the ketchup commercial with that song?

Another thing: if you offer a refund guarantee, it takes the pressure away. After all, they really don't know what they're getting; they just know that you've promised them some pretty amazing benefits and they want those benefits. So you take all the pressure away by saying, "Hey, I know I haven't given you all the details — but remember, there's a money-back guarantee. Take 30 days to look it over. If you don't like it, send it back. We'll give you your money back *and* you'll keep this free gift just for checking it all out." Taking that risk away from them makes a blind offer even more appealing.

NUMBER EIGHTEEN: the "ten-fold readership path." Basically, you take your main benefits and express them again and again, in as many different ways as possible. I got this idea from Dan Kennedy. He calls it "the double readership path," where you take all the main benefits and express them at least twice. But we took that and cranked up the volume full blast. We keep hammering those benefits home again and again. Are my sales letters redundant? Yes, they are. But people read in a very passive, apathetic sort of way. Most people aren't staying up till three in the morning reading that 20-page letter; they'll barely read it at all. They skim through it, and that's all they do. So that's where the repetition really comes in. If you have the same benefit expressed ten different ways, hopefully even the apathetic reader will read it at least once. For some readers, it really does take that repetition just to get it into their head. Saying things over and over again helps to get your message across, and it helps convert sales in the long run.

As I write this, I'm looking at a 44-page sales booklet we used as an example during the original seminar this book is based on. It's pretty lengthy. Most people aren't going to read it all the way through. They'll read the front page, maybe they'll thumb through it, they'll kind of scan it a little... maybe a sub-head catches their eye, and they'll read for a couple of paragraphs and

then they'll flip through it some more. Oops, that catches their
attention, and they'll read a little bit. And then they'll flip back;
they'll look at the back cover, and maybe they'll read the P.S. and
try to figure out how much it costs. Maybe they'll look at the lift
piece you added. Maybe they'll go straight to the order form.
People read all over the place. Very few will read your 44-page
sales letter from the opening word all the way to the end. People
don't read that way. They skim and they scan. And so, if you use
this ten-fold strategy and employ ten different readership paths,
you're more likely to snag their attention. Some people are going
to scan and they'll read the sub-heads all the way throughout it,
so you want your sub-heads to kind of tell a story. You want to
say things enough, in different ways, so that as people are
skimming they pick up on the main points, even though they're
not reading the whole letter.

To summarize: Different people take different readership
paths through your sales copy, and you want to try to present
your message in enough ways, enough times, to catch them
regardless of which readership path they're on. If they're
scanning, skimming, reading different pages, just flipping
through it, you want them to be able to get the main points
without having to read the entire sales letter from front to back.

And last, but not least, NUMBER NINETEEN: segment
your list and be aggressive with it. You *have* to segment your list,
because not all customers are the same. People who spend more
money are showing you they're more serious, and that's how you
have to interpret that spending. So always separate people by the
amount of money that they spend, and also by how recently
they've bought. Make them offers while they're still what I call
"in heat." I don't know how else to say it. That's when they're
the most passionate, the most enthusiastic about what it is that
you offer. You've got to strike while the iron is hot! You have to
realize that timing is essential here. Nothing drives me crazier

than when we've got leads that are just sitting there.

I was in the grocery store at lunchtime recently getting some snacks when Keith Banman, the man who owns that store, asked, "Well, T.J., you going to take the weekend off?" I just looked at him and he goes, "No, you're not, are ya?" We'd just gotten our first lead in two days for a new promotion we were doing, and I knew it would drive me crazy if I didn't have that thing ready to go by Tuesday. Here's the metaphor I use: "When it comes to leads and getting things to people fast, today's salad is tomorrow's garbage." You've got to get them while they're hot! Every day you sit on those leads, every day you're not sending stuff out to the people who requested it, you're shooting yourself in the foot. You have to realize that right after someone buys, they're willing to buy more. So they're putting the pressure on you to have something to send them, which is the pickle I was in on the weekend I was just telling you about. I had leads coming in, so I had to get that sales piece ready to go so I could get it to the printer and then to shipping so it could be mailed out.

So segment by the type of product that they bought from you, by the dollar amount, and by how recently they purchased. Another good way to segment is by the frequency of their purchases, because people who buy more often are telling you things about themselves that, if you're a smart marketer, you're paying attention to. Segment that list! And you *must* have a list. I know people who've been in business for several years now, and they don't have a very good list. Some don't even know how to keep a good list. Well, it's easy. Most computers come with a database program that's adequate for someone starting out in direct-response marketing. As your business grows, you're going to need a stronger database that can do a few more things in the query and sort department, and spit out the kind of information that you want. But with most of the programs, like

Microsoft Excel, you'll be able to keep track of customers and generate the types of lists you need.

The main thing about segmenting your list is to make sure you're keeping one. If someone's responded to you, they need to be on a list that says what they responded to. If they bought something, they need to be on the list that tells you what they purchased. Before you can segment, you have to *have* a list, so start building it! And then attack it. Be aggressive. Stop worrying about mailing to your customers too much. Yeah, you'll probably make some of them upset; but if that's the case, get rid of them and keep the pressure on. If a customer's upset, it means they don't want what you have to offer anyway — and if they aren't attracted by your offers, they've got no pressure. The pressure comes from the desire to buy what you have to sell, and the conflict in their minds that they don't want to spend money, or they don't believe it's real, or they don't believe you're really going to give them the benefits you're offering. So the pressure is on them when they feel like you really do have something that they want, but they're conflicted for a number of reasons. If someone's just upset with you and they want off your mailing list, they're probably not going to be a customer anyways.

So segment your list. Purge it of the people that decide to not do business with you. Continue putting pressure on the ones who do through more offers, more mailings. You can't mail to your customers too much, as long as you continue to provide them with valuable products and services and as long as you do it in the right way, using the right methods. I haven't heard of anybody who over-mails their customers; most people don't do it often enough.

# CHAPTER EIGHTEEN:

# One Last Thing...

I want to tackle one last subject before I call it a book, and that's the subject of getting started. Years ago, in our "Blue Jeans Millionaire" seminars, I remember that when it came time for Q&A, the only question anybody ever had was, "How do I get started?" My wife, who has a sarcastic sense of humor, used to say, "You get started by getting started!" And that's the whole thing. People say, "Well, I don't know how to get started. I don't know if I can." She would throw something on the floor and say, "Try to pick that up, right now. Just try! There's no 'trying' to pick that up. You'll either decide to pick that up, or you'll decide *not* to pick it up."

I know that's a little sarcastic, so I want to give you a better answer than that. What I want to tell you is, a lot of this stuff becomes much clearer when you actually have customers who have responded to one of your offers, and now you've got two or three hundred people to work with. I was consulting with a client recently, a doctor. For 30 years he's had a little marketing business with only a hundred customers, and a lot of them have been with him for a long time. Our friend Jeff Gardner made millions with 282 customers. That's all he had: 282 customers. But he did all the things I've shared with you in this book with those 282 people. He stayed in touch with them constantly, he kept coming up with new things that were related to what they bought the first time, and he built relationships with them that were deeper and deeper all the time.

All of this really does become so much easier and simpler. It goes from being just a concept or an idea to actually being something that you implement and put it into action, and you see it make you money. That's when you get excited about this business. You have to believe it before you see it. You have to accept these ideas and know that they're true and will work for you, and then go ahead and put them into action and make them work. My best idea is that you need something to bring in some new customers, and you need to make sure they're well qualified. When you're just offering something for free, the good news is, a lot of people will respond. People love free stuff. They go crazy over it! The bad news is that they don't convert very well. They don't end up being very good prospects at all.

I've got 30,000 really good customers, and about a million prospects in my database. We have what we call Primo-A at the very top, and then B and C and D. We kept lowering our standards of what it took to actually get on our Primo-D list. It used to be that you had to spend two or three hundred dollars. Every year we lower the bar a little, so now somebody just barely jumps over the little bar and they're on our list. Once you have customers, you have to become dedicated and committed to serving them and giving them more of what they bought from you the first time. This means staying in touch and building a relationship and letting them get to know you, and then offering them additional products and services. All this becomes so simple that a lot of the confusion goes right out the window. Do you still get confused sometimes? Of course; I know I do. I fact, I often don't know how I'm going to do something until I do it! Now, I have the benefit of 20 years of experience, so I've done it a few times before. But I'm still figuring things out as I go along, and I strongly suspect I'm not

One Last Thing... 🖼

the only one. I'm probably just the only one to admit it to you.

I would counsel you to look closely at the two-step marketing model, and then go out there and choose a mechanism where you're going to a) generate some leads and b) qualify those leads so that you don't spend a lot of money mailing to or communicating with leads who haven't really jumped through a hoop. For example, if they're responding to an ad for a 24-hour recorded message, in the message you can say, "The price of this opportunity is somewhere in the neighborhood of a washer and a dryer." Or, you can say something like, "If you're not able to spend four to five hundred dollars, this opportunity is not for you." Make sure you say that at least three times, so that once they've listened to that recorded message... well, if they go ahead and leave you their information, at least they've heard it. They're not going to be such a tire kicker. They answered the ad, they listened to the message, and they went ahead and left their information. That way they've at least jumped through a hoop or two before you take any action other than putting the infrastructure up to have that ad and recorded message in place. Now, you're to the point to where you're going to send them some sales material. And hopefully you have that ready to go once the leads start coming in, and you mail it out right away. Some might say yes, and some might still say no. You look at the process, and keep doing exactly what I've been telling you. Keep that pressure on them with a follow-up piece, and have the confidence to do it!

Chris Hollinger used to coach basketball, football, and track. And invariably, he says, he would go down to the local restaurant on Saturday-morning after a Friday night game, and would hear the Saturday morning quarterbacks talking. He'd hear them say, "Well, they should have done this and they should have done that. *I* would have done it. Damn coach!" Right. When you're in the heat of the game, sitting on the bench,

could they have made that decision *at that moment*? Who
knows? Maybe they could have. As a coach, you can let those
Saturday morning quarterbacks bug you, or you can ignore
them. The point here is that in the heat of the moment, in the
heat of marketing, you need to be able to make the necessary
decisions. You need to ask yourself, "Okay, what's my follow-up
going to be?" You also have to decide to take the responsibility
for your own success at some level. To go out there and to
launch something like that, and to have it come back and the
sales weren't where you wanted, can be crushing. You have
these high expectations and you think, "Oh, this is really good!"
You're really into the offer — but they didn't respond to it. Well,
just go back and tweak it again. Make them that next follow-up
offer and see if you can do a little better. Or change something
— some of the nuts and bolts that I've been talking about.

   You don't need the Saturday morning quarterbacks. You're
going to be your own second-guesser in your own marketing.
Make those decisions in the heat of the moment, and you go with
them. Put your best foot forward, do the best that you can, and
you learn. And use all the resources available to you! The proven
ideas that have worked for others are there for you to use, too.
Keep in mind that it won't be easy; don't let anyone tell you that.
The best things in the world aren't always the easiest things. A lot
of people are addicted to easy — but the truth is, the things we
value the most in this world are often the things that require the
biggest price. We see that in other aspects of our lives.

   I want to encourage you to take the time to learn how to do
copywriting. We call it the #1 marketing skill for a reason; and it
*is* a skill, and therefore it can be learned. But it's not always
easy. It can be fun, and I've tried to suggest some things to you
that will make it even more fun. Just find that one time in the
day that's best for you, and get to it.  It doesn't have to be for
more than an hour or two a day. For me it's the morning hours;

that's when I do my best *new* creative work. And then in the evenings, when I'm relaxing at night, I'll have a laptop right there on my lap and I'll be half-watching some program and my wife will be right there, and the dog will be right there, and I'm doing other kinds of work. It's fun. It's creative. It's rewarding. But it's still difficult at times.

I'm married to a very stubborn woman, and she can be quite bossy. Sometimes I say to her, "Eileen, when are you going to be subservient to me?" As if! Her job as CEO was to boss people around. Even though she's not CEO now, she still bosses me around sometimes. When I ask her, "When am I going to be the boss, and then you do whatever I tell you to do?" She tells me, "T.J., if I was that way, you'd get bored with me so fast it's not even funny!" And she's kind of right. I've thought about it. Sure, I would like for her to do it for a week or two; that'd be fun. But afterward...

Sometimes it's the challenges in life, I think, that keep us going. Although they're challenges, although they're difficult, good things can come out of that difficulty. To me, easy is boring. And the worst thing for me is to be bored. I can take a lot of things, and I have: just bring it on! But boredom? I don't do well with boredom at all! I've made some of my biggest business mistakes when business was really good, when the sales were rolling in and there was nothing much for me to do. I think part of the reason I did those stupid things is because I was just bored. I can't stand boredom! And when things are too easy, they're kind of boring. It's one of the reasons we like living in Kansas, because the weather constantly changes.

Here's something that Chris Hollinger tells me he's been adopting into his writing and thinking about a lot lately. I think it's a good idea. It's just this statement: "If it sounds good, people are going to hear it. If it looks good; they're going to see it. If it's marketed well, they're going to buy it. But if it's *real*,

**297**

they're going to feel it." I think that's something you can shoot for in your copywriting. Make your reader see how positive you are, how positive this offer can be for their life and their financial situation, and really make them *feel* it.

I've talked a lot about being genuine with people. It allows you to be yourself and express yourself freely. It will separate you from all those marketers who are trying to be perfect, even though that quest for perfection is hurting them in a number of ways. First of all, it takes a lot more energy to be perfect than it does just to be yourself. And two, what people really want is to do business with other people. In fact, the logo for direct-mail marketing used to be just two hands clasping, surrounded by a circle, people saying, "Hello. It's good to meet you. Thank you. I really appreciate it." Then they changed it, of course; I guess somebody decided it was too old-fashioned. But it was a good logo — just one person trying to communicate with another person, by means of direct mail.

Let me leave you with one final idea/concept. Whenever someone purchases one of your products or services, use this very simple strategy. It goes a long way towards the next sale.

Just say "Thank you."

LaVergne, TN USA
17 December 2010

209153LV00001B/93/P

9 781933 356273